THE WORLD RELIGIONS SPEAK
ON
"THE RELEVANCE OF RELIGION IN THE
MODERN WORLD"

WORLD ACADEMY OF ART AND SCIENCE

6

THE WORLD RELIGIONS SPEAK
ON
"THE RELEVANCE OF RELIGION IN THE
MODERN WORLD"

edited by
FINLEY P. DUNNE, JR.

Editorial Committee
Dr. STUART MUDD
Dr. HUSTON SMITH

1970
DR. W. JUNK N.V. PUBLISHERS - THE HAGUE

Published under the auspices of the
World Academy of Art and Science

PRINTED IN HOLLAND BY KONINKLIJKE DRUKKERIJ VAN DE GARDE N.V. ZALTBOMMEL

Papers and Commentary

presented by
leaders of the world's great religions
at the
First Spiritual Summit Conference
Calcutta, India,
October 22–26, 1968

Table of Contents

SECTION II

TOWARDS INTER-RELIGIOUS COOPERATION

APPENDICES

At sunrise beside a lotus pond in Calcutta's beautiful Botanical Gardens on the Ganges, the delegates joined their many voices in one universal prayer for peace and the welfare of humanity.

Left to right: Swami Lokeshwaranda, Belur Math, Calcutta; Mrs. Dickerman Hollister; Sardar Sher Singh "Sher", Shadeed Sikh Missionary College, Amritsar.

Left to right: the late Father Thomas Merton, Abbey of Gethsemani, Kentucky; Pir Vilayat Inayat Khan, Paris; Mrs. Sanford Kauffman, Old Greenwich, Conn., representative of the National Council of Churches, U.S.; Professor Wei Tat, Hong Kong.

Left to right: Rev. Pierre Fallon, S.J., Calcutta, representative of the Vatican Secretariat for Non-Christians; Finley P. Dunne, Jr., Executive Director, the Temple of Understanding.

H.S.H. Princess Poon Pismai Diskul, with Mrs. B. K. Birla.

Left to right: Professor Amiya Chakravarty, State University of New York;
Swami Madhav Goswami, Gauriya Math, Calcutta.

Preface

by

FINLEY P. DUNNE, JR.
Executive Director, The Temple of Understanding, Inc.

For centuries it has been more or less assumed that the different religions of the world could have little communication with one another. This assumption seemed particularly valid as between religions separated geographically or along ethnic and linguistic lines. What, for instance, would American Baptists have to say to Buddhists from Thailand, and vice versa, about matters with which their religions might be concerned? It has also held true in many localities where members of different religions were citizens of one country, spoke the same language and even went to the same schools.

The religions themselves have often contributed by trying to keep their members isolated from the presumably dangerous doctrines of other creeds. There have been some good examples of fruitful dialogue, notably the effort in the United States to eliminate prejudice between Christian and Jew, and the recently created Congress of Religions in Ceylon, which is helping to reduce traditional tensions among the Buddhists, Christians, Hindus and Moslems inhabiting that island country. But for the most part the great religions have indeed followed separate paths, and have learned little about one another.

Perhaps in days gone by, although the sad history of the many wars that have been mainly religious in motivation argues otherwise, the world could look upon interreligious separatism without too much concern. A Christian in America or Europe might comfort himself with the thought that he did not need to bother about what Hindus in India or Buddhists or Shintoists in Japan were thinking and feeling. If he felt compelled to do anything about them, he might support missionaries bent on converting them. Nothing more was necessary. Now the circumstances are radically changed. In respect to travel-time, Calcutta, Bangkok and Kyoto are not nearly as far from Dubuque or Mid-Europe as they were. Nor are they as distant ideologically, economically and politically. The prospect is that they will be even closer in the future. With the threat of atomic warfare

hanging over the world this means that none of us can afford any longer to
ignore our neighbors in the world. All of us must learn to see one another
as members of the family of man, taking into account our weaknesses and
failures as well as our strengths and successes. We must learn to cooperate
and to understand. Nothing else will do. It is understand or perish. Nowhere is this more deeply the case than in the sphere of the great religions,
with their 2,500,000,000 adherents.

The central purpose of the Temple of Understanding, Inc., is directed to
these circumstances. It aims to open new windows of understanding between and among the great religions. A part of its plan, from which the
organization takes its name, is to construct a Temple of Understanding,
which will be a center for interreligious study and where visitors of every
faith may learn about other religions, their fundamental creeds, sacred
scriptures and rituals. Its educational program, world-wide in scope, seeks
to replace age-old isolation, indifference and prejudice with the constructive communication that is necessary before understanding in any meaningful sense can be achieved. This purpose, it must be made clear, is not
syncretic. There is no intention of trying to combine any religion with any
other, no thought of changing the elements of creed and faith, ritual and
scripture, ethics and cultural content that give each religion of mankind
its distinctive character. Rather, each religion is honored for its own
special ways of going and doing, its own unique traditions. The differences
among them, far from being deplored, are to be cherished, both for themselves and the sanctities and beauties they reveal, and for the insight they
give us into the true nature of each of them.

The Spiritual Summit Conference in Calcutta was an example of these
purposes and policies in action. Several notable features distinguished it
and made it memorable. First, it brought together representatives of no
less than eleven major world religions: Buddhism, Christianity, Confucianism, Hinduism, Islam, Jainism, Judaism, Sikhism, Shintoism, Zoroastrianism and Baha'i. Secondly, these representatives, coming from many countries, were singularly well qualified to speak for their own religions; they
were recognized spiritual leaders, scholars and philosophers. Thirdly, in
the subject they came to discuss, "The Relevance of Religion in the Modern
World", they were dealing with one of the great questions of the present
time, a question which is troubling men and women of every generation
in every part of the world.

Is religion as we have known it relevant to life as men are now living it
on this planet or may expect to live it in the decades to come? Has science,
in the process of reducing some of our ancestral lore to the cheerful
package of myths it is, also destroyed the concept of divinity? Is religion a
back number, no longer able to help us as we struggle with the things that
are obviously wrong with our world? Has it been nothing more than an
opiate for the masses? Were it not that so many people, especially so many of

the younger generation, in the United States and abroad, appear to have a-
dopted a distinctly negative posture, one might dismiss these questions as
frivolous or politically motivated. As it is, we are persuaded that they need
to be faced and if possible answered. Unless unequivocal answers can be
supplied, man is in danger of losing what has been his most reliable steady-
ing-sail, his assurance that there is something in the universe greater,
wiser, more enduring than himself. He is in danger of drifting helplessly,
without direction, at the mercy of every wind of emotion or storm of
passion, and at last being engulfed.

Relevance, a word which has fairly recently leapt into common use –
or indeed into excessive use – needs to be somewhat carefully defined in
our context. Too many immature people are using it as an excuse to rebel
mindlessly against legitimate authority, which they declare irrelevant to
what they consider their needs. Too many politicians, whether leaders of
revolt or defenders of privilege, declare that the ordinary rules of civilized
behavior are irrelevant to modern conditions, and so ask to be applauded
for violating them. What we mean by relevance was set forth in a brief
paper that was mailed to the delegates in advance of the conference:

Relevance obviously must always mean relevance to something. Thus, the
wind is relevant to the tree whose branches it sways, and the tree is relevant
to the wind, but a tree in Bombay is only remotely relevant to the glaciers
of Alaska, nor are the glaciers immediately relevant to it. In the case of our
Conference, its theme being The Relevance of Religion in the Modern
World, we are thinking of the ways in which the various religions, with
their ancient histories and their modern practices and observances, are
applicable to the fate of man in the second half of the Twentieth Century.
How do they contribute to the growth of mankind in an age which features
scientific development, material advancement and political power and
seems so often to overlook the needs of the spirit? What lessons does
religion have to offer to those who have been led to place their faith in the
computer and its offspring, the Inter-Continental Ballistic Missile,
the moon rocket and the miracles of telecommunication? What can
religion say to the countless young people in every land who have seen
how unable we are to cope with injustice, war, famine and racial and
religious prejudice, and who therefore are tending to pull away from our
institutions?

We are asking these questions of the individuals who will come to the
conference as members of the different religions. We are not hoping that
any of them can speak authoritatively for the whole of his own religion,
because this sort of requirement would compel him to talk in generalities,
or in dogmatic terms. Our thought is, rather, to let each delegate attack
these questions as an individual member of his religion – as a scholarly,

informed, inspired and, in some cases, hierarchical member of his religion, but still as an individual person with his own personal views.

Although the papers collected in this volume represent the personal views of the authors, we believe they afford a very fair and acceptable insight into the positions of the religions themselves, justifying the title, "The World Religions Speak".

Of course, the delegates who came to Calcutta did much more than merely present their views. They also, for the better part of a week, mingled with one another in an informal and spiritually enriching way. The hours of participation in the regular sessions of the conference were greatly outmatched by the hours they spent in intimate and animated conversations, in small and large groups. What resulted was a communication that, in the words of THOMAS MERTON, who was deeply involved in all of it, was "not communication, but communion." There grew up, under our eyes, a transcendent spirit of brotherhood, emerging from the mutual discovery of one another by men of true and abiding faith, each in his own religion.

There was present at all times a warm current of religious feeling, which found expression in many ways, but most of all in the prayers, mostly quite spontaneous, and led by men of different religions, in which all the participants joined at the beginning and end of every session.

Finally, as the reader will see, this book has two main Sections. Section I comprises the papers given at the conference, as well as some extemporaneous remarks. Section II is devoted to action taken by the delegates to activate what was brought forth and perpetuate what was created at the conference. As stated in the Final Declaration, the delegates voted unanimously to request the Temple of Understanding to hold another such conference as soon as possible: and further, to ask it to explore the feasibility of establishing a world body of religions dedicated to continuing and extending the kind of communication among the world religions that was initiated at Calcutta. We consider that a mandate. We shall do our best to comply with it.

Washington, D. C. 1969

Foreword

by

STUART MUDD, M. D.
Vice President, World Academy of Art and Science

Since our hominid ancestors first evolved to become human, thoughtful men have observed and pondered the world about them. Even the most primitive men could observe the ordered progression of the stars about the poles with each diurnal cycle and their movement through each season. They could observe, even though with only simple understanding, the marvelous self-regulating capabilities of living beings to perpetuate themselves and to adapt to changing conditions through progressive evolution. Primitive peoples sought to interpret the forces of nature in animistic terms intelligible within their own experience.

The emergence of the prophets and founders of the world religions gave men more enlightened conceptions of the universal order and its mysterious and all pervading harmony. As a practitioner of natural science, I regard the prophets and saints of the world religions, and those who have followed them, as predecessors in the search for enlightenment.

To understand the cosmic order is the goal of science. Can we truly understand the microcosms of the atoms, with their unimaginable complexity of electrons whirling about their nuclei? Can we truly understand the complexity of the atomic nucleus, with its protons, neutrons and powerful binding forces? Whence the regularity, the stability, the order in these incredible microcosms? Can we adequately comprehend the ordered evolution of cosmic clouds, stars and galaxies in the macrocosmos?

Can we really understand a living cell, even a microbial cell? We visualize with the electron microscope cell membranes, cytoplasm, a nuclear area, with its skein of deoxyribonucleic acid bearing the genetic blue print. We even break the genetic code and discern how the alphabet of four base-pairs is translated into the alphabet of twenty amino acids, and these in turn into the catalysts which regulate structure and function. We isolate the enzymes and their substrates, and reconstitute their several functions one by one. But the microbial cell, invisible to the naked eye, can carry out simultaneously and in a few minutes an ordered succession of chemical interactions, transformations and syntheses which the most modern laboratory in a scientific world cannot duplicate. Whence the logistics, the ordered sequence, required for survival? Whence, indeed, the urge in religionist and scientist alike to probe the ultimate mysteries and to achieve a harmonious relationship to the divine or cosmic order?

At the core of every scientific problem into which I have ever inquired in sufficient depth, is mystery, the profound mystery of order and adaptedness. I aspire to gain in understanding of this mysterious cosmic order by the procedures in which I have been trained as a natural scientist: observation and experiment; induction; deduction; verification.

To the religionist who aspires to gain in understanding of the ultimate mysteries of the spirit and its relation to the divine order, by whatsoever means of inspiration, meditation, devotion prove effectual for him, should the scientist not say:

We are both seekers. May we both gain in understanding and in achieving harmony with the mysterious order in which we live.

A great contemporary scientist has written: * "To pursue science is not to disparage the things of the spirit. In fact, to pursue science rightly is to furnish a framework on which the spirit may rise.... Science has a simple faith, which transcends utility. Nearly all men of science, all men of learning for that matter, and men of simple ways too, have it in some form and in some degree. It is the faith that it is the privilege of man to learn to understand, and that this is his mission."

The understanding to be sought embraces the ecology of our entire planet, the well-being and quality of life of all mankind. This understanding should include the religious insights and aspirations of man, the verified discoveries of science, the useful applications of technology. The goals should be optimally viable economic and social organization in relation to the entire planet, the good life for all mankind; for the unit of survival in the presently emerging world is not one particular religious, ethnic or political group, but *mankind*.

The primary purpose for which the World Academy of Art and Science is chartered is to provide a forum for the discussion, without bias, of matters of concern to all mankind. Certainly the world's religions are of profound significance and relevance to man.

As an observer at the Spiritual Summit Conference from the field of natural science, it has been profoundly reassuring to me to see that all religions share the common aspiration to gain in understanding of the divine or the cosmic order, and to bring man into harmonious relation to that order. As a working scientist, this is also my aspiration. It is reassuring, also, to see that the orientation to human conduct of all religions stresses justice, compassion, love. There is thus a common human basis of aspiration and behavior for all men of good will.

* VANNEVAR BUSH, 1968. THE SEARCH FOR UNDERSTANDING. *American Scientist* 56: 298–301.

Special Prayers Offered
at the First Spiritual Summit Conference

Opening Prayer: Mrs. DICKERMAN HOLLISTER:

We thank Thee, heavenly Father, for gathering us under Thy wing, and for the steady out-pouring of Thy love and Thy light. We ask only that Thou continue to guide and protect us in this holy endeavor to create a Temple of Understanding. Ignite our hearts and minds with the force of Thy creative action, that upon this beautiful planet, for the weary children of earth, we may light this flame of understanding. We ask only that this symbol of illumination may never dim, but be fed by Thy constant and our constant care. Amen.

An Invocation: Dr. V. RAGHAVAN:

He who is Brahma, Shiva, Vishnu, and the Sun to the followers of the Veda; the impersonal absolute, Brahman, to those who follow the path of knowledge. He who is Buddha, Anri and Ahura Mazda to the followers of the traditions of Buddhism, Jainism and Zoroastrianism. And for those who are the followers of the Jews, of Christ, and Mohammed, He who is Yahweh, God and Allah. The same one which is in diverse forms, that one truth we adore.

Closing Prayer: Father THOMAS MERTON:

I'll ask you to stand and all join hands in a little while. But first, we realize that we are going to have to create a new language of prayer. And this new language of prayer has to come out of something which transcends all our traditions, and comes out of the immediacy of love. We have to part now, aware of the love that unites us, the love that unites us in spite of real differences, real emotional friction. ... The things that are on the surface are nothing, what is deep is the Real. We are creatures of love. Let us therefore join hands, as we did before, and I will try to say something that comes out of the depths of our hearts. I ask you to concentrate on the love that is in you, that is in us all. I have no idea what I am going to say. I am going to be silent a minute and then I will say something. . . .

Oh God, we are one with You. You have made us one with You. You have taught us that if we are open to one another, You dwell in us. Help us to preserve this openness and to fight for it with all our hearts. Help us to realize that there can be no understanding where there is mutual rejection. Oh God, in accepting one another whole-heartedly, fully, completely, we accept You, and we thank You, and we adore You, and we love You with our whole being, because our being is Your being, our spirit is rooted in Your spirit. Fill us then with love, and let us be bound together with love as we go our diverse ways, united in this one spirit which makes You present in the world, and which makes You witness to the ultimate reality that is love. Love has overcome. Love is victorious. Amen.

SECTION I

THE RELEVANCE OF RELIGION IN THE MODERN WORLD

Introduction:
The Relevance of the Great Religions
for the Modern World

by

HUSTON SMITH

Professor of Philosophy, Massachusetts Institute of Technology, Cambridge

This paper, here presented as an Introduction, was delivered by Dr. Smith as the concluding address of the First Spiritual Summit Conference, Calcutta, October 1968. In this its edited form it is dedicated by Dr. Smith to Thomas Merton whose death a month after the Conference underscored how much his presence there had meant.

Religion can, of course, be irrelevant and often is. No human endeavor is immaculate, and one that traffics with millions is bound to emerge a mixed bag. In this respect religion is no different from other corporate enterprises – education which quickens and represses, government which orchestrates and restricts. Religion has been revolutionary and conservative, prophetic and priestly, catalytic and incubus. It creates barriers and levels them, raises church budgets and raises the oppressed, makes peace with iniquity and redeems, in part, the world. We acknowledge this mottled record right off for it would be a sad miscarriage of our Conference intent if in the act of assembling religion's delegates it were inadvertently to widen the gulf between them and their critics – between those for whom "religion" is a good word and those for whom it is not. No representatives from the Socialist nations are here. In view of their Marxist premise that religion is opiate this is not surprising, but it is none the less a lack. So to this absent third of the world we say: whereas the ecumenical movement's first phase sounded the potential unity among Christendom and its second phase is exploring the unity latent in religions, we look to a third phase that will seek the unity latent in man, the unity underlying the ideologies that divide him into secularist, socialist, religious, or by "isms" whatever.

I

Religious relevance takes different forms according to the period in question. I propose to distinguish three great ages through which man has passed with an eye to what religious relevance has meant in each.

1. The first age, by far the longest, was the archaic. It lasted, roughly, up to the first millennium B.C. In this Archaic Period, during which man was rousing out of his animal innocence, his chief spiritual problem was time. Lower animals are oblivious of time for they possess neither foresight nor hindsight, neither anticipation nor memory. When man first acquired these time-binding faculties he found their implications terrifying: the future, he discovered, was contingent, and the past impermanent. His recourse was to blink these terrors; insofar as possible simply to turn his back on them and deny their existence by attending to their opposite. This opposite – Great Time – was in fact timeless. It consisted of momentous, originating acts which, his myths told him, had brought order out of chaos and established the patterns for meaningful activity: creation of the world itself, the first planting, the first mating, each act accomplished by the gods in epic proportions. For archaic man, being *was* these timeless, paradigmatic acts which were significant, secure, and impervious to time's decay. His religion consisted of replicating these acts through rites that were myth-ordained and myth-prescribed. Through these rites his life fused with Being. It merged with the meaningful and the real.

Note how little ethics entered into this first, originating phase of religion. The reason is that at this stage ethics didn't pose much of a problem, little more than it does for subhuman animals. Men were living for the most part in small groups, in tribes or tiny villages wherein everyone knew everyone else and cooperated pretty much as do members of a normal family.

2. Following the terminology of KARL JASPERS, I shall call the second period the Axial Age, for during it human history took a marked turn, a giant swing on its axis so to speak. This is the period that witnessed the rise of the geniuses the world still honors: the great prophets of Israel, Zarathustra in Persia, Buddha and the Upanishadic seers in India, Lao Tzu and Confucius in China. This burst of religious creativity across the full arc of the civilized world, an extraordinary proliferation of prophetic genius diffused in space but condensed in time and amounting to nothing short of a mass religious mutation – this remarkable phenomenon has often been described but never satisfactorily explained. I submit that it was at root the spirit's response to a marked change in man's condition, a crisis in human evolution.

By the first millennium B.C. or shortly before, agricultural improvement had advanced population and settled existence to the point where men were dealing regularly with persons outside their primary group. As a consequence, familial feelings no longer sufficed to keep society intact. Perceptive souls – we call them prophets, seers, rishis, sages, magi – saw this and summoned religion to emerge from its archaic phase to help meet the problem. Rites and rituals are no longer enough, they said in effect.[1]

1 "I hate, I despise your feasts, and I take no delight in your solemn assemblies" (AMOS 5:21). "*Lower*...knowledge (is) of...ceremonials" (MANDAKA UPANISHAD) (Italics added).

You must give an eye to how you behave toward your fellows. For flawed human relations can reduce life to shambles. Religion isn't exhausted by inter-personal relations, but it stops in its tracks if it tries to skirt them. *Yogas* (spiritual techniques) must be prefaced by *yamas* (moral precepts), *dhyana* (meditation) and *prajna* (wisdom) by *sila* (ethical observances). "If you are offering your gift at the altar, and there remember that your brother has something against you, leave your gift there before the altar and go; first be reconciled to your brother, and then come and offer your gift" (Matthew 5:23–24). For "he who does not love his brother whom he has seen, cannot love God whom he has not seen" (I John 4:20).

Hence the Golden Rules of the great religions which we have reaffirmed this week: Christianity's "Do unto others..."; Judaism's "What doth the Lord require of thee but to do justice, love mercy..."; Jainism's *ahimsa* and *aparigraha;* Buddhism's *metta* and *Karuna*, its "boundless heart toward all beings"; Hinduism's "highest [yogin] who judges pleasure or pain everywhere by the same standard as he applies to himself" (Gita, VI, 32); Islam's man who "gives his wealth...to kinsfolk and to orphans and to the needy and the wayfarer...who sets slaves free... and payeth the poor due"; · Sikhism's "humility to serve"; Confucius' human-hearted *jen*. These expressions of personal concern for the well-being of others have been the glory of the religions during their axial periods. They account for a good half of the resonance across credal lines that has characterized this Conference, for in the altruism of their ethics the great religions are much alike.

3. This brings us to the third great period in human history. I shall call it simply the Modern Age and mark it as having been inaugurated by the rise of modern science in the Seventeenth Century and the Enlightenment in the Eighteenth. Our Modern Age differs from its predecessors in many ways, the pertinent one for us here being that it sees social structures as malleable. In previous ages institutions – family systems, caste and class, feudalism, kingship, chief and emperor – were assumed to be divinely ordained; irrefragable, ineluctable, of a piece with the order of the universe. Modern man sees them as contingent, and by the same token fallible! The corollary is immense. For if society *can* be changed, it often *should* be changed, in which case its members are responsible for seeing to it that it *is* changed.

Obviously this new perspective enlarges the scope of ethics enormously. Whereas religion's ethical dimension was minimal in the Archaic Period and personal in the Axial Period, today it has become both personal and social, both individual and collective. For to repeat: if social structures can be good or evil and are subject to man's will, man is responsible for their quality.

II

Against the backdrop of these three stages of human history the question of religious relevance becomes more manageable. What makes religion relevant depends on the age in question. Archaic religion was relevant without containing much in the way of ethics at all, for ethics wasn't then a major problem. But if religion had idled ethically in the Axial Period when ethics had become a problem, we wouldn't be assembled this week as its representatives. Having lost step with relevance, it would have disappeared.

Similarly today, social ethics having emerged as man's new responsibility if religion doesn't assume its share of this responsibility it will lose the relevance it has thus far enjoyed. Personal kindness is no longer enough. Institutions affect man's welfare no less than do interpersonal relations. This being so, enlightened compassion calls for social responsibility as much as for face-to-face good will.

Item: It is now an established fact that if a child does not get a certain minimum of protein before the age of six he will be mentally deficient for the rest of his life. Our Conference is meeting in a city in which 100,000 inhabitants have no homes but the streets, where gutters serve as bathrooms and sidewalk corners are at once bedrooms for men and stables for beasts. Here in this Calcutta where "Above the packed and pestilent town/Death looks down" no amount of personal kindness is going to insure that all children will receive the protein they need if for no other reason than that most of the persons who are in a position to see to it that they do live geographically removed. Direct, face-to-face kindness (the "cup of water given in my name") won't solve the problem, but indirect, organized institutional kindness (UNICEF, or Save the Children Federation, or more equitable trade agreements) might.

Item: It took all of human history up to the middle of this century to develop an economy – that of the United States – capable of growing at the rate of $2\frac{1}{2}\%$ per annum. Such a growth rate, if sustained, would enable children to be roughly twice as wealthy as their parents. Less than twenty years separate us from 1950 and already two economies (the West German and the Japanese) are pushing 10% per annum growth. If economies sustain this order of growth, children stand to be roughly six times richer than their parents and thirty-six times richer than their grandparents. These figures point up the fact that after capital accumulation reaches take-off momentum it increases exponentially. This places nations that take off early at an enormous advantage; they leave other nations not just behind but increasingly behind. The gap between them and less developed nations widens. The consequence is that if events proceed on present course, the world is going to become in the remainder of our century even more unbalanced in wealth and power than it is already. As the population explosion is centering in the "have not" nations, the "have" nations will re-present a decreasing proportion of the world's population while possessing an increasing proportion of the world's wealth and power. Pointing as this does towards a world composed of islands of affluence off a mainland of misery, the situation is neither just nor healthy.

Item: Ten years ago it came clearly to view that for the first time in human history enough metabolic and mechanical energy is available to provide high standards of living for everyone in North America almost immediately and everyone in the world within forty years despite the population explosion. All that stands between us and such universal affluence is invention of the social institutions needed to effect the requisite distribution.

Man's well-being has always been conditioned by his social matrix. The point of the above examples is to emphasize that this matrix, which now can be controlled, needs to be controlled. We have reached the point in history where to be indifferent to social structures is, in the last analysis, to be indifferent to people.

Is the moral that religion should convert to social action? Not precisely. Religion should take up social action but not confine itself thereto. More-over, in becoming active toward society it should be active in a special way. These distinctions are not simple but they are important, sufficiently im-portant to occupy us for the balance of this paper.

III

Religion has three dimensions: transcendental, personal, and social. To some extent all three have been present from the start, but they have come to prominence successively. Archaic Religion kept religion's tran-scendental component at stage center, attending almost entirely to ade-quating man's finite, ephemeral acts to the heroic paradigms that lodged them in eternity. Axial Religion added personal concerns to the repertoire and sought the education of conscience, compassion, self-know-ledge, and forgiveness. In adding social responsibility to its preceding agen-das Modern Religion effects a third great extension.

But it must be an extension, not a replacement – everything turns on this distinction. If in the Axial Period religion had relinquished eternity for love of neighbor it would have cashed in religion for ethics. It did not, of course, do this; statements like "We love, because he first loved us" (I John 4:19), and "It is not for the love of creatures that creatures are dear; but for the love of the Soul in creatures that creatures are dear" (Bhidad-Aranyake Upa-nishad, II, 4) make clear that the ethics of Axial Religion was in direct touch with its religious source. Whether the social thrust of Modern Religion is genuinely religious or only seemingly so (being in actuality indistinguish-able from secular social action) depends on whether it represents an ex-

tension of religion's transcendental and personal concerns or has relinquished these.

The distinction, timelessly important in deep-lying, imperceptible ways,
is about to become politically important. The United States is a case in
point. Churches are tax exempt, political organizations are not. But clergymen are becoming politically active, marching on Washington, destroying draft records in Milwaukee, abetting revolutions in South America. A
paradox in the making, one that could develop into a major contradiction.
The Supreme Court has already been invoked and the problem is still in its
infancy.

Nothing can save the Court from the headaches that are in store for it,
but the principle that should guide it in its decisions seems to be clear. It
is the one just stated. Social action is religious when its agents are equally
at work on religion's personal and transcendental dimensions.

These three dimensions figure so prominently in this discussion that it
behooves us to take a moment to identify them a little more precisely than
we thus far have.

Religion's social dimension is reasonably self-evident. It consists of its
efforts to change social structures (create world government, pass fair
housing laws) or affect the influence that flows through structures already
in existence (foreign aid appropriations, or whether in the U.S. $ 6.6 billion
will go into anti-ballistic-missiles or the ghettos).

Religion's personal dimension reverses the direction of concern, chan-
neling it toward the self and its inward journeyings. It is antithetical to the
religious outlook to see all life's problems as externally originated; so to
see them diminishes the soul's status, reducing it to a pawn that could be
manipulated into fulfillment or defeat. Given the soul's vulnerability, it is
conceivable that defeat might be engineered, but fulfillment never. For
fulfillment cannot be bestowed; even with grace it must in part be won.
Hence *sadhanas*, spiritual exercises, disciplines ranging from prayer and fasting to *zazen*. To characterize these as inward journeyings is accurate in that
they seek to change one's own self, but it would be a mistake to assume that
they involve a retreat or withdrawal from the world. On the contrary, the
paradoxical object of most soul searching and spiritual homework is to
unbar the dungeon of the self to enable it to open to life more freely, fully,
and joyfully.

The central object of personal religion is to strike contact with religion's
transcendental dimension, but the latter needs to be separately identified
to make clear that just as there is secular social action, there are secular
self-improvement programs: psychoanalysis, sensitivity training, what have
you. Religion's eternal dimension is fundamental; both personal and
social religion proceed from it and continue to draw from it. It is also
elusive. Historically in the West we could have identified it by invoking the
word "God", but in our century the contours of that word have blurred,

beyond which stands the complicating fact that it has no exact equivalent in Afro-Asian faiths. Eternal religion is hung up on "why" questions, beginning with why anything exists rather than nothing. It deals with the individual's stance toward his world, whether he feels at home in it or alienated from it – the ways he belongs to it and the ways he does not belong to it but is separate from and stands over against it, pointing thereby to an ultimate beyond it. Eternal religion grapples with the failure that in one form or another visits everyone – how we can live with ourselves and feel acceptable when in so many ways we are not. Its root concern is in some way with time: how everything can matter, as we feel in some sense it does, when in the long run it would appear that nothing matters. Running throughout is the question of meaning; how life can be meaningful when so much of it reads like an idiot's tale. Eternal religion knows that there are no discursive answers to these questions. It ranges time and space for insight – *prajna*, vision, a revelation which, by-passing words, will disclose directly why we exist and the world is the way it is in something of the way loving explains why we are male and female.

IV

Even Communists now concede that "faith for the Christian can be a stimulus for social commitment," [1] a marked qualification of their original perception of religion as the opiate of the people. It would be pleasant to think that religion's transcendental and personal dimensions protect it against the special dangers to which social efforts are heir – fanaticism, projection, means-ends casuistry, and discouragement – but nothing turns on this. With such safeguards or without them, religion must join the world.

Its social efforts differ from those of secularists primarily in their personal and transcendental roots but there is another difference: religion's guiding social goal must be general. Images of a new heaven and a new earth, of lions lying down with lambs, of messiahs and *maitreyas* and swords beaten into plowshares are vague, but in this case savingly vague. For sharpened much further they become ideologies. Ideologies have their uses, but sooner or later all are surprised by history. One or another may merit qualified support at a given moment, but to become tied to any would be to lose the freedom and flexibility religion needs if its social voice is to be timelessly contemporary. Probably no social goal more specific than that every child of God have an equal chance at life's opportunities deserves unqualified religious endorsement.

Though I have argued that religion must now include all three of the components enumerated, it would be foolish to contend that everyone should

1 HEINZ KLOPPENBURG, in: "THE CIVILIZATION OF THE DIALOGUE", an Occasional Paper published by the Center for the Study of Democratic Institutions, Santa Barbara, California, p. 21.

attend to them equally. People are irreducibly different; in religion this makes for priests and prophets, for hermits and crusaders. It is even appropriate that there be sects that highlight the components differently, as did Confucianism, Taoism and Buddhism in traditional China. But in a tradition or culture as a whole the three should be reasonably balanced.

V

I have argued two theses: to remain relevant religion must become socially active; to remain religious such action must retain its ties with religion's earlier concerns. It happens that with respect to these theses East and West have, today, complementing strengths and weaknesses. When in May, 1968, the "Ceylon Daily New" quoted the eminent Buddhist authority Dr. WALPOLA RAHULA as asserting that development of a sustaining economy for all of the people is as much a religious duty as any other, and that "cultivating a farm properly is better than building many temples," it showed that Asian religions are not unmindful of the need to involve themselves deeply in their adherents' struggle to pull themselves out of the straightjacket of hunger, under-employment and indebtedness. Throughout Asia swamis, monks, and laymen are changing the image of Hinduism and Buddhism. Religious leaders of many stripes write tracts on problems of modernization, encouraging laymen and fellow leaders alike to participate in economic and social development. In much of Asia we seem to be witnessing of something like a Protestant Reformation in its Weberian sense. If MAX WEBER were living today he would have to revise his judgement of the Asian religions; he would find "worldly asceticism" beginning to operate in them too to break barriers to economic, social, and political modernization. But the qualifying phrase "beginning to operate" is important. By virtue of their strong prophetic heritage and even more because industrialization has shown them how much society *can* be changed, Western religions can still help Afro-Asian faiths to see the necessity of social participation. Meanwhile Asian religions can alert those of the West to the danger that threatens them, the danger of focusing exclusively on society, neglecting religion's personal and transcendental roots and becoming in consequence unrelievedly secular. In registering for a sizeable proportion of Western society a "nagging residual disappointment in good, honest, liberal, generous Protestants," TIMOTHY LEARY shows how real this danger has become:

They have lost the fire somehow. They have lost the pulse. Their thing was dying and they knew it. The Protestants just weren't religious. Their great thing was their social instinct, their sense of equality. But in their protest against the superstition and authoritarian priesthood they had lost the magic. When they threw out the statues and the incense and the robes and the chanting (all sensory), it became social and rational and senseless.[1]

1 HIGH PRIEST (New York: New American Library, 1967).

Some clergymen are beginning to agree. In "Up to Our Steeple in Politics," two ministers chide their fellow Christians for swallowing the prevailing American assumption that "the political order...is the *only* source and authority to which we can and ought to repair for relief from what ails us....Politics has become *the* end. We have been gulled into believing that whatever ails us...can be cured exclusively by political and social nostrums."¹

"If there be East and West/It is not wisdom," sang that delightful, Tibetan saint Milarepa. In view of what East has to learn from West today about religious *relevance* and West from East about *religious* relevance, his words acquire new meaning.

1 WILL D. CAMPBELL & JAMES Y. HOLLOWAY, CHRISTIANITY AND CRISIS, XXIX, 3 (March 3, 1969), p. 36.

The Relevance of Hinduism

by

Dr. V. Raghavan
Professor of Sanskrit, University of Madras

On the subject of the relevance of Hinduism today, I desire to place before you my ideas from a special as well as a general point of view. Although I say this to make a start, I am sure I will not be able as I go along to keep the two points of view separate. In fact, what I want to say on behalf of Hinduism will, I hope, gain strength from the latter point of view; for it is on the general, the fundamental and universal aspects of Hinduism that I propose to concentrate my short exposition so that its relevance and validity may be seen in their true proportions and depth.

Modern developments have brought the peoples of the world together for good and bad. To make good or bad out of these developments is solely in our hands. One of the results which should be deemed good, or out of which we should still try to derive as much good as possible, is the meeting of cultures and the study of the writings and religions of other peoples. The study of Hinduism by those not professing that religion – as also by those who profess it but have come under the influence of the theories and interpretations of the former – may be considered to have had, so far, three phases: The first began with the academic orientalist; and the second was what the missionary cultivated as part of his proselytization. The third is a recent development, indeed a part of a phenomenon which embraces the whole of Asia.

It began with the end of the Second World War and the disappearance of colonialism, accompanied by the waking of the several countries of Asia into their new freedom, in which they have been faced with problems of developing their economy, industry and production and extending the benefits of the welfare state to as large a sector of their people as possible. The development of these countries became the concern of those more affluent, with whose aid these new programs have been undertaken. In the wake of these extensive aid programs, economists and social scientists, particularly from the biggest aiding country, the United States, had been visiting the aid areas and carrying out, in their own way, field work and textual and contextual studies to assess the impact of the aid given, the tempo of the process of development and the quantum and nature of the achievement. Among these economists and social scientists, so far as India is concerned, and with rare exceptions, we find the latest critics of Hinduism.

A considerable literature has grown up on the theme of tradition and modernity, with several variations of this title. Some of the authors of these works, as also their students and followers in this country itself, have been extremely vocal with their own findings about the incompatibility of religion and technological growth, and about Hinduism as (in their view) an impediment to progress and all that modernization implies. India itself, under the leadership of the first prime minister of the country after Independence, opted for such planned development. Although the influence of western civilization had, during the British period, made itself felt on the Indian mind, on its modes of thought and on its patterns of westernized behavior, the impact of modernization has been most patent since Independence by reason both of its acceleration and its sweep. Even so comparatively detached a student of Hinduism as the present Spalding Professor of Eastern Religions and Ethics at Oxford, Professor ZAEHNER, says in his book HINDUISM (London 1962): "The struggle between the old and the new in which it seems the new must in the end triumph, however protracted and bitter the struggle, is still going on. Hinduism is living through a time of crisis which threatens the very pre-suppositions on which it has hitherto been built, and it is too early yet to see how and in what direction it will transform itself; but transform itself, it must . . ." What Professor ZAEHNER gives as his own final answer, we shall come to later.

The apprehensions which those who attach value to religion have formed are the subject of discussions in numerous books by leading thinkers of a different and larger background in the West, which is the mother and *guru* in modern times of all the new ideologies and movements leading to the orientation of human efforts to scientific and technological development and growth of production, trade and affluence, and finding expression not only under the capitalistic system but also under that of socialism and communism. The industrial revolution, the increase of machinery and automation and the attendant social, moral and intellectual changes have been analysed with great concern and wisdom. One wonders if the apostles in the West as well as their counterparts in the East, who want to alter the entire face of the East and change the very structure of its society and re-fashion its mode of thought, pause to listen to the other voices of the thinking West, the elite there, and profit by their warnings about the other side of the picture, about the attendant and growing evils of this system as it effects individual life, social conduct and state policies. For example, MEREDITH TOWNSHEND, writing some time back, asked in the chapter on The Standard of Comfort in India, in his book ASIA AND EUROPE how it was

fair, or justified or worthwhile, to tamper with the value-structure of India
on the basis of one's own inbred conviction that comfort and civilization
are identical. The recent book THE MONKEY AND THE FISH: CULTURAL
PITFALLS OF AN EDUCATIONAL ADVISER, relates in this connection the oriental
fable of a monkey seeing a fish in water, thinking that it is uncomfortable,
and out of a humanitarian desire to save it, lifting it out of the water; the
fish being hardly grateful for this, not being able to live at all outside. The
American social scientists, mentioned earlier, who have pronounced
Hinduism a stumbling block to economic and industrial development,
have generally been guided by the principles of the German sociologist
MAX WEBER whose works have gained a fresh vogue with them. We shall
therefore examine the basic ideas of the Weberian thesis.

In his RELIGIONS OF INDIA: THE SOCIOLOGY OF HINDUISM AND BUDDHISM
(1958, The Free Press) WEBER wrote; "The spirit of Capitalism cannot find
congenial motivational sources or support in the 'spirit of Hinduism'. It
could not have occurred to the Hindu to see the economic success he had
attained through devotion to his calling *as a sign of his salvation*....." (Italics
ours). What does WEBER mean by salvation here? Could any religion see
this or have such a conception of salvation? Elsewhere he defines the
capitalist spirit as the temper of single-minded concentration on pecuniary
gain. To the assignment of such an over-riding importance, such single-
minded devotion to pecuniary gain, Hinduism cannot of course subscribe;
in fact, to be solely motivated by material gain is considered reprehensible.
Rama, at the time of the disturbance of his proposed coronation, tells his
brother Lakshmana that one to whom material gain is the be-all and end-all
of his life is to be detested – "*Dvesyo bhavatyartha-paro hi loke*". In his BASIC
CONCEPTS IN SOCIOLOGY (English translation, London 1962), WEBER speaks
of a "goal-oriented course of conduct or behaviour" and a value-oriented
conduct, i.e. conduct according to one's notion of how he feels called
upon to act as required by a sense of duty, honor, beauty, religiosity,
piety etc. Here, of course, he widens the bases of conduct from the pure
profit motive to duty, beauty, piety and so on. In fact, he is unconciously
referring to the whole gamut of the springs of human action which the
Hindu concept of the four *purusarthas* explains adequately. The Protestant
ethic that WEBER postulates as the most potent basis of the profit-making
urge and all that ensues out of this enterprise may also be examined: To
quote ALDOUS HUXLEY (ENDS AND MEANS, pp. 240–1)" ...the first and most
ruthless capitalists were men brought up in the tradition of Calvinism.
Believing that good works and inner life were without any eternal significance, they gave up charity and self education and turned all their attention to getting on in the world," an attitude which in India we refer to as
Charvaka. The Protestants have not been the only successful business mag-
nates and entrepreneurs. In his essay "A Criticism of Max Weber and His
School" in the collection THE WEBER THESIS AND ITS CRITICS (Edited by

ROBERT W. GREEN, Pennsylvania State University), H. M. ROBERTSON quotes
from French Catholics to show how the Catholic faith, too, affords enough
motive force for action and the discharge of one's duty, which thereby
become sanctified.

It has been alleged that Hinduism is a life-negating religion, laying a
premium on abstaining from things, venerating renunciation, considering
life a misery and pleasures evanescent; and that this whole mental set is
hardly conducive to a new ideology of an abundant life. Elsewhere I have
examined in detail, and answered, the criticism of Hindu culture as being
otherworldly. The very continuation of Hindu culture and the survival
of Hindu society comprise an adequate answer to this notion. The criticism
springs from an incomplete knowledge and understanding of Hinduism,
for in Hinduism different ideas refer to different stages of life and different
stations or vocations; they have an absolute significance and also a relative
or practical field of operation. Thus there is a basic dictum – "*Nivrittis tu
mahaphala*" enunciated by Manu (V. 56). To abstain from a thing is indeed
great and is of the highest good, but having a thing within limits or without
violence to other principles is not only not prohibited but is also approved,
for human nature has needs, like eating, drinking and sexual enjoyment,
for its very sustenance. In every religious act that the Hindu performs he
prays for welfare as much as in the hereafter, *aihika* and *amusmika*. The Vedas
are full of prayers for the good things of life, for cattle, wealth, progeny,
long life. A whole section in the Yajur Veda enumerates all the economic
requirements and also all other things whereby life could be enriched and
enjoyed. Another prayer in the same Veda mentions the concept of adding
to and conserving one's possessions and asks for both of them – "*Yoga-ksemo
nah Kalpatam*". KAUTALYA'S ARTHASASTRA on the science of polity states that
none should deny himself pleasure, *Na missukhah svat*. The Ramayana declares
that the world flourishes and prospers through economy and commerce –
"*Vartayam samsritah tata loko' yam sukham edhate*". Of the four classes of society,
the third, the *vaisya* or merchants, have their legitimate duty of acquiring,
the duty of the second class, *kshatriyas* or rulers, being to foster and promote
the growth of wealth.

In ancient times, India could boast not only of philosophy and thought
which spread abroad but also of her famous commercial products and
goods which went over the seas and drained foreign markets of their gold.
The commercial traditions, as also the arts, crafts and productive occupa-
tions flowed continuously up to the time of the rise of the British power.
The correct Hindu attitude can easily be understood in the scheme of four
purusharthas or aims of man's action, *dharma, artha, kama* and *moksha*: virtue,
material gain, enjoyment of desires and spiritual salvation. These four
which are prayed for in all rites and rituals, are legitimate pursuits and they
cover the whole field of human activity and aspiration. Hinduism therefore
does not deny profit or pleasure; but it includes virtue and the final

spiritual aim, which together form the fundamental aspirations of man.
Virtue and the religious or spiritual ideal exercise a chastening influence
on the pursuit of profit and pleasure and it is here that the difference
comes between Hinduism and Weberism and the new cult of gearing
up the whole people and the whole process of life to industry and production.

The above ideas within the framework of Hindu thought provide enough
basis for building up and developing our economy with the aid of modern
technology. To have some basis in one's own tradition for accommodating
new ideas is an excellent thing, for it neutralizes an allergy to new ideas by
making them, through identification or interpretation, integral parts or
continuations of parts of one's own tradition. It smoothes transition and
avoids revolution or sudden deracination. TRADITIONAL CULTURES AND THE
IMPACT OF TECHNOLOGICAL CHANGE by GEORGE M. FOSTER (University of
California at Berkeley) has the following wise observations embodying the
same valuable idea:

When new tools and technical innovations can be adapted to traditional motor patterns,
the probability of acceptance is greater than if no attempt at accomodation is made.
(p. 89)
... in all societies traditional institutions have recognized roles; if new forms can be
integrated or associated with these traditional roles, they have a better chance of being
accepted than if there is nothing to tie to. (p. 162)
DUBE speaks of how in India there is a tendency in cultures to reinterpret the profer-
red innovation in terms of the dominant themes and existing needs of society. (p. 175)
The point of view is something like this: No culture is all good or all bad. Basically all
cultures are reasonably good; otherwise they would not have survived...real progress
is made when it springs from and builds on the good things already existing in a culture,
rather than when it is defined in terms of an approximation of the American way of
life. ... All could be greatly improved within the economic limitations of each country
building on what existed rather than by trying to approximate to standards that had
been developed for Americans in the U.S. (pp. 202–3)
Further he does not believe that industrialization must produce a carbon copy of
Western social institutions; different kinds of social and political institutions can
support an industrial economy as is clear from the Russian example.... This is not
simply the morality of cultural relativism. It is not simply tolerance and broad-
mindedness. It is basic wisdom for the technical agent. For in every culture there is
reason for every element. Sometimes the reason is no longer valid: change then will
not be dangerous. At other times the reason is still valid and change may spell disaster.
(p. 267)

The normal Hindu is the householder, the *grhastha*, one in the second of the
four stations of life. This second station of life is praised as the highest, as it
supports the other three, the student and the two classes of those who
have retired from active life, *brahmacharin*, *vanaprastha* and *sannyasin*. To support
these sections of society, the householder must have sufficient resources.
Hospitality is enjoined as one of his primary duties, and this, along with the
important concept of *dana*, making gifts and helping the poor and the
unfortunate, and *istpurta*, setting up charitable establishments and works of

public utility, tanks, wells, parks, avenues, trees, and so on – all these form part of the Hindu conception of socialism or the social obligations of man, by which the more affluent is made to share his wealth with the less fortunate. There is a Mantra in the Rigveda which says that he who cooks or eats for himself alone eats sin. The Bhagavata puts it with an edge when it says that he who covets more is a thief fit to be punished – "*Adhikam ye abhikankseta sa steno dandam arhati*". The *smriti* of Yajanavalkya states that to attain salvation, it is not necessary to renounce life or leave the house but if a man as a householder earns wealth by righteous means, is well-grounded in the knowledge of the ultimate principles, is hospitable to guests, performs his duties by his ancestors and is a speaker of truth, he too is liberated.

Nayagatadhanah tattvajnananistho' tithi-priyah/
Sraddhakrt satyavadi ca grhasto pi hi mucyate/ /

What is more relevant today than the philosophy of *svadharma*, the performance of one's appointed duty devoutly as an act of adoration of the Lord, which the Gita taught (XVIII) – "*Svakarmana tam abhyarcya siddhim vindati?*" The injunction of Veda and Dharma Sastra that one has to perform his ordained duty and that its neglect is to be atoned for imparts sufficient seriousness to work; it is further sanctified by the Gita in the doctrine, quoted earlier, in which every act man performs as his duty is a flower with which he adores God. It is interesting to note some Catholic parallels: In the NEW WHOLE DUTY OF MAN, CONTAINING THE FAITH AS WELL AS PRACTICE OF THE PRESENT AGE, we read: "... the man that serves God by continual application to the duty of his calling and state of life, besides the comfort of a good conscience which is of all others the greatest happiness, such an honest and industrious laborer may entirely depend upon the goodness of God, that he will always take care of him" (Gita, *Yogakseman vahamiyaham*). H. M. ROBERTSON, who quotes the above in his criticism of MAX WEBER's thesis, quotes also the following: "There are duties to be performed in all conditions of life and it is in acquitting oneself of these duties that one is sanctified." The great epic the Mahabharata, brings out the dignity and sanctity of one's calling in two deservedly famous stories which the grand old man of the royal house of the Kauravas, Bhisma, narrates to King Yudhisthira, the stories of the merchant Tuladhara at Banaras and the virtuous hunter, Dharma Vyadha, in the forest. In each of these two cases a Brahman, proud of his learning and austerity, is made to go to the merchant and the hunter for enlightenment on the secret of *dharma* in actual practice.

The conception of performing one's duty in a disinterested and perfect way, unmindful of gain or loss of advantage, as acts which one has to perform, constitutes the teaching of *karma-yoga* in the Bhagvad Gita. It is this which formed a powerful inspiration to some of our greatest leaders of public life in modern times, TILAK and GANDHI. Such a conception of action and duty effects also a synthesis between the secular and the sacred.

This doctrine of *Svadharma* is part of the functional organization of society, the *varnas*, usually referred to as caste, and often attacked these days and considered by the social scientists referred to above as an impediment to the advancement of the country. The *varna* or caste of Hinduism need not engage us for long now, as it has figured in several books and discussions. I shall content myself with only one quotation on it, from MEREDITH TOWN-SHEND's ASIA AND EUROPE (p. 72): He says "I firmly believe caste to be a marvelous discovery, a form of socialism, which through the ages, has protected Hindu society from anarchy and from the worst evils of industrial and competitive life – it is an automatic poor law to begin with and the strongest known form of trade unionism." The *varna* is comparable to an orchestra in which, irrespective of the nature of the instrument one plays, all contribute to a common end of a rich and perfect symphony. There is no high and low in this. The fisherman in KALIDASA's play SAKUN-TALA, when the city guards ridicule him for his calling, replied that however reproachable from other points of view, one's calling is not to be abandoned. "*Sahajam kila yad vininditam na khalu tat karma vivarjaniyam*" (Act VI prelude).

It is one thing to point out how, within the framework of Hinduism, there are concepts and beliefs which could form an adequate basis and motive force for modern developments, so that it is not necessary to throw Hinduism overboard for this purpose. It is quite another thing to accept wholesale the new doctrine that economic development is the sole aim of our life. What is the difference between this doctrine and the Marxist ideology? As has been shown above, on the basis of the concept of *purusharthas*, religion and spirituality are as much the legitimate and natural impulses and aspirations of man as economic gain. No apology is needed on behalf of religion. Nor does sovereign religion have to bow to the new master, adjust itself to its gradually declining positions, and eventually fade out.

The assumptions, on the basis of which the changes that have been coming on are taken for granted as if inevitable, are themselves not proven or universally accepted. First among them is the idea of a linear progress. Many doubt whether there is such a progress at all. Some see rather a rhythm of ebb and flow. Some, with the Hindus, see the movement as cyclic. Some, taking their stand on the second law of thermodynamics, consider that energy is running down and order passing slowly into disorder. "And we should expect after ever-increasing complexity of life", says KARL JASPERS in his PERENNIAL SCOPE OF PHILOSOPHY, "a return to simplicity ... science itself might show us the way." (pp. 258–9) If all this change is justified in the name of history, one may with authority say that historicalness is not a value (ALDOUS HUXLEY, ENDS AND MEANS) and what has to be done inevitably is not necessarily what ought to be done. Religious truth is beyond time and history and any attempt to bring it up-to-date will only dilute or distort it. In the modern context, for example, it is being made into something merely "humanistic" – almost a sociological form, nay "a kind of idealism whereby the world is to become an easier and more pleasant place to live in." (LORD NORTHBOURNE).

It is sometimes said that Hinduism is much engrossed in individual salvation and does not attach much importance to working for others' salvation. Nothing can be farther from the truth. Such an assumption would negate the whole history of the *acharyas*, saints and mystics of Hinduism, and the role they have played. Attention can be drawn to several contexts and ideas in Hinduism and its writings which speak of men of knowledge and realization still functioning for the benefit of the world, *lokasamgraha*, and being as active after attaining knowledge as during their striving for it, with this difference; that their present activity is free and unbinding. The realized souls continue in our midst for our welfare, as KALIDASA says of his sage Kanva. Krishna has explained this clearly in the Gita, pointing to himself as the example of one continuing to be active, although free from any objective of personal gain. This is the ideal of a *jivan mukta* that has been taken by some of our thinkers as an ideal for the selfless public worker. Nor is there real substance in the argument that Hinduism suffers from a pessimistic outlook. To know the real value of material things is not pessimism. He is a fool who thinks that merely by multiplying one's wants or goods one is adding to his happiness.

The more the wants and desires are fulfilled, the more they grow, says Viyasa, even as by gratifying fire, you do not quench it but only inflame it more:

Na Jatu Kamrah Kamanam Upa – bhogena samyati / Havisa Krsnavartmeva bhuya evopa ciyate.

The discoveries, remedies or new aids to enjoyment are not unmixed blessings; they bring on other reactions, dreamt of or undreamt of. The real remedy to this is the religious ideal, of chastening the course of the second and third *purusarthas*, *artha* and *karma* by the first *dharma*. In fact as embodied by Rama and Yudhisthira, and as expounded inimitably and with unending variation by Vyasa, *dharma* has, on the active plane, been the most inspiring ideal of Hinduism. It is still a potent force animating the nation. ZAEHNER, whose question about the survival of Hinduism I quoted at the beginning of this paper, answers the question by saying that so long as this *dharmic* ideal is there, Hinduism will not disappear. ZAEHNER says that this *dharma* is "what gives Hinduism in all its phases its peculiar bitter-sweet flavor – the flavor too of a thirst for righteousness in an unrighteous world and a constant yearning for truth wherever it may be found. This flavor is embodied as nowhere else in the legendary figure of Yudhisthira, the gentle compassionate 'King of righteousness' and in the historical figure of MAHATMA GANDHI who declared that 'Truth is God'."

"... a system of which the essential basis is production for profit", observes J. D. BERNAL (National Scientific Research – Progress 1934), "leads by its own impulses into the present highly unstable and dangerous economic and political situation where plenty and poverty, desire for peace and the preparation for war exist side by side." The situation is best reflected in that country which is the model for the whole world now, the United States. Guided by its own ideals and time, tested by the concepts of its religious culture, some of which have been explained in this paper, India should strive to evolve her own type of modernization. That this is quite possible is what strikes a foreign student of India and Hinduism – WILFRED CANTWELL SMITH, who asks in his MODERNIZATION OF A TRADITIONAL SOCIETY (Indian Council of World Affairs, Delhi): "Can the U.S. and the Soviet Union both be modern but in different ways? Are we sure that modernity will not be (or cannot be) multiform? Could India become modern in quite a different way yet"? (p. 9) If such a third way evolves in this country, we may say, it will, once again, be by the triumph of the role and relevance of religion, of *dharma*.

In the course of its long history and its handling of different schools, Hinduism gave certain scientific analyses which are also relevant today when we are in the midst of many religions and want to understand them. Religions grow in particular times and countries and among particular peoples, and take on different backgrounds and social and cultural features. When they expand over further areas and are accepted by more peoples, more such features become incorporated into them. For example, in the Hibbert Lectures of Dr. EDWIN HITCH, INFLUENCE OF GREEK IDEAS AND USAGES UPON THE CHRISTIAN CHURCH (London, 1907), one reads the story of how the simple Sermon on the Mount took the creed of Greek philosophers, and thus something Semitic came under Hellenistic influence. It is the duty of the discerning to see the core, through the external and the historical.

This insight helps us with real understanding, transcending names such as Christianity, Islam, Buddhism, Saivism and so on, names which may produce mutual allergy during discussions in a colloquium.

In its laboratory, Hinduism has given us a threefold scientific analysis of all religions. No religion can escape these three characteristics. Just as all food, from whatever area and of whatever substance, color, taste, form of consuming, etc. has to be assimilated as carbohydrates, proteins and fats, so also have all religions to be analysed into the three approaches or *margas*: *karma*, *bhakti* and *jnana*. As *bhakti-marga*, several of them cut across their historical and cultural milieu and come together under one process. Their appeal or applicability also gets widened accordingly, leaving behind race, geography etc. Men take to these approaches by character and mental attitude and other endowments and equipment, which Hinduism calls *adhikara*. *Adhikara*, meaning fitness or competence, is another idea which is relevant in the context of understanding the genius of Hinduism and its organization of its multiple cults and practices on a ladder scheme, each of which is not untrue for the aspirant, but is transcended when the higher one is reached in his upward progress.

Hinduism makes a rational approach to man and his capacity, need and qualification, and instead of prescribing the same treatment to all, gives each what suits him or will be fruitful to him in his stage. As LORD NORTH-BOURNE says in his RELIGION IN THE MODERN WORLD (London, 1963), "There are degrees or planes of reality...There is no discontinuity between the planes of reality...the lower is always a symbol of the higher and as such can suggest or evoke it." (pp. 32, 33). The classical exposition of the three paths, or *yogas* as they are also called, is in the Bhagvad Gita. In the Bhagvata, the most popular and powerful of the *puranas*, the same Krishna, in the course of his discourses to his kinsman Uddhava, prescribes this receipt for persons of different character and equipment: "The path of *knowledge* is for those who are weary of life; those who have yet desires should pursue the path of sublimation through *works*; and for those who are not completely indifferent nor too much attached the *devotional* path bears fruit."

The implications of *karma-yoga* and its relevance as an inspirer of action have been stressed already. All action done in a devout spirit, as discharging one's duty and as participation in a divine program is not only a form of adoration; it is also a great aid to the disciplining of oneself, a *sadhana*. *Bhakti* is the most widespread form all over the world and it appeals to the bulk of humanity for reasons adduced by the Bhagvata. But it has some attendant features which have to be overcome in the larger interests of religious understanding. To love one form only and to believe that that is the only road to salvation breeds sectarianism and the urge to convert others. History is too full of the wars and the destruction of cultures in the name of such religions. To quote ALDOUS HUXLEY in his ENDS AND MEANS, "It is the business of the rational idealist to harp continually upon this all-important fact. In this way, perhaps, he may be able to mitigate the evil tendencies which history shows to be inherent in the way of devotion and the belief in a personal deity."

The third and highest path is that of knowledge, which does not eschew either acts or devotion but includes them and eventually transcends them. Knowledge also idealizes acts in the form of rites and rituals, by giving them symbolic and esoteric interpretations which are meaningful as meditative exercises. This intellectualizing of acts began with the Brahmanas and Upanishads and was developed later as a regular interpretative scheme to bring out a higher meaning from the myths and stories of the epics and cult-acts, thus taking the former out of historicity and saving the latter from vulgarity. This deritualization, as a social scientist would designate it, serves as a golden link between action and knowledge, and devotion and knowledge. The best-known of these rarefied acts is *japa*, mentally revol-

ving a sacred name or formula, as a higher substitute for a physical performance or worship, etc. The relevance of this will be appreciated today when
on the one hand we encounter the possibility of duly performing the rites
and rituals in the midst of the many preoccupations of modern life, and
on the other, the intellectual attitude of the age which prefers such an
approach.

There is another department of acts as a *sadhana* which should be mentioned for its universal relevance. Whether it is action, devotion or knowledge that we choose, discipline of the senses and concentration of mind
are necessary; these are of utmost necessity in the path of knowledge, but
they are of use in the path of devotion also. Knowledge and its dawning
on one is no matter of mere talk or profession; it involves strenous effort
and it is one of the unique gifts of Hinduism, the *sadhana* called *yoga*, which
the world has accepted for the physical as well as spiritual benefits it can
bestow.

The final Hindu standpoint with which I want to close is perhaps well-
known, but would bear repetition. For it is the most fundamental tenet,
and one whose relevance has grown in importance today when all religions
have met and they have to live together and understand each other. This is
neither a slender voice in the chorus of Hindu doctrine nor one of later
development. The most ancient and primary expression of Hinduism
embodies this as part of the intuition of the first sages. In the first book of
the Rigveda, we hear the declaration, "Truth is One, the Wise expound
it diversely; that one Truth they call by different names, *Agni* and so on."
The Vedanta gave this its firm metaphysical basis in the ultimate reality or
supreme Being, the One, Absolute, impersonal Brahman of the form of
Existence, Consciousness and Bliss, *Sat, Chit* and *Ananda*. It is the source of
the universe of name and form, which has its manifestation, being and
dissolution in it. It comprehends all forms including those personal manifestations, Saguna Brahman, through which it reaches out to those who seek
it through these forms because they are easier to grasp. These forms may
be any or many but all of them lead to the same one Summit. The Upanishads employ also the analogy of many rivers flowing from different regions
and reaching the same one ocean, an illustration which poets and hymnists
like the great KALIDASA and PUSHPADANTA employ. In the Bhagvad Gita, the
Lord declares that in whatever form men seek him, in that form he reaches
out to them, and whatever form of His a devotee adores in faith, in that
form he strengthens his faith.

The thesis of this supreme self with which all individual selves, themselves mutually identical, are one, places even ethical acts on a better and
higher philosophical basis, and love of fellow beings or charity towards
them becomes really sensible, without appearing to be sentimental or dis-
dainful. In his RELIGION IN THE MODERN WORLD, (London 1963) LORD NORTH-
BOURNE observes (pp. 78–79) "... in the last analysis and in its only pure

form, charity is the recognition of the fundamental identity of myself and my neighbor. Thus true charity is by no means synonymous with altruism, for altruism as such tends to be more separative than unitive."

It was on the basis of this one fundamental impersonal being with diverse personal forms, that Hinduism organized and reduced to understanding all the numerous forms and modes of worship that continuously manifested themselves. The universality and the eternal validity and vitality of Hinduism rest primarily on this fundamental. If Hinduism can call itself *sanatama dharma philosophia perennis*, it is because of this truth. There has been a continuous tradition of the philosophy of gnosis among all nations; the Greek philosophers, too, spoke of the one God with many names. The great relevance of this today is that it provides a key for the great religions to unlock their inner unity and not only understand each other better but also divert their energies spent on criticism or conversion to a common effort against irreligion, pseudo-religion and social, political and national substitutes for religion. The appreciation of this Hindu standpoint is gradually growing on students of religion and comparative religion all over the world, holding forth perhaps, in the not very distant future, the hope of the emergence of a world religion based on this universal principle.

In the book THE COMING WORLD CIVILIZATION, (New York 1956) WILLIAM ERNEST HOCKING speaks of this eventuality: "In all religions there are 'unlosable' essentials which appear in history in different forms and interpretations. With relations between religions thus relieved of confusion, at once by the growing unity of their unlosable essences, the understanding acceptance of variety follows." It is our hope that this understanding, the solvent of the many chains of troubles besetting humanity, will grow in relevance and depth and be strengthened by the work of the Temple of Understanding.

Parasparam bhavayantah
Sreyah param avapsyatha – Gita

"Cherishing each other, let us achieve our common goal of supreme welfare."

Christianity in a Pluralistic World

by

The Rev. PIERRE FALLON, S. J.
Calcutta; representative of the Vatican Secretariat for Non-Christians

The Rev. PIERRE FALLON, S. J.
Calcutta; representative of the Vatican Secretariat for Non-Christians

A QUESTION

Is the Christian religion still relevant today? Can it still give us, men and women of the Twentieth Century, the *Faith* we need in order to go on believing that reality is infinitely more than what appears to the eyes of our practical wisdom; the *Hope* that will illuminate our hearts and minds, and make us feel confident that human life has a meaning and leads somewhere; the *Love* which, redeeming us from the isolation of our self-centered individualism, will inspire us to work in fraternal collaboration with all our fellow-men to the building up of a new world of peace and justice and universal brotherhood?

Many people around us ask themselves this question: Has not modern science destroyed the very foundations of religious faith? Has not modern philosophy demonstrated that life is absurd and meaningless? Has not modern sociology made it clear that the City we have to build must be a profane and secular one, where human relations will be strictly functional and impersonal? Besides, has not history itself sufficiently exposed the inanity and irrelevance of the Christian religion? A dream, a beautiful dream it was. But has not that dream failed to materialize, and Christianity proven inadequate to its task of establishing peace, justice, and brotherhood?

It is a fact that many modern men and women of Christian heritage are inclined to regard the Christian religion as a thing of the past, a precious heirloom, a rich treasure-house of poetic images and symbols, a certain way of life inherited from their forefathers, with a familiar cycle of feasts and rituals and perhaps a code of personal conduct, but no longer the stupendous message that was to transform the world, the Divine Revelation which called men to freedom and joy. Like the two disheartened disciples walking away from Jerusalem towards Emmaus, they too would probably say: "We had great hopes, but....".

A DISTINCTION

Let us first of all distinguish clearly two very different questions: what is the relevance, influence or vitality of Christianity as the religion of the Western world? And, second, what is the relevance of Christianity as a world religion? Although born in Jerusalem, the Christian religion soon spread westward and its history came to identify itself to a large extent with the history of the Western world. For many centuries, it gave our Western world its spiritual unity; it gathered in its living and growing body the treasures of Graeco-Roman culture as also the varied traditions of the many barbarian ethnic groups which, under its tutelage, gradually developed into the nations of the West. Christianity did indeed mightily contribute to the education and the civilization of the West; it has, at all levels of life, profoundly influenced our ideals and institutions, and individual men and their social and political communities. Questions as to how far the religion of Christ today is still relevant to the life of the Western world: what is its vitality or influence in the various countries of the West, and which are the problems it faces there, are, of course, of the highest importance. But I judge that the scope of this Conference is broader.

It is the relevance of Christianity as a world religion that we must consider; and I do not speak here as a Western Christian, but in my role as a representative of Christianity as a "catholic", i.e. a universal, religion. In fact, from its very first origins, the Christian religion was never within the limits of the Western world; we know it well here in India, where Christianity struck its first and most indigenously generated roots long before the West became Christian. Let us therefore think of Christianity world-wide and not only of its Western expression.

THE ESSENCE OF CHRISTIANITY

What is Christianity? The whole Christian religion can be expressed in the simple formula: *Jesus is the Lord*. These few words proclaimed the central mystery revealed in Christ, the mystery of the Incarnation. Not a new metaphysical system, not a new ethical code, not a mystical gnosis or theoretical idea! A fact, an event, at once historical and transcendent: *The Word was made Flesh*. The humble reality of our earthly and human existence becomes one with the eternal and absolute plenitude of light and life and joy. Jesus, the Jew, who lived and taught, suffered and died in Palestine, is the Lord, Yahweh, the One whose name is ineffable, the One-without-a-second, to whom the Prophets have witnessed in all ages and nations. Jesus, the God-Man, the Way, the Truth, and the Life, the Saviour who died for the sins of all, and rose on the third day to lead men into the new life, calling all to be reborn in faith as sons of the Father, to live in the freedom of the spirit as the members of one family, one people of God!

I think this is Christianity.

THREE OBJECTIONS TO THE RELEVANCE OF
CHRISTIANITY AS A WORLD RELIGION

Has this Christianity still any relevance for the men of our times? Does not its historicity restrict its universal significance? Does not its proclamation of Jesus as the Lord and Saviour of all make it necessarily intolerant, and therefore unsuited to the secular and pluralistic world in which we now live? Does not its supernatural call to sacrifice and redemptive death make it alien to the modern spirit of humanism and the growing preoccupation of men with the earthly tasks that must be attended to here and now?

HISTORICITY AND CATHOLICISM

According to our Christian belief, God chose to come and enter into our human history. Jesus, in whom dwelt the plenitude of divinity, was a Jew who spoke the language of his time, who accepted the traditions and customs of his people; not the universal man of the philosophers, but a particular man at a particular moment of history.

Yet we know that he died precisely because he stood against the narrow particularism of the religious and political leaders of his nation: Jesus preached a gospel of salvation that was not to be restricted to any particular race or people. The history of the Christian religion has continued the history of Jesus: because it incarnates itself deeply in the various societies and nations that accept its message, Christianity becomes historically conditioned and limited in its outward forms. But it always remains greater than any one of its particular expressions; it has never allowed itself to become the exclusive monopoly of any one race or nation. It is continually entering into new forms of vital synthesis with the new cultures and traditions of the people who profess it. Therefore, though always concrete and historical, it remains of universal significance.

In recent times, we have all witnessed the considerable effort of *aggiornamento*, i.e. renewal and adjustment to modern conditions, that has been undertaken by the Christian Church in the Second Vatican Council: ancient liturgies and traditional systems of theology, administrative structures and institutional forms, practical codes of conduct and discipline, all these historical legacies of human origin have been, and are being, re-examined in the light of Christian Gospel and with regard to the changing conditions of our modern world.

INTOLERANCE AND PLURALISM

But, we asked ourselves, is not the Christian religion radically unsuited to the religious pluralism which, more and more, becomes normal in our modern secular societies? Does not its very claim to universalism or catholicity make it naturally intolerant and even perhaps fanatical? Is it not a fact that, in the past at least, the Christian Church rarely participated in inter-religious conferences, and that it showed little respect for non-Christian religions?

It is certain that religious tolerance has rightly come to be considered as one of the most precious achievements of the modern mind. Here, in India, in a very special manner, intolerance is thought to be incompatible with genuine religiousness.

Is the Christian religion in fact intolerant? And what is its attitude towards religious pluralism? These questions do not concern Christians only; they concern all sincere believers: how to reconcile, without compromise or falsehood, a deep attachment to our own religious beliefs and a cordial attitude of respect towards and fraternal collaboration with men professing other beliefs? How to keep in harmony the healthy and normal desire to share with others that which is for us a source of inspiration, and which we firmly believe to be truth of universal value, and that tolerance which is the necessary expression of our respect for the spiritual and personal freedom and dignity of our fellow men?

In our modern world, this question has assumed a very great importance. Men belonging to different religious traditions come every day into new forms of association; believers and unbelievers, theists, agnostics and materialists must meet and collaborate in a thousand ways. The days are past when there was a close link-up, a nearly inseparable unity, between religion and culture, the profession of a particular faith, and social or political membership in a state or community. The "closed society" has had to make room for the "open society" Uniformity of religious belief and practice can no longer be imposed by modern secular societies.

In the 19th Century and during the first decades of the 20th, the answer most commonly proposed to the problem of religious pluralism was that of *syncretism*. Under various guises, this syncretism prevailed in many places. It was often well-meant, generous and idealistic, but it was in fact confusing, and it could not but be distressing for all sincere believers. Christianity could have no truck with it. It was in fact the outcome of the philosophy which, directly or indirectly, dominated much of western thought for a long time: the metaphysical idealism of Hegel. Religion came to be regarded by many as a branch of philosophy, and the various religions of the world were supposed to be nothing but varied manifestations of the universal religion which, like the Idea of Hegelianism, objectivated itself in time and space through some dialectical process. Positivism and agnosticism came in the wake of idealism. Comparative religion and the first attempts to establish inter-religious conferences and parliaments long suffered from the dominating influence of scholars who were too often idealists, positivists or agnostics, philosophers rather than personal religious believers. Syncretism may have had its good points: it broke some barriers, it brought together some people who formerly had lived in complete ignorance of each other. It is today, like so many other 19th Century ideologies, a thing of the past.

True pluralism is an altogether different thing. It does not aim at promoting a new religion artificially constructed. It simply approaches the diversity of religious traditions with respect and an effort at positive understanding; it fosters an attitude of dialogue and collaboration, without asking anyone to abandon or belittle what is sacred and true to him. It is not based upon a philosophy and it does not reduce living faiths into categories of a preconceived system. The tolerance it teaches is not the agnostic's or the pragmatist's theoretical relativism, but the personal and existential respect every man owes to his fellow-men and the freedom of his conscience. With this pluralism Christianity is in complete accord.

The last Vatican Council, in an official Declaration on the attitude of the Church to the non-Christian religions, clearly stated that Christians should "through dialogue and collaboration with the followers of other religions ...recognize, preserve and promote the good things, spiritual and moral, as well as the socio-cultural values found among those belonging to other traditions"; the same Declaration invites us to consider "what men have in common and what draws them to fellowship." The religion of Christ is not out to destroy any of the precious values found in the various spiritual and cultural traditions of mankind.

I may add that Christianity, because of its belief in Christ Jesus, the God-Man, is opposed to all forms of fanaticism and intolerance. Christians do believe that Christ is the Word of God who illumines every man, that his salvific grace reaches far beyond all the visible limits of the historical Church which he founded, and that no man of good will is outside the influence of his life. That is why there can be no impatience in our zeal to proclaim his gospel; we know him to be there, already invisibly at work in the hearts and minds of all men.

Besides, true pluralism means freedom from social and political compulsion in religious matters. Christianity has again and again opposed various forms of spiritual totalitarianism and regimentation. The separation of Church and State, the clear distinction between temporal and spiritual realms, the sacred principle that religious faith must be the free assent of man to what in conscience he believes to be true: these are essential values in the eyes of all Christians. This is why genuine pluralism is in perfect harmony with Christian doctrine.

OTHER WORLDLINESS AND HUMANISM

Our third question was whether Christianity was not incompatible with true humanism; whether a modern man, intent on his responsibility here and now in the world, should not find irrelevant a religion that preaches the Kingdom of Heaven, that insists on the sinfulness of man and his need of supernatural grace; that affirms the primacy of spiritual values; that recognizes suffering, poverty, and detachment as ways especially blessed by God. The other-worldliness of Christianity may seem to set it against the spirit of our modern age. I am sure that much of this is not peculiar to Christianity: all the religions of mankind may, in various manners, face the same challenge. Is the need of a religious faith what truly matters most in the Twentieth Century?

What are the great problems that beset the minds of men today? The sub-human misery of vast masses of men, and the under-developed condition of many regions of the world: the racial hatreds that divide men; the terrible anxiety caused by the possibility of nuclear warfare; the population explosion; the wide-spread dissatisfaction of youth, and the growing attraction of violence. Has religion a vital role to play in the solution of these agonizing problems? Has Christianity any relevance in our modern world context? Do men today still need religion?

I believe that the first thing which men stand in need of today, and lacking which they can never solve this century's earthly problems, is a strong and inspiring sense of *hope*. Only religion can give this hope. This religious hope is not the consolation to which men resort when everything else has failed them; it is not a Utopian optimism based upon some romantic idea of the natural goodness of man; this hope does not bypass the world, it looks at the world and man in the world with realism and a keen awareness of all that is evil in the world and in the heart of man, but it vanquishes all despair about man and about the world because it is founded upon an unshakable faith in God as creator and redeemer of the world. It gives us confidence and courage to accept our task in the world with joy and determination. Science, sociology, psychology, economic planning, all the technological resources of modern times, must be marshalled to solve our problems, but all these would be of no avail if, deeper than all these, a living hope were not there to inspire men. Modern man is anxious; he is frustrated in the midst of plenty, or desperate because of material insecurity and misery; he hungers for meaning, purpose, a constructive and prospective answer to his present unrest. I sincerely believe that religion has never been as relevant as it is today to the solution of our most vital human problems.

The second thing which our modern world needs today, a thing which again religion alone can give, is *respect for man as a person*. Man is more and more reduced to a mere number in a series, a creature whose personality is threatened by the machines and institutions which our technological age has created. He feels small, a small cog in an immense and impersonal machine, and he is often treated as a mere object, a thing manipulated by powerful forces that crush his human dignity. I believe that religion is the only real safeguard of true humanism because it alone proclaims the unique greatness of man. For a religious believer, every single man, whatever his rank or his intelligence, his race, his power, is worthy of infinite respect because he is loved by God, called by God to share in the divine life, because he is a temporal creature with an eternal destiny, a material being endowed with a spiritual soul. This personal and spiritual dimension of man is often lost sight of nowadays; this is why so many solutions proposed to our human problems fail to solve them: they do not take into account the total reality of man.

If religion is needed by man to keep his hope alive and to safeguard the respect due to him as a person, religion again is vitally needed by modern man to protect his *freedom*. And, first of all, religion clearly affirms this spiritual freedom against all the doctrines and ideologies based upon determinism. It further educates man to freedom, this freedom having to be conquered through a life-long struggle against the compulsions of passion and instinct. Religious faith alone can free man from all the impersonal forces that enslave his mind and his heart: our modern world, with all the power of mass propaganda techniques, makes it difficult for us to keep mentally and spiritually free. Public opinion, fashion, political ideologies, practical materialism with its commercial idolatry of money, sex and pleasure, these are tyrannical masters; to remain free, we must maintain in our lives a clear awareness of absolute values. Only through being firmly anchored to the absolute can we fight successfully against these impersonal tyrannies. I should add, and this takes us even deeper into the very reality of religious life, only through our humble and loving reliance upon divine grace can we possess our souls and minds in freedom.

But, most important of all, *love* is that which the world requires if the problems that face us today are to be solved. Not the sentimental philanthropy of romantic dreamers, not the facile and abstract "love of humanity" preached by philosophers, but the dedicated and self-sacrificing love which only religion can inspire. Men today realize better than before how much all are organically united in the human family, and yet bitter conflicts still set man against man in our modern world. The very individualism of modern society has painfully increased the competitiveness of men. The 19th Century doctrine of enlightened self-interest has proved shallow and deadly. If our racial hatreds are to be surmounted, if justice and some equality are to be brought about among the people of the world, if our functional and mechanical life is to be made humanly livable, we need more and more men who can love. But love does not come easily to man; without religion, all human loves tend to become selfish and narrow.

I was expected to speak of the relevance of Christianity in the modern world. The things I have said just now are true, I believe, of the Christian religion; they are true also of all the great religions represented here. This is why I have purposely abstained from presenting them as exclusive characteristics of Christianity. To save men from anxiety and despair, to preserve and foster the respect man is entitled to as a person, to help him in his struggle against all that would enslave him, and untiringly to call all men to love, this is the duty of all religious believers, and in the fulfilment of this sacred duty we must all fraternally collaborate.

WAYS OF MAKING RELIGION RELEVANT IN THE MODERN WORLD

That religion is relevant today is clear to us. Yet there are many all around us who question or deny this relevance. It is therefore important that we ask ourselves why many modern men and women find religion irrelevant.

One reason may well be the fact that, often, the language of religion, its conceptual representation and imagery, have become meaningless for many. A constant effort has to be made to re-interpret our religious beliefs in terms clearly intelligible and significant to people living in the world of today.

Another and more fundamental reason is that, in the minds of many, religion is associated with social and political conservatism. Great religious leaders and dedicated believers have always been rebels who refused to compromise with injustice and untruth, but there have been numerous others who never practised their religion whole-heartedly. At various times, political leaders have exploited religion by patronizing it; religious believers have also sought in various ways the support and alliance of wordly forces, thus compromising the spiritual purity and freedom of their religious action. Besides, the condemnation by religion of all forms of violence and hatred has created the impression that religion is hostile to social change.

It is the duty of all religious men today to work uncompromisingly and fearlessly for social justice, peace and true brotherhood among men of all races and nations.

Thirdly, religion is looked upon by many modern people as unscientific and irrational; this is mainly due to the long and unjustified prevalence of last century's rationalism and positivism. We have seen that contemporary philosophers have denounced the geometrical simplifications of rationalism and many leading scientists today recognize that the seeming conflict between science and religion was the result of a misunderstanding. The acknowledgment of "mystery" and transcendence has come back into the very midst of modern thought, including scientific thought. Masses of people, however, are still dominated by the popular prejudices which the philosophers and scientists of yesterday created against religion. This widespread error can be overcome only if religious believers will enter into a cordial and respectful dialogue with unbelievers, so that these prejudices may be removed and all may perceive that religion gladly accepts the discoveries and certitudes of genuine science and never asks from man the abdication of his intellect.

CONCLUSION

Is the Christian religion still relevant today? Is modern man still in need of religious faith? As a Christian priest living in close touch with young Christian people, as a college teacher who has known personally many students belonging to different religious traditions and communities, I can answer without hesitation that religion has never been as relevant as it is today in this world which is, all around us, searching for a way to more justice, more freedom, more love and brotherhood.

In spite of many revolts and denials, in spite of much bitterness and frustration, the youth of our time is hankering for faith, hope and love. I believe that the world that is growing under our eyes is, more eagerly and sincerely than ever before, searching for absolute values. Men, young and old, are in fact more "religious" than men have ever been before.

Whether they will or will not find the answers they are now anxious to discover may greatly depend upon the manner in which we believers not merely teach them our religious doctrines, but bear witness to them through our lives.

The Four Noble Truths and the Eightfold Path

by

H. S. H. Princess POON PISMAI DISKUL
President, The World Fellowship of Buddhists, Bangkok, Thailand

Throughout history the practice of adherence to and belief in religion has been a virtually universal aspect of human society. And, as a rule, the increase in complexity and sophistication of a given culture bore with it an accompanying increase in the level of ethical and philosophical development of that society's religious thought.

Today we find mass atheism, skepticism and indifference. True, these anti- or nonreligious attitudes existed in earlier times, even back in ancient Greece and India. But in olden times they were largely confined to select groups of philosophers or other exclusive minorities. Today these ideas have penetrated to nearly all social levels (regardless of education) among the advanced nations of the world. In Europe and America they have insidiously encroached upon the traditional forms of religion. Educated members of the free Asian nations have begun to follow in the same direction.

It is not religion alone which seems threatened. Ethics, philosopy, metaphysics and mysticism also appear to wither before the onslaught of industrialization, science and psychology. Such concepts as justice, virtue, Infinite Being and Transcendental Absolute which occupied the minds of the ancients are now challenged as being hypothetical at best. At worst they are pure verbiage and syllogisms lacking empirical and experiential verification. Spiritual experiences now take the status of psychological phenomena and sometimes can be better induced by chemistry than by meditation or prayer. Ethics as a philosophy suffers the same fate as metaphysics. Ethics as a behavioral code for conducting one's life, is, in the eyes of traditional moralists, becoming mocked and disregarded.

Such are the features of the modern age. What then of religion? Even the newest of the existing major religions, Islam, is well past its first millennium. Christianity rapidly approaches its two-thousandth birthday, while Taoism, Buddhism, Confucianism, Zoroastrianism and Jainism all share roughly contemporary origins dating around 500 B. C. Judaism and Hinduism extend even further back into antiquity.

Our religions, then, are all products of bygone eras. They arose at a time when men thought in terms of magic, spirits and myths. Insanity was demon possession; hallucinations, messages from the divine. The sun moved around a stationary world, and one's fate could be altered by magic rituals or by flattery and offerings to supernatural powers.

Banana leaves as wrappings and thatched grass for roofs have been used for centuries. With the advent of paper, plastics and sheet metal they quickly fell into relative disuse. Will the same happen to religion as men learn to modify and control their environment and unlock the mysteries of creation? Will devout congregations be sought out and scrutinized by anthropologists and psychologists in the same manner that these scholars now pursue the Australian aborigines?

Each religion must endeavour to answer these questions and challenges on its own. As a Buddhist, I shall endeavour to answer these questions within the framework of Buddhist thought.

First of all, before any meaningful approach can be taken towards a Buddhist position, one must clarify what form of Buddhism one is considering. The religious movement started in the Fifth Century B. C. by Gautama Buddha has, in the intervening centuries, taken on diverse forms and paths of development as it spread to new lands and cultures and intermingled with local beliefs and practices. Thus, I wish to confine my discussion to the form of Buddhism known as Theravada, which is the prevailing religion of Ceylon, Burma, Thailand, Cambodia and Laos. But I must be even more specific than this; for I do not wish to discuss the various local traditions, ceremonies and later schools of thought which have become attached to Theravada. Rather I shall discuss the earliest known form of Buddhist thought – the teachings of the Buddha as recorded in the Pali language scriptures known as the Suttas and Vinaya.

If one confines his attention to these earliest known Buddhist scriptures, the western reader is often surprised by the contemporary ideas contained in writings which date back over 2000 years.

Perhaps most appealing to the modern mind (whether scientifically oriented or not) is the Buddhist emphasis upon free and rational inquiry. "Do not believe out of blind faith, do not believe out of scripture, do not believe out of tradition", said the Buddha. "Do not believe me just because it is I who speak. But when you have seen, examined and experienced for yourself, then believe." Only the mind freed of vested interests and prejudices will really be able to see and truly understand. Thus we read, "If others speak against me or against our order, be not angered or dejected. If they praise us, be not elated. Rather analyze what has been said and weigh its merits." Unlike the mystics of his time, the Buddha made full use of logic, debate and reasoning based upon experiential data rather than metaphysical. He placed experience before logic in his quest for truth, and thus when he did use logic, it was based upon facts readily admitted by all.

Instead of commenting upon Ultimate Reality, he spoke of craving and sorrow, of ordinary human experience. For, he explained, it is in the here and now that we can act and thus affect our destinies. Moreover, the Buddha never claimed a monopoly on truth. The truth was there for any man to find. His authority lay only in the fact that he had discovered it first and could show others the way to this discovery.

In order to explain the central concepts of Buddhist teaching and practice we should first note the way in which Buddhism views man and his relationship to the world about him.

The Buddha regarded the question of ultimate beginnings as irrelevant to the problems of life in the present. Change and cause and effect are the paramount features of the Buddhist concept of the universe. All things mental, physical and social go through an unending process of birth, growth, decay and death. Nothing finite is static, immortal or unchanging. Whatever has an origin is subject to cessation, be it man or mountain, consciousness or constellation. And what is it that regulates this unending flux and mutation? The answer is cause and effect. Each existing condition becomes the cause of future conditions, and these effects in turn become the causes of conditions which arise after them. Even the world itself will, after great eons of time, wear away but other worlds have existed before, and others will continue to arise into the unending future. There need not then be a beginning or an end to time but rather eternal cause and effect with world evolutions and dissolutions stretching back into the infinite past and continuing into the infinite future. All of these concepts are clearly stated in the Pali scriptures and require no degree of alternation or reinterpretation to find compatibility with the view of modern science.

Such is the way in which Buddhism views man and the world. How does this relate to the religion as lived and practiced?

In Buddhist thought the central issue in life is neither philosophical in the sense of resolving ultimate mysteries nor religious in the sense of worship, rites and ceremonies. Rather the prime concern is happiness and sorrow. There are moments of true happiness and fulfillment and moments of sorrow, frustration, irritation and despair. All this comes about through cause and effect, and pleasurable and displeasurable mental states are no exceptions. Thus the solution to living is to understand those factors which produce desirable or undesirable states of mind and with this understanding to guide our lives in such a way as to minimize the unwholesome while developing the wholesome to its maximum possible realization. Consequently the central teaching of Buddhism is the Four Noble Truths.

The first of the Four Truths simply states that suffering, frustration, discomfort and unwanted experiences in general are an inherent aspect of life. The second states that the primary cause of such discomforts is desire or misdirected pleasure seeking. Third, we are told that suffering can be overcome; and fourth the means by which this is done.

The last of these Four Truths, known as the Eightfold Path, thus forms the basis of Buddhist practice. It includes the disciplines, the practices and the insights by which one may grow spiritually.

Feelings and desires determine our behavior and also our consequent happiness or sorrow. Therefore, the purpose of the Eightfold Path is to produce, by means of self-training, a new and better human being and to enable one to progressively mature towards the relative or absolute realization of the Noble Truths. These practices are both negative and positive. On the negative side one seeks the eradication of greed, hatred, egotism, delusion. The positive ones are to cultivate and develop kindness, compassion, equanimity, wisdom and insight. Greed, hatred and other unwholesome mental states are not only predisposed to sorrowful consequences; in addition they are in and of themselves agitated and discomforting. Conversely, kindness and compassion are more than forerunners of happy conditions; by their very nature they are rich and rewarding experiences.

It should be noted that Buddhism regards the human mind as a compounded phenomenon of various attributes and qualities. Consequently the techniques for development and purification of the mind must likewise be multi-dimensional and varied in accordance with individual needs. Educating the mind to right understanding; guiding speech, habits and profession into harmonious life patterns; cultivation of discipline and energy and meditative stilling of the mind to bring about awareness of subtle thoughts and feelings that normally escape awareness – these are the techniques by which one progresses along the Eightfold Path. This is the practice of Buddhism as originally taught by the Buddha himself.

Now, acknowledging that actions are preceded first by thought and motivation, we see that good and evil originate from the mind. Thus a mind which has realized the Buddhist goals of subduing greed, hatred and egotism while developing kindness, wisdom and compassion is a mind which will have a natural and spontaneous virtue. The need for arbitrary rules of conduct will be greatly lessened and one's goodness will be genuine rather than enforced.

It may be seen that while Buddhism proceeds from a very different set of premises than most other religions, we note a nearly complete agreement as to the standards of ethical conduct: love, kindness, charity and generosity are universally hailed by all of man's great religions regardless of what concepts their doctrines are built upon, and Buddhism not only teaches us to be kind; by psychological practices it tells how to achieve the genuine feeling that is kindness. For kindness and compassion, like all other aspects of the mind and this universe, arise through cause and effect.

In our discussion of Buddhism to this point we see it as a system of psychological principles and practices which an individual can apply to the benefit of his own spiritual advancement and emotional well-being. Thus the prime value of Buddhism in the modern world is that it shows one a way to happiness and peace of mind regardless of the political and social environment. However, it would be erroneous to assume that the Buddha's doctrine was personal to the exclusion of concern for human relationships and society at large.

The reason for emphasis upon individual development was founded upon the principle that the blind cannot lead the blind; or as the Buddha stated, "One, himself sunk in the mire of greed and delusion, cannot pull another out of that mire." One should first purify oneself to be able to show the way to others.

We can only have a better world when we first have better people. Fear, jealously, egocentrism, hatred and greed are the original cause of human strife, be it petty crime or global war. Education, legislation and arbitration, while useful countermeasures, will not suffice to penetrate to the core of human motivation and alter one's basic feelings. Buddhism is structured to do just this. In fact such is its primary concern.

Personality cannot be separated from society. While the sum total of personalities determines the character and quality of a given society, conversely society influences and formulates the development of personality. This fact was readily acknowledged by the Buddha. He did not advocate social reforms such as we think of today but did deal directly with the social injustices of the time. Perhaps the best example is the caste system. He did not advocate a social revolution to replace this system, but any person who became a Buddhist ceased to have caste identity and thus was no longer subject to caste regulations. He thereby afforded men and women a way to escape from this social injustice. In similar manners he opposed slavery and elevated the social status of women.

Recognizing that civilizations have flourished under a variety of different political systems and that because of the universal law of change no society or culture will endure forever, the Buddha did not advocate any particular type of government. When speaking of monarchies he said the responsibility lay with the king, and the king should cultivate justice, charity, compassion and virtue both for the prosperity of the nation and as an example for the government officials and common citizens. A few democratic states existed at the time of the Buddha, and of these he said that they would continue to flourish so long as the citizens could assemble and meet in harmony and maintained good moral standards.

In the centuries following the Buddha, his followers built hospitals and rest houses in accordance with his teaching of compassion. The great Indian Emperor, ASOKA, in the Third Century, B. C. as a result of his conversion to Buddhism, stopped all wars and conquests, built wells and carried out other acts of public welfare. Other Buddhist rulers have followed this example.

And of illness he said: "Whosoever would honor me, whosoever would follow me, whosoever would take my advice, he should wait upon the sick."

And to his disciples he said, "Go forth into the world to spread the Teaching for the benefit, welfare and happiness of all beings." Once kindness and compassion gain prominence in human motivations, then will men strive to better the world in whatever way their immediate environment affords, be it food given to a hungry stranger or a multi-million dollar campaign against world hunger.

Thus, we Buddhists are trying to follow his sublime steps.

May all beings be well and happy in a just peace.

Religion in the Twentieth Century with Special Reference to Islam

by

Dr. Syed Vahiduddin
Professor and Head of the Department of Philosophy, University of Delhi

Unto Allah belong the East And the West and whithersoever ye turn, there is Allah's countenance.
   Lo! Allah is All-Embracing, All-knowing. (Koran-II, 115)
   O mankind! Be careful of your duty to your Lord Who created you from a single soul and from it created its mate and from the twain hath spread abroad a multitude of men and women. (Koran-IV)
   O mankind! Lo! We have created you male and female, and have made you nations and tribes that ye may know one another. Surely the noblest of you in the sight of God is the most God-fearing of you. God is all-knowing, All-aware. (Koran-XLIX, 13)

Religion changes its aspect in the varied context of history and it may even have different meanings in different phases of an individual's spiritual development. If at one time the dogmatic content seems to be decisive; at other times it is the emotional attitude or moral commitment which expresses best the meaning of religion. But it is futile to consider any one aspect as exhaustive of the religious life or (to speak the language of Indian tradition) to consider *karma*, *bhakti* or *gayana* as exclusive expressions of religious awareness. Even dogmatic involvement cannot be isolated from the attitude and behaviour of the religious individuality. Dogmas offer metaphysical commitments which others can accept or reject. It is a peculiarity of the religious situation that dogmas cannot be accepted or rejected on purely rational grounds.

This is indeed true of all metaphysical propositions. Their claim to truth does not rest on theoretical evidence, and religious metaphysics has seldom pretended to offer any rational verification. Reason has only a two-fold function. It clarifies concepts and delimits the area of their application. The claim to truth goes beyond the arbitration of reason, and reference is made to non-rational evidence through nonrational means. Even when rational theology has brought out arguments in support of its contentions, these arguments have not been absolutely decisive. Their intention has been to create an atmosphere in which the dogmatic contentions became relevant.

Hence a religion is bound to be a multi-dimensional structure and its socio-moral character involves features which enable it to respond to the challenging situations of life from its own resources. Its dogmatic content is essentially an expression of its metaphysical commitment. But its metaphysical elan is not wholly expended in its dogmatic understanding, and the intellectual changes wrought by time force every religion to reassess the dogmatic formulation of its basic metaphysical position. This makes every religion a dynamic growth in the understanding of its living content. Every age has its own understanding and there is no reason why the classical formulations should be considered final.

Even the attitudes which are associated with any religion change with the tempo of historical change. The militant attitude which characterized earlier generations might give way to contemplative inwardness, or pietistic passivity might be forced to take up arms in response to the unexpected and unpredictable challenges of life. There is no reason why any one phase of religious life should be characterized as alone expressive of its own inner dynamic. The multifarious possibilities which a religion hides within itself leads to a shift in its characteristic expression. When such a reassessment happens within the framework of a religion it is often construed as a betrayal of the religion's original ethos or it may be viewed as having been determined by extraneous facts or having resulted from foreign infiltrations.

The very fact that a religion survives as a living force which determines the life and actions of untold members of the human community, which brings solace in suffering and which gives man principles to live by in every age, shows that it has relevance beyond the confines of the community which is its historic mouthpiece. This universal relevance is what we are interested in at present. When we emphasize the transcommunal relevance of religion we go beyond its dogmatic formulation to the basic roots. In contemporary reference we can say that it is the existential impact of religion which makes it relevant to the crisis of civilization. Recent attempts to evaluate the human situation have taken man as we know him empirically, and have taken into account his helplessness and the fact that he is an unfinished product and an incomplete animal who has to complete for himself what is not given to him beforehand.

No wonder man's first emergence appears to him as a state of being "thrown" on earth in a state of existential helplessness. WHITEHEAD once defined religion as what man does with his solitariness. But simple solitary isolation cannot produce any religion. In religion, solitariness is transcended and man feels that even in apparent loneliness he is not alone. The Koran expresses this dramatically when it says: "Three men conspire not secretly but He is the fourth of them, neither five men but He is the sixth of them, neither fewer than that, neither more, but He is with them, whatever they may be." (Koran-LVIII).

The sense of loneliness can only be overcome by the awakening of consciousness of an all-abiding Presence and a primordial communication with

God. Religion is not born of fear nor is it a reaction against fear. The fear of natural objects which gives rise to defense mechanisms in primitive man has often led to the wrong conclusion that it is fear which provokes religious consciousness. What gives rise to religious consciousness is really something else – the pervasive dread (*Angst*) which persists as a basic condition of man even when no objects are associated with it. It is of course true that this dread is basically the dread of death; all that potentially or actually threatens life evokes it. But even when man is mortally afraid there is not necessarily a religious response. Modern existentialism is carried by a genuine religious motive: to encounter man in his ontological nakedness and isolation. But what religion means is the realization that man is not basically isolated. It reveals to him that existential isolation and solitariness can be countered by a metaphysical realization of divine participation. What comes first metaphysically is not isolation, but participation and communion, although in human knowledge isolation takes precedence over participation. Hence the development of scientific consciousness can eliminate fear, but it cannot overcome dread. Dread can only be transcended in religion and only so is isolation ultimately overcome. The knowledge of my own self has a transcending movement and leads beyond personal isolation. Thus in religious consciousness man is not forsaken and forlorn but participates in a cosmic life, though this participation in a cosmic process is given varying expressions in different religions. In one religious perspective, man is a ceaseless itinerant in life's march, laden with the responsibility to make good the errors of the earlier manifestations. In another religious perspective, what is to come is determined by what we do here and now. In any case, man's life is not wholly expended in the spatio-temporal manifestations which we call our earthly career, and it is necessary to maintain a close watch on our thoughts and doings, for these are the stuff out of which our pattern of life is molded on the next plane of our existence.

Hence the relevance of religion in our times is its existential relevance, its capacity to enable man to hope against heavy odds, to stand firmly when to all appearances the situation seems hopeless, not to accept defeat in any circumstances and to feel that no defect can ever be ultimate. Islam now has a meaning for us only in its existential relevance, in its perpetual insistence on the grace of God that never fails, however belated it might appear to the impatient soul of man. Man is characterized as a creature given to haste, as a being who always is prone to rush ahead of due time and thus to precipitate disaster. But hope is the sign of faith. In the Islamic perspective hope and faith are knit together and the loss of hope is the loss of faith. None despair of the grace of God but the faithless.

Now, the consciousness of being thrown into the universe appears only as an initial consciousness. In fact, in the Islamic perspective, both self-consciousness and world-consciousness involve God-consciousness'. Psychologically the consciousness of self and the consciousness of nature may claim priority but ontologically the God-consciousness is basic. As has been observed since Aristotle, what comes first to our knowledge need not be first in itself.

The relevance of religion is shown by the answers that it can provide in the stresses and strains of modern life. Life has always been a challenge and the ability to meet it adequately is what guarantees its preservation. These challenges are not directed to man's physical existence alone but to the totality of his being. Again we may refer to the existential character of these challenges. Inadequacy of response leads to mental disequilibrium and ultimately to disintegration of the personality. Life seems pale and bloodless and devoid of meaning and significance. Art and religion both make the insignificant significant but this transformation is much more profound in religion. The seemingly insignificant does not become significant only in so far as it is informed with meaning in an aesthetic framework. What religion does is not only to make the insignificant lose its insignificance but also to expose all hollow pretensions to value and significance. In other words the seemingly insignificant is shown to be insignificant only in a temporal context, and to be significant in terms of eternity.

The relevance of religion is not confined to any one level of human existence. It ranges from the lowest to the highest levels, from the economic to the metaphysical level. But it must be conceded that it is metaphysical conviction that determines even economic attitudes and behaviour. Islam's attitude to wealth and the hoarding of wealth is a classic example. In spite of the common notion that Islam is a naive world-affirmation, there is a strong negative note in the Koran: "What else is the world but an illusion, and a sport and play". This does not mean that the world is nothing but an illusion; only that it has developed a strong illusory aspect. And this illusory aspect is created mostly by over-emphasis on economic worth, and rivalry in wordly increase. The distinctions of wealth are not substantial, nor are the divisions made by race, religion, language or genealogical descent. The one most respectable before God is the one who fears the Lord and the best provision for what is to come is piety. Thus it is always the transcendental reference that is decisive.

Thus religion cannot claim any viability if it cannot maintain its relevance equally in the lowest and the highest human reference. The religious and the secular man are distinguished not only by the absence or the presence of the transcendental reference, but by the extent to which the transcendental is made effective. The pragmatists rightly emphasize that a religion which is not relevant for action is dead, though they ignore the fact that the transcendental reference has its own validity, and the human commitment makes no difference to it. Thus in Islam there is a close and inseparable bond between faith and action. A faith which does not work and which is ineffective in life cannot lay claim to any recognition; so far as human judgment is concerned man is judged only by what is accessible to our knowledge. Poets are taken to task for not being able to live up to their visions, for divorcing the vision from action. The inward life is accessible only to God. Thus in this recognition of the inaccessibility of man's inward life to external scrutiny there is involved a commitment to the uniqueness of personal existence and its sanctity. Man exists in his own right as an autonomous being. In spite of the fact that he cannot live outside social, regional, linguistic and national affiliations, he is still something more than any of these contingent associations in which he is called to play his role. This naturally awakens in man the right sense of values, leading him to eschew over-emphasis on goods, which have only an instrumental worth and which by no means touch the intrinsic merit of man. Islamic *Weltanschauung* is based on the concept of man according to which he is precariously poised between his divine origin and his eventual alienation, between his innate goodness and his propensity to evil.

When the Koran affirms that man was created in the best of forms and then thrown into the lowest depths it is referring to the idea of man who is created in the image of God and his subsequent failure to live up to his divine image. Human beings are divided into categories, some fulfilling the divine purpose and others betraying it. Indeed, from God we come and unto God we return, but the question is how we return. For us it is important to realize our original roots and then to strive to move back to the origin in a way that is consonant with the divine purpose. What is important to note is the idea of humanity as an organic unity, as one community. Men are created from a single self and, "Whosoever killeth a human being for other than manslaughter or corruption in the earth, it shall be as if he had killed all mankind, and whoso saveth the life of one, it shall be as he had saved the life of all mankind." (Koran-V, 32).

The Koran is addressed to man as man, to man who is unique in creation, and who has been assigned a mission which he himself ventured to choose without of course fully realizing the consequences of what he was choosing. In a remarkable passage, the Koran speaks of man as opting for a responsibility which nature refused to accept. "Lo! we offered the trust unto the heavens and the earth and the mountains, but they shrank from bearing it and were afraid of it. And man assumed it. Surely he has proved a tyrant (against himself) and foolhardy!" (Koran-XXXIII, 72).

What is it then which distinguishes man in creation? It can only be something from which all his other activities follow and which makes him qualified to create beauty and to become a moral agent capable of judging his own actions. It is reason which includes both theory and practice, thought and deed, that enables man to lead his life according to his own insight, without seeking guidance from nature and without being entirely predetermined in his activities.

What is then wrong with the world we live in? What ails the modern mind? The relevance of religion is brought home most emphatically when it is confronted with the problems of modern man. Man has become a problem for himself. Strangely enough, in spite of the fact that technological advances have brought men nearer and nearer, there has been no corresponding growth in men's spiritual relation to one another. Scientific advancement in the sphere of human welfare is nothing compared with man's advance in self-destruction. Death which is a most natural and spontaneous culmination of man's career on earth is artificially invoked by scientific ingenuity, and the mortality that should be accomplished as a matter of course is now brought about as a matter of force. But the question is not only how long a man lives and to what distances in the infinite space he can fly, but how he lives in the short span of life granted to him as an individual. The same may be said of nations. Every man has his own term, and every nation has its own termination. The question is how an individual or nation disposes of its potentialities within its own temporal frame-work. Two ways are open to either: to cooperate with God in establishing a meaningful order, or betray the purpose of creation and fall to a 'state which is worse than that of an animal. If man is created in God's image he should reflect those basic attributes of God which have human relevance and the principle which should govern human relations should be one of cooperation and goodwill and not of revolt and resentment. Before the vision of a God who encompasses all that is, the world we know and the worlds we know not, human wrangles and squabbles on petty issues lose their significance and man is called to know what he is, in order to do what he ought to do. Islam takes into full account sex, wealth and the will to power as the main drives of human life which can take hold of man to the detriment of his spiritual growth. As the Koran puts it: "Beautified for mankind is love of the joys (that come) from women and offspring and stored-up heaps of gold and silver, and horses branded (with their mark), and cattle and land". (III, 14).

But if man is given only to the satisfaction of his instinctive drives, his perspective of values is distorted and this twist in his value-consciousness leads to moral pathology, to socio-economic imbalance and mental disequilibrium. Inward peace, which the Koran refers to as *raza* or reconciliation, is the condition in which man is reconciled with the order of the universe and the condition in which he should breathe his last. Religion then has a double function to fulfill. It is to insist on man's supra-temporal destiny, his uniqueness which is inexhaustible in this world and at the same time to awaken in him the consciousness of unity with the whole of creation. Mankind is one whole or as the poet SADI said, human beings are parts of one another inasmuch as they belong to one substance. Islam inculcates the sense of human community by invoking the historical consciousness, by bringing to mind the panorama of nations succeeding one another and coming to their end, not so much by mechanical necessity as SPENGLER would say, but by a teleological necessity which compels nations to take to wrong ways, when they have achieved plenty. They are then puffed with power and tend to exploit the weaker and even to annihilate them in their own interest. The fall of nations and the extinction of civilizations has been man's own responsibility. Hence if man is not to repeat his own past history and is to escape the possibility of total annihilation which is being brought constantly nearer to realization by the new developments in scientific inventions, he must awaken in himself a new consciousness of unity, and if a new civilization is to emerge we have to learn to live not only with one another but for one another, or else there will be none left to mourn the fate which man will meet.

Islam has a dual aspect. It is not only a message which became historically effective and vocal through the Prophet at a certain period of time, but equally a message which was proclaimed in every period of history through the different media of divine consciousness whom we call Prophets. The burden of the whole message is insistence on divine guidance and human responsibility, an exhortation to good words and a call to good deeds: "Every soul is a pledge for its own deeds" (Koran-XLIV, 29). "Unto Him good words ascend and the pious deeds doth He exalt" (Koran-XXXV, 10).

What is most abhorrent is the mischief that is done in the name of re-form, and the confusion that is created on earth after it has been given to us as an ordered whole. The pattern of life of the man who follows the straight path, and who alone can truly prosper, is given in unambiguous language. Committed as he is to the transcendental vision, "he gives his wealth, for love of Him, to kinsfolk and to orphans and to needy and the wayfarer and to those who ask, and to set slaves free, and observeth proper worship and payeth the poor due. And those who keep their treaty when they make one, and the patient in tribulation and adversity and time of stress. Such are they who are sincere. Such are the God-fearing." (Koran-II, 177).

Thus what the world needs is neither the birth of a new man nor the return of the old but the reawakening in man of the divine consciousness which is eclipsed more and more by worldly distractions and the will to power. Only when they help one another "unto righteousness and piety", and "not unto sin and hositility" can nations and individuals attain *falah* or inner prosperity. Then only will this world become an abode of peace where all individuals or groups will be free to follow the pattern of life which is consonant with their genius.

Judaism and its Relevance to Modern Problems

by

Rabbi MORDECAI WAXMAN
Temple Israel, Great Neck, Long Island, New York

SECTION I

The question we are considering (The Relevance of the World's Religions) in the form in which we are considering it, already bears the stamp of a secular age. It implies that the scale in which we weigh our respective religions is the scale of contemporary problems. Religions then stand or fall by virtue of their ability to supply answers to problems which are not of their own making and which, indeed, they might not choose to consider as the preeminent problems of human existence. Another age might have faced the question in precisely the opposite way – have accepted the religious outlook as beyond argument and employed it as a scale in which to weigh contemporary problems.

This caveat is suggested for two reasons. On the one hand, it is a reminder that the weight of a thing may vary depending on the world in which you weigh it. Thus in weighing myself on the scales in the planetarium of New York City, I found that I weighed some 2,700 pounds on one scale, 37 pounds on another and about 170 pounds on the third scale. In the first case I was weighing myself on the planet Jupiter, in the second case, on the moon; in the third case I was being weighed on earth. Nonetheless, the essential "I" remained the same no matter what the ostensible weight, although the ability of that "I" to function might be radically different on each of the three bodies. Similarly, a religion would retain its essential quality under different situations of time and circumstance, although it might function more effectively in one period than another or in one set of circumstances than in another group of circumstances. Secondly, we ought to bear in mind that most religions address themselves to a wide variety of problems, social and personal, eternal and temporal, human and divine. A request that a religion be interpreted in the light of one set of circumstance, inevitably means that the response will be, in some degree, unbalanced and distorted and involve an emphasis upon one or several aspects of the religion to the apparent neglect of other facets.

Nonetheless, it is fair to say that to the problems of contemporary society Judaism offers an approach born of a long and unique history. Its emphasis has always been on man in cooperation with his society and man in the midst of society. Its greatest figures have always been men who labored in the midst of society rather than men who withdrew from it to seek individual holiness. It has doctrines and laws set forth in the Old Testament, the Bible, which have been elaborated and developed in a vast literature in many languages over the course of several thousand years. Because it is the outlook of the Jewish people which has had the unique experience of living dispersed among other peoples for 2,000 years, almost always under conditions of persecution, without losing its identity or being brutalized by its experiences, it has acquired perceptions and emphases which have been denied peoples living under more normal circumstances. A major theme in its history and beliefs has been an optimism about the world and about the responsibility of men to cope with social circumstances. All of these elements have been combined in an unusual and possibly unique melange of faith, theology, history, culture, peoplehood, law, ritual and skepticism.

It would be possible to consider Judaism fruitfully under any one of these headings. I propose to consider it, in the light of our topic, as a system of personal and social ethics and behavior, and to make only glancing references to these other approaches. As background elements, however, I propose to present some broad brush-strokes about the Jewish conceptions of God, Torah, man and the Jewish people before proceeding to a consideration of what I am calling the Jewish system.

GOD

Judaism starts with the assumption that God is one and unique and concerned with man. The nearest thing to a creed that is offered is the Biblical verse, "Hear O Israel the Lord is our God, the Lord is one" which has become the central declaration of the Jewish prayer book. Ancient Judaism understood this to be a denial of all idolatries, of all multiple conceptions of God and of all assertions that God has various manifestations or aspects which are harmonized by a fundamental unity. It elected a pure monotheism. And modern Judaism, holding to the same tenet, is equally opposed to the whole gamut of secular idolatries including the philosophies which turn the state or society or man into God.

How man comes to know God is, of course, a key question in any religion's outlook. While Jewish philosophers in relatively late periods in Jewish history, like SAADISH in the 9th century, HALEVI in the 11th century and MAIMONIDES in the 12th century, offered variants of the rational proofs of God, the Biblical source of Judaism proposes other views. It suggests that God is apprehended by man in two ways. On the one hand, God reveals himself to aspiring and gifted individuals like Abraham, Moses and the later prophets and, at Mt. Sinai, to the Jewish People as a whole. What this revelation actually means is subject to much dispute in Jewish religious literature.[1] The essential points, however, are that God shows his concern with man through this historical revelation and that the only way that aspiring man can know God is if God reaches out in turn. A concurrent notion would be that revelation is forever taking place in the world, that it is open to all men, Jew or non-Jew, and that the precondition for it is that men have the capacity to attune themselves to it. The analogy that presents itself is that of radio waves being sent from distant stations. Only finely attuned short-wave radios can receive them.

The other aspect of the Biblical approach is that God reveals himself through history. The Biblical view is that the redemption of the Jewish people from the slavery of Egypt is a revelation of God working through history and that the subsequent experience of the Jewish people and other peoples reflect God's footprints in history for those who have eyes to see. Even very skeptical Jews, of whom there are many, find it hard to avoid a certain mystique about the sheer survival of the Jewish people under the most untoward of circumstances and about the reestablishment of Jews in the Land of Israel after a separation of 1,800 years.

Both these views of apprehending God have significant results for Jewish social philosophy. They offer a basis for belief that God is concerned with human destiny and that human existence and history have meaning and purpose. It is out of these convictions that the Jewish Messianic notion that man and society can be brought to some state of perfection, was built. This notion that history has a destination which will be achieved within history and society, which is a natural development rather than a supernatural imposition, has been a key factor in Jewish thoughts.

The vision of God which Judaism presents has another facet. God is understood to be a perfectly ethical being. He is not anethical, like the Greek gods, or morally ambiguous. He is the abstract standard by which we judge human ethical behavior. The goal of man is the imitation of God – "Ye shall be holy, for I the Lord your God, am holy" (Leviticus). Clearly one cannot undertake to define the ethical qualities of God with any real knowledge, but we are free to assume that as one expands his ethical horizons and deepens his ethical understanding and compassion, he approaches closer to God. Thus, in Judaism, the ladder by which one climbs to God is the ladder of ethical behavior. Nor is it assumed that God is above and beyond the canons by which we ourselves are bound, Abraham's challenge to God over the destruction of Sodom is "will not the judge of all the earth do justice?" and Job's complaint to God is that He is acting unjustly. If the answer is that God's view of justice and man's view may differ, the plain

---

1 For varying points of view on revelation: ABRAHAM HESCHEL, TORAH MIN HA-SHAMAYIM B'ASPEKLARIA SHEL HADORET;
MORDECAI KAPLAN, JUDAISM AS A CIVILIZATION.

conclusion is that, nevertheless, God Himself is self-bound by His ethical nature and cannot discard it.

These challenges to God, contained in the Bible, reveal another strand of Jewish thought and that is a skeptical strand. There is no such thing as blind belief and undemanding faith. Man's role is to wrestle with God and with belief as his role in nature is to wrestle with the universe. It is only through this sort of challenge and response that man can grow and win through to some understanding of God and of human destiny. Thus, in a sense, God grows, and takes on different dimensions as man grows and understands more. It is for this reason that science and the expansion of scientific knowledge have never been regarded as a threat to the Jewish outlook. More knowledge is simply a stronger base from which to engage in an assault on meaning and purpose and to understand them more fully.

This doctrine also has its consequences in social philosophy. It means that social institutions ought to be approached with the same spirit of skepticism and with the conviction that unless they serve to better man's lot and to direct his purposes to good ends they ought, properly, to be challenged.

THE TORAH

Hand in hand with the idea of God goes the Torah. The term is applied, in a limited sense, to the first five books of the Bible, – the five books of Moses. These volumes which are a combination of a poetic myth of creation and of the origin of man, of the early history of the Jewish people from the time of Abraham through the days of Moses, of personal and social law and of rituals, are the first of the sacred texts of Judaism.

From the point of view of social philosophy, however, they are very much more specific. They incorporate a constitution for the Jewish people to apply in setting up their society in the Land of Canaan to which they are moving. While they contain broad general principles for personal and ethical behavior, they include detailed regulations for the social ordering of the society.

By themselves, however, the five books of Moses never constituted the sole basis by which Jews sought to live. The books of Moses were the base of an inverted pyramid from which a far reaching literature of interpretation developed. Judaism is a religion not of The Book, but of books. The rest of the Bible, the Apocrypha literature, the Talmud, the Codes, the commentaries, the legal and ethical treatises, represent an expanded Torah. The whole corpus of Jewish learning and of Jewish historical experience is what is really meant when the term "Torah" is used in its fullest sense.

The essence of the Jewish Torah is that it is, in a figurative sense, a vertical text. A man reading the words of the Bible does not get a picture of the Jewish outlook. It is the way that the Jewish people undertook to understand the text and to live by it that is decisive. Thus, for example, while the Bible speaks of "an eye for an eye and a tooth for a tooth", the corpus of Jewish law and lore called the Talmud interpreted this to mean monetary damages and proceeded to spell out how these are to be computed. The Talmud is decisive, not the Biblical text.

The tradition of Jewish law was that the five books of Moses represented the revealed word of God and were intended as a guide for man's behavior. However, as has already been indicated, works like the Talmud which represented the summarized views of generations of sages did not hesitate to override the very text of the Bible. They did so with the double conviction that the injunctions of the Bible represented conclusions which could also be attained by the use of reason and that the interpretation of the tradition undertaken by the majority of a properly constituted religious and judicial body, like the Sanhedrin, equally reflected the revealed word of God. The bent of the scholar sages who held themselves to be the successors of the prophets is reflected in the Talmudic story of the sage who represented a minority viewpoint and who called upon Heaven to validate his view. A voice from Heaven promptly intervened to proclaim his point of view as the correct one. The majority group responded by quoting the Biblical statement, "the Torah is not in Heaven" and going on to say that since the Torah had been given into the hands of men, the responsibility lay with them and that they operated by majority rule and that Heaven had no right to intervene. The Talmud goes on to represent God as being delighted with this ruling.

This excursus on the Jewish conception of Torah is necessary to make two points. On the one hand, it may clarify the difference between the Jewish and Christian approach to the same old Testament which both of them hold sacred. Christianity abandoned the legal regulations of the Mosaic Books which include the social laws. Judaism held them binding upon itself and proceeded to develop a great vertical text in the attempt to explicate the laws. On the other hand, that vertical text, the Talmud and all the works of the centuries, is the key to the Jewish social philosophy.

Judaism was not content to abide with abstract ethical principles and not even with detailed social regulations unless all other implications had been fully explored. It recognized that, in its own ancient world, it shared certain ethical principles with the Greeks and others and yet lived in a different way and with other emphases and it concluded that life patterns had to be spelled out in detail. The situation is analogous to one suggested by ARNOLD TOYNBEE. TOYNBEE records a trip that he made from London to Delhi by jet plane and notes that the only things he actually saw in his entire trip over one half of the globe were the London airport, the Delhi airport and one Alpine peak which poked its head above the clouds. He goes on to observe that a native of India travelling from a nearby village to Delhi by ox-cart saw more of life and history and experienced more than he did in girdling half the globe. In the same vein, one might observe that on the jet-plane level most religious and ethical systems say much the same thing. The distinction comes in the ox-cart journey over the rough terrain of daily personal and social living. It is on that ox-cart journey that Judaism concentrated in its expanded Torah.

Because Judaism was a system which made no distinction between religious and social life, it undertook to legislate, religiously, in its classic texts, such decisive things as the laws of torts, of charity, of agriculture, of social reform, of the limits of governmental power, of advertising and of monopoly. Most of this legislation is the product of the Biblical period and of the early centuries of the Christian era, much of it was applied internally until a century ago in Jewish communities which enjoyed semi-autonomous status within larger communities. And from this legislation and the manner of formulating it, one may readily extrapolate Jewish views on social problems and may discuss the tone of social attitudes which prevails within the Jewish community today.

THE CONCEPTION OF MAN

The Jewish conviction that God guarantees purpose and meaning to the universe and to the human endeavor and that the Torah is a guide to living is accompanied by a distinctive conception of the role of man.

Fundamental to the Jewish conception is the notion of the dignity of man and of the uniqueness of the individual. It is set forth in myriad ways in the Jewish tradition. Man is represented as created in the image of God, (Genesis) that is as a possessor of reason, and, therefore, every human being is precious. He who kills one man, we are told, destroys an entire world and he who saves one man saves the entire world (Talmud: Sanhedrin). Further, we are advised, that only one man was created so that no man might say, My father is superior to yours; that man was formed of clay of many colors so that no one might say, My color is superior to yours, that the King of Kings, unlike human kings who stamp out coins each one identical with the other, stamps out many coins (souls) but each one is unique. (Talmud: Sanhedrin and Midrash: Bereshit Rabbah).

The Jewish tradition approaches the question of man and his role from another significant direction. It proposes the notion that God and man are partners in the creation of the world. Man has been given the capacity and the direction. It is his responsibility to bring the world that ought to be into being. This doctrine is linked to the doctrine of free will and is regarded as a partial answer to the problem of evil in a world in which God is held to be good. However, its major concern is to indicate that the world of man is still coming into being and that man is a co-creator with God.

The humanistic emphasis of the Jewish tradition is quite plain in these and other treatments of the role of man. The human being is central and

nothing that degrades the human is tolerable. It is in this vein that MARTIN
BUBER, the modern Jewish philosopher, insists that one must continually
seek the "thou" in the universe as against the "it". Men must be treated on
every level of relationship as a "thou" ,never as an "it" to be employed for
someone else's advantage. It is in this light, too, that one must judge the
role of states and societies and of technology and science in our lives. They
exist to benefit the individual man, subject to the rights of other men, and
they cease to fulfill their proper function if they become a Procrustean
bed to which the individual must conform.

A humanistic outlook often involves conflict with religious viewpoints.
In Judaism the attempt is made to make them interdependent. Thus the
Talmud portrays God as saying "It is all right if they desert Me, but let them
observe my Torah". In a similar vein, the Talmud (Tractiate Berachet)
discusses the question of when the Shema prayer asserting that "God is
One" is recited in the morning and suggests that it is not recited until a
man can see his pillow in the glimmering dawn at a distance of four paces.
Thus it makes the point that God is not one until man is one. Perhaps the
most significant phrasing of the concept of man's role is the famous passage
in the Sifra (a first century rabbinic text) which interprets the phrase in
Isaiah "ye are my witnesses, saith the Lord" to mean "if you are my witnesses, then I am God, if you are not my witnesses, then I am not God."
This apparently heretical passage was intended to make the point that the
God of metaphysics does not need man to affirm his existence. He is self-
sufficient. But the God of religion, that is the revelation of God in the
world, depends upon the meditation of man. Thus not only does man need
God, but God needs man.

THE JEWISH PEOPLE

To understand the play of Jewish ideas, one must know something of the
self-image of the Jewish people and something of their history. Judaism
does not exist in a vacuum. It is the body of spiritual and intellectual ideas
which is carried by the Jewish people and constitutes their national purpose.
Ideas, of course, have no boundaries. They are the common possession of
anyone who chooses to accept them. But what ideas come to mean in
practice depends upon the society in which they are nurtured and applied.

The early Biblical view of the role of the Jewish people is quite plain.
Abraham breaks through to an awareness of God as the one and only God
of all the universe. He rejects the idols and idolatries of the highly sophisticated world of the 18th Century B. C. in which he lives, and dedicates himself and his family to the worship of the one universal God and to making
Him evident in the world. God, in turn, enters into a covenant with Abraham through revelatory visions, the content of which is that Abraham's
descendants will prosper and inherit the Land of Canaan in which Abraham

has settled. Some generations later, after the experience of slavery in Egypt, and in the process of redemption from that servitude, that covenant is renewed under the leadership of Moses, at Mt. Sinai in the desert. That covenant is now expanded to include a group of laws and moral precepts by which the Jewish people undertake to live, personally and as a society once it is established. It does establish itself in the Land of Canaan and founds its society. This is the theme of the five books of Moses.

In this conception, the Jewish people become at once "a chosen people" and "a choosing people". They become a people selected by God to live by certain laws and canons, which extend far beyond the ritual and embrace every aspect of personal and social life. They also become a people which has elected to live in this manner. They are thus, in Isaiah's sense, witnesses to God in the world. The quid pro quo is that they will enjoy the favor of God and know prosperity. However, as the Biblical story unfolds and as the prophets expand the original theme, the obvious advantages fade away. It becomes clear that God's goal is that all the world come to live in peace and harmony and enjoy prosperity. If nations are righteous, whether or not they are clearly aware of the one God, they will prosper, since God is equally the God of all peoples. That is the burden of the Biblical book of Jonah in which the great city of Nineveh is portrayed as on the road to doom and destruction because of the evil of its ways. God sends Jonah, an Israelite prophet, to warn them of their fate and they see the error of their ways, repent and are spared. And the concluding line of the book makes the point plain that they are spared simply because there is both human and animal life in Nineveh. "Should I not have pity on Nineveh, that great city, wherein are more than six score, a hundred and twenty thousand persons that cannot discern between their right hand and their left hand, and also much cattle?"

It is important to note that Nineveh is spared not because its people have become Jews or worship the one God or accept the Torah, but simply because they repent of wicked behavior and adopt a social attitude and morals which are what the Talmud characterizes as the seven laws for the children of Noah, that is, Laws of Natural Reason. The Jews on the other hand are expected to conform to all the detailed regulations of the Torah and to the exclusive worship of the One God, in order to win redemption. If they fail to do so, the prophets contend, they are subject to heavy national punishment at the hands of God. Jewish history is fraught with tragedy – the shattering of the State of Israel and Judaea in Biblical times, the destruction of the central Temple in Jerusalem, exile from the Land of Israel, dispersion among the nations and unending persecution. Nonetheless, through all these experiences the essential prophetic theme is maintained, that these events occur because the Jewish people had failed to live up to the high standard which had been set for it in the Torah.

The bargain struck at Sinai thus becomes a very dubious proposition,

Obviously the advantages to the Jew are negligible. In this world all nations
are ultimately expected to share in peace, harmony and prosperity. Even
if we speak in terms of an after-life or the Messianic world to come, the
Jewish thesis, as it is developed in the Talmud, is that "the righteous of all
peoples have a share in the world to come". It is only the Jews who are
called upon to live by the Torah and to adhere to the exclusive worship
of the One God in the modes established by the Jewish tradition. In short,
the Jewish thesis becomes that once a person has been shown a high purpose, both personal and national, he is culpable if he fails to aspire to it and
to achieve it. And the only prize, it emerges in the words of the Talmud
(Ethics of the Fathers), is that "the reward for a *mitzvah* (ethical Torah precept) is the *mitzvah* itself" or by extension the capacity to perform other
mitzvet.

Oddly enough, the Jewish people have clung to this outlook through
centuries of adversity. Since the ethical tone of their personal and social
life was often measurably higher than that of the people among whom they
lived, since for most of their history they were victims and not victimizers,
they doubtless had misgivings about the thesis. Certainly, the Hitler period,
which involved the ruthless and barbaric slaughter of one third (6 million)
of the Jewish people by supposedly civilized nations and which was acqui-
esced in by other civilized peoples, raised serious theological and ideological
problems for Jews. However, twenty years later, the Jewish people still
seems dedicated to the proposition that the human obligation is to live by
the highest standards which one can conceive. With this conviction goes
the parallel conviction that such living will eventually yield a world,
here on earth, which can be characterized as "God's Kingdom".

The social consequences of this sort of thinking and the directions for
living which come out of it are obvious. But there are also lessons to be
learned from the unique Jewish experience of the last nineteen centuries.

For nearly 2,000 years, the Jews have formed a unique political community, dispersed throughout the world, without a central religious or political
authority and without a central land. They constituted a Diaspora, but the
central country existed only in historical recollection and in aspiration.
The hope of an eventual return to the Land of Israel and the reconstitution
of an autonomous Jewish community in which the forms and the values
of Jewish life might be applied was central to Jewish thought. That such a
visionary expectation could even find partial fulfillment as it seems to have
done in this generation by the establishment of the State of Israel is in the
nature of a miracle which has no significant parallel in history. However,
whatever Israel may become there are significant social lessons to be
learned from the unique Jewish experience of the past two millenniums.

The Jewish people formed a unique political community because they
devised a way of maintaining national unity and identity while they were
in a scattered state and while they lacked any governmental authority.

They became citizens of "a portable fatherland", of the world of ideas and practices which constituted the expanding Torah. Citizenship in this portable fatherland depended upon literacy, upon a willingness voluntarily to accept ideas as binding elements and upon common practices. This was buttressed by the creation of communities all over the world which, for centuries, had similar institutions, such as synagogues, schools, public welfare funds and internal courts which rendered judgment according to Jewish law. These institutions were accompanied by a vibrant internal creative life which enabled the Jewish tradition to change and grow as it faced new conditions.

There are obvious parallels to this situation. Any religion which is world-wide is engaged in uniting its adherents by common ideas and practices, even while they give political loyalty to the state in which they reside. What gives the Jewish situation a special cast is that it was maintained by a small group, living in a variety of cultures under conditions of persecution. It involved few apparent advantages and many obvious disabilities. It, therefore, required more deliberate decision and it depended very heavily upon creating a community highly literate in the Jewish tradition.

The social implications of this experience are particularly significant in a world in which the threat to human existence is so monumental that the need for peoples to live together in amity is greater than it ever was before. The Jewish experience is a reminder that if people living under diverse circumstances can be brought to adhere to common ideas about the nature of man and society and of the responsibility of every man to a portable fatherland of ideas, the quality of international social life may be improved. These need not be necessarily religious ideas, although one significant line of approach is to explore the social ideas and ideals which religions have in common. At the same time, however, they must be more than vague ideals to which all give casual and meaningless assent. To be effective in motivating men to sacrifice immediate and apparent advantage to long range goals which are capable of yielding greater advantage, they must enjoy the authority and cogency with which religions have been able to invest them in the past.

One further aspect of the Jewish historical experience is worth pondering. For close to 2,000 years, Jew have not possessed governmental power. That experience has shaped and directed their attitudes. Having observed empires rise and fall, they have come to distrust the effect of power and the uses of power. Having seen violence rampant for long periods in many countries, they have come to believe that violence destroys and never builds. Having observed extremists through the centuries, they have come to believe that while extreme dedication to great ideas may be admirable, extremism in action is rarely admirable or useful. Holding to the truth of their own religious vision, they do not hold that it is an exclusive truth nor deny that there are many facets to truth and many ways to understand

God. Experience has taught them that the qualities in man most to be cherished are moral concern combined with an ability to live and let live. And the Jewish test for a society is whether, whatever its beliefs about immortality and an after-life, it is prepared to deal with the problems of man in this world in terms, first of all of justice, and then of compassion.

SECTION II

The combination of Jewish theology, thought and experience which has been sketched above indicates the direction and emphasis of Jewish social ethics. Clearly, we are not talking about specific programs. They are political matters which vary with time and circumstance and possibility. We are speaking of the spirit in which a religion approaches the problems of existence and society and of the demands it makes upon its adherents. Thus the Biblical programs for dealing with poverty, including such laws as leaving the corners of the field for the poor and the obligation to lend money or seed to a fellow Jew without interest and the laws of the annulment of debts in the sabbatical year are merely guide-lines to a philosophy of social responsibility for the impoverished. They were succeeded, as times and economic circumstances changed, by a series of community chests and funds and taxes for public welfare. The line of concern and responsibility for the needy, however, is clear in the Bible and becomes the basis for different solutions to the same problem.

Some of the central social ideas of Judaism which have been understood and applied in different ways at different times are the following:

> 1. *Every human being is sacred because,*
> *however figuratively this is understood,*
> *he has been created in the image of God*

The Talmud records a debate between two of its great figures as to the most significant statement in the Bible. Rabbi Akiba endorses the verse "Thou shalt love thy neigbor as thyself" (Leviticus); Ben Aza proposes the statement, "In the image of God created He man" (Genesis) because it implies the inherent dignity and equality of all men.

The corollaries which flow from these statements, as they are formulated in Jewish law, are many and varied. Men are to be treated equally before the law. One man must not be sacrificed for another nor even for the whole community. "How do you know", says the Talmud, "that your blood is redder than his?" Murder is, of course, forbidden although it is recognized that there are situations where the issue is one of unavoidable self-defense. However, the concern with human life ultimately became so strong that by the first century the Jewish religion's courts had virtually abandoned capital punishment.

These are the grosser implications of the doctrine of the sacredness and dignity of human life. The more significant applications are in the nuances of ethics. Murder is defined as anything which shortens a man's life. Stealing involves stealing a man's mind or opinion as well as his purse. Taking advantage of the disadvantaged – the blind, the deaf, the lame, the servant, the aged – is held to be a crime. Obviously, not all ethical crimes can be handled by the courts. A great many of them are in Jewish law, but other things, more subtle, are described as "deeds free in human law but guilty by Divine law" or as "acts exempt from punishment but forbidden."

The positive side of the conception of the dignity of man is very far-reaching. Society owes man an opportunity to live. He is entitled to the basic necessities of life as a matter not of charity, but of justice. ISRAEL ZANGWILL's novel, KING OF THE SCHNORRERS (Beggars) makes the point ironically. The Jewish beggar patronizes the Jewish banker on the grounds that he, the beggar, is enabling the banker to do his duty and thus earn merit. In broader terms, however, the conception of dignity and sanctity of personality means that even help must be given with due regard for the feelings of the recipient, and so MAIMONIDES speaks of the eight rungs of just giving, in which anonymous giving to an anonymous recipient and helping a man to help himself are at the top of the ladder.

Since man does not live by bread alone, the welfare of his body and soul become the concern of the community. The Jewish community, was, therefore, frequently organized to provide medical services and special care for the aged and the orphaned. More important still, it established the pattern of universal compulsory education for boys from the age of six on, as early as the First Century.

A concept which starts with the dignity and inherent worth of man clearly has no limit in its application. If it is taken seriously, it becomes a spur to social reform until the point is reached where the society does proper justice to every individual. In the formulation of BUBER it means that every individual must be treated as a "thou" – a subject of ultimate concern, even as God is treated as a "Thou" by man and man is treated as a "thou" by God.

In the complicated life of our day, this doctrine acquires new nuances. It implies not only that social justice is a burning moral obligation, but also means that the human consideration must come first. In an age where technology, computerization, the manipulation of men and the minds of men and the regimentation of men for the functioning of society are becoming a commonplace, the idea of the sanctity and dignity of the individual needs renewed emphasis.

2. The goal of religion, in the view of Judaism,
is to establish the Messianic society in this world

Many ancient mythologies had a vision of a golden past which had been lost to man by virtue of his failings. Judaism too starts with the image of the Garden of Eden, but it was dedicated to the idea that a golden future is the goal of history. It believed that however stumblingly man approached the goal, he would ultimately achieve it because God has so ordered history.

This notion pervades all aspects of Jewish life and thought. It is a recurrent theme of the prophets; it engages the legalists and the philosophers; it is embroidered by folklore and it was the leaven in the sour dough of Jewish existence for long centuries. Most strikingly, it is the theme of the Kaddish prayer which is recited in memory of the dead. Judaism believes in immortality, but its highest testimony to the deceased is the assertion that he may have contributed in some way to the advancement of God's Kingdom on earth.

Judaism entertains the vision of perfectable man and perfectable society because it is very much a "this world" religion. It would contest the notion of WHITEHEAD that "religion is what man does with his solitude" even though it has its own very considerable mystic strain. It would deny that man's primary business is to make his peace with God, although it believes in immortality, or rather it would say that he best fulfills the will of God when he fulfills his obligations to his fellow men. Thus the Kol Nidre prayer, the prayer of the 24-hour Yom Kippur day, which is devoted to prayer, fasting and introspection, asks forgiveness for the vows made to God and not fulfilled. It assumes that God will forgive. But Jewish law specifies that vows made to men are never forgiven unless they are fulfilled (Mishnah Yema).

The belief that both society and man can be perfected does not grow out of any overly sanguine notion of human nature. Judaism recognizes that man has a capacity for great evil, although it does not believe he is immersed in original sin. But it believes that he has a capacity for great good, too, and that the business of man is to make the good prevail over the evil. The materials for the good life are available to man in the world about him and in his own capacity to master and refashion nature. Judaism is sanguine that he can master human nature and social nature, too.

The Messianic age to which Judaism points is one in which justice will prevail within man and society, one in which there will be peace between nations and within man himself, one in which harmony will be achieved in the natural world and in which "the knowledge of the Lord will cover the earth as the waters cover the sea."

Judaism is not alone in this vision. Christianity, its daughter religion, took over the same hope for the future, although its theological premises differ and its Messianic vision has a supernatural cast as against the naturalistic bent of Judaism. The result, however, is that Western civilization bears the imprint of the Messianic idea.

A Messianic vision is no guarantee that there will be a Messianic outcome. And certainly the Jewish Messianic expectation has become much more diffuse than it was in the past. But it has lent a tone to Jewish life and to Jewish social goals which continue to be pervasive. It at least leads Judaism to stand in opposition to the dis-utopias which hold out little hope for the future or which envision the future in terms of HUXLEY'S BRAVE NEW WORLD or ORWELL'S NINETEEN EIGHTY-FOUR.

In social terms, the Messianic tone in Judaism means a commitment to what is called the liberal political point of view. It means laboring for human rights, for freedom of opinion and freedom of investigation. It means a belief that knowledge and education are stepping-stones to better personal and social life. It involves a commitment to social justice, a conviction that with will and energy society can and must solve problems of want and scarcity, a laboring for peace and an opposition to discriminations. It means a belief that most problems can be solved by peaceful means, a tolerance of opposing points of view and an opposition to violence.

This set of attitudes, and the attendant actions drawn from a belief in the worth of the individual and a commitment to a Messianic future are, I believe, characteristic of the Jewish stance in the world today. They may be confirmed by observing the voting patterns of Jews in the countries where they live and by noting the causes to which they commit themselves.

3. The keystone in the arch of
Jewish social attitudes is Justice

HEINE's statement that "since the days of Moses, justice has spoken with a Hebrew accent" is a reflection of the fact that the Bible insistently harps upon the theme of justice, that the great Jewish holidays are built upon the theme of God sitting in judgment of man and man sitting in judgment of himself. From the statement in Deuteronomy, "Justice, justice shalt thou pursue", through the cry of Amos "let justice well up as the waters", through the demand Job levels against God for just treatment, justice is a recurrent concern of the Bible. It is not that Judaism is unconcerned with love or compassion. The love of God for man and of man for God, the love of neighbor and love of the stranger are insistent themes in the Bible and in all of Jewish literature. And the concern for compassion is no less. The insistent injunctions throughout Jewish writing "as God is compassionate, so be you compassionate" and the concern for "the least of all living things" is very great. In the Jewish view there may be the key to personal relations and perhaps the key to relations between man and God. However, for Judaism, justice constitutes the best base for the social structure and love and compassion are graceful adornments.

Judaism is rather pragmatic about the working of society. It believes that justice is a measurable quality and that love and compassion are not. It recognizes that love is rarely given to the stranger, often not to the neighbor and sometimes not even to oneself, but that justice can be rendered even without liking. Thus in Biblical teachings it insisted that a court owed equal justice to rich and poor alike. It should not be swayed by the power of the rich and it should not be swayed by the plight of the poor. Even in the case of the poor, it should first render justice and then, as a matter of grace but not of right, act with compassion.

Justice, of course, goes beyond mere law. It was to the knotty problem of how to translate abstract ethical principles into just law that the Jewish religious genius addressed itself. In consequence, Hallachah, the system of combining law and ethics, is the high water-mark of Jewish literary creativity after the Bible. That it often achieved triumphant results may be seen in the passage from Talmud Sanhedrin, quoted earlier in this paper, in which the court in exhorting witnesses in capital cases to be very cautious in their testimony presented a philosophy of the uniqueness of every human personality as part of its ordinary proceedings.

It is a sense of realism that led Judaism in the past and in the present to believe that the effective remedy for social ills is justice rather than love. It is simply easier to infuse law with justice than it is to displace hate or indifference with love. It is easier to maintain just laws than it is to retain the emotions of love. It is easier to unlock the doors of the court or the parliament than to unlock the doors of the human heart.

But if justice is to be real justice, it must have compassion in its train. An old Jewish legend has it that God first attempted to build the world on the principle of absolute justice. It failed. He then attempted to build the world on the principles of absolute mercy. It too failed. Our world is compounded of a mixture of the principles of justice and mercy. It goes stumbling on.

SECTION III

In discussing some of the social attitudes of Judaism, I have been tacitly accepting the thesis that if one changes the world one changes man. This is only a fraction of a religious outlook. The fundamental purpose of any religion must be to present answers to ultimate questions and not only to social and often transient phenomena. It must, in short, deal with man's relation to God, with meaning and purpose in the universe, with the nature of religious experience and with man's relation to himself. Here the mystical and the natural, prayer and ritual, life temporal and life eternal all join hands.

Much of this subject is outside the scope of this paper. But I propose to suggest that a fundamental emphasis in Judaism, as in most religions, is that the way to change the world or to generate the attitudes which change the world is to change the individual. For that purpose, Judaism has devised a system which is the heart of its religious outlook.

There are two fundamental religious ways of becoming a changed man. One, a way which Christianity has elected, is that if you believe strongly enough, you will become a changed person. The other, the Jewish position, is that if you become a changed person, you may become capable of belief. In Judaism, therefore, religious faith is a summit and not a base.

This Jewish view is born out of a belief that religious capacity is an art form. A genius for religion or a talent for religious experience are at least as rare as genius in music or painting or literature. The same holds true of genius or talent in the realm of ethics. There is no reason to assume a democracy of ability in these realms any more than in the realm of the recognized arts.

While it is possible to live meaningfully without being talented in one of the arts, any religion would deny that it is possible for man to live significantly as a full human being without religious and ethical capacity. The question then becomes, how does one take the ordinary man, untalented in these realms, and develop his capacity? In the realm of the arts, the procedure is clear. Enough instruction, training and direction and persistent practice will convert a non-pianist into a fair or competent pianist. It will not, of course, make him a talented pianist unless the extra touch is there.

Judaism has sought in the same vein to develop a system to take ordinary human beings who may have the desire but not the talent for religious and ethical life and to make them competent in those realms. Its goal is not to convert every man into a Moses or an Isaiah but rather by dint of detailed training, instruction, practice and discipline, to make men more sensitive spiritual and ethical human beings.

The system hewed out over the course of the ages reaches into every aspect of a man's life. It touches every aspect of a man's life, his prayers, his dress, his personal habits, his sexual relations, the division of his day, the expenditure of his money, his relations to his family, his friends and himself. It bids him on the one hand to immerse himself in sacred texts, to devote some hours to such study throughout his life, and it bids him on the other hand to immerse himself in water and learn how to swim.

Obviously, no one observes the system in its entirety. No one could, even if we were not living in a pluralistic society with various systems competing for our attention and concern. But it is clear, too, that in the past and in the present those who live in large measure by the system develop a "Jewish character." They become capable of reacting automatically in ways endorsed by the religion, or spiritually and ethically sensitive to the varied exigencies of life. We all face so many ethical decisions a day and have so many life experiences in a day that we have no time to reason about most of our problems and experiences. It is the total character, the built-in attitudes, that finally speak in any given situation.

The thrust of the Jewish system might be seen in three rather casually selected examples.

The first is the injunction that a man ought to recite a hundred benedictions of God each day. The occasions for the benedictions are varied – putting on a new suit of clothes, beholding a wise man, hearing thunder, rising to confront the dawn, the process of excretion. The intention of the injunction is to make man continually aware of the extraordinary in the ordinary, to force him to take a few seconds at each encounter with life and to make him recognize the awe, the wonder and the mystery of existence.

The Sabbath affords another example. Here the Jewish tradition has manipulated time to shape man's attitude. In sidereal time each hour is the same as any other. In personal time, an hour may be an eternity. Judaism invented the notion of taking one day a week out of the routine of life and giving it a different character in the hope that the experience would set the tone for the other six days of the week. Thus many things are forbidden on the Sabbath. Labor and purchasing and riding and a whole host of daily routine activities are prohibited. But the Sabbath is not merely a day off. It is a totally different day, for other things are enjoined. It is a day for extended prayer, for speculation, for study, for the cultivation of friendship, for closer family association, for familial dining and chanting. It is in short a strenuous day, but the demand is upon the spirit rather than the body. And because it is impossible to order that a man change his outlook at 6 p.m. the whole day is surrounded with rituals, the lighting of candles, benediction over the wine, special foods and the like. And when the Sabbath is observed, the purpose is achieved. Man is removed from the routine of events and made conscious that he belongs to the realm of the spirit.

The dietary laws of Judaism offer a third example. They reflect another aspect of man's life – the fact that he is an animal, subject to physiological needs, passions and lusts. The great problem in human life is how to spiritualize the markedly animal elements of our life. Judaism makes one attempt among others through a spiritualization of a frequent animal action, the process of eating. It bids a Jew wash his hands with a benediction as a reminder that a table may be an altar, it calls for a benediction before eating, for a lengthy value-studded benediction after eating and it limits what foods a man may eat.

These examples illustrate the interest of the entire elaborate system and that is to brain-wash or soul-wash an ordinary man into increasing sensitivity to the spiritual and ethical implications of living. At the end of a life-long struggle he may be capable of religious experience or he may not, but he will have realized his capacities.

The interrelation between this method and the social ethics of Judaism which has been discussed before should be obvious. It is easy to formulate social values. It is difficult to get people to live by them. Practical and political solutions to problems change as conditions change. How then does one get a man to elect the right things, to distinguish between justice and injustice, to elect the humane, to strive to perfect society rather than to despair of it? Judaism has sought a formula which would make the ordinary man as well as the spiritually and morally gifted man capable of responding in the right way to the problems of personal and social life. It is a method which for periods of time has produced whole communities of pious and sensitive men who, if they were not prophets were at least in the tradition. Religions which can do that – and Judaism is certainly not alone – are relevant to any time.

SECTION IV

Having responded, however inadequately, to the question of what is the relevance of religion to our time, a religionist is entitled to raise the contrary question. Ours is essentially an irreligious age. It is an age which daily challenges old values, which asserts that all values are relative. It is an age of great technological and scientific virtuosity, but one in which man is being bent to the demands of technology rather than bending technology to his needs. It is an age in which scientific truth is the criterion by which we live, but it is also the age in which it has become clear that science is dedicated to a truth which is not concerned with moral responsibility or life values. It is an age of great and golden potentialities, but it is also an age of great violence, brutality and unending war.

BIBLIOGRAPHY

This is a short list of books which serve as a guide to Jewish thought and experience.

I Encyclopedic Works
BARON, SALO – A Social and Religious History of the Jews, 12 vols.
FINKELSTEIN, LOUIS – The Jews, 2 vols.
WASMAN, MEYER – A History of Jewish Literature, 5 vols. (in 6 parts)

II Theological Works
AGUS, JACOB – Modern Philosophies of Judaism
GORDIS, ROBERT – The Root and the Bough
HESCHEL, ABRAHAM – Man is Not Alone – The Prophets
JACOB, LOUIS – Principles of the Jewish Faith
KAPLAN, MORDECAI – Judaism as a Civilization
MOORE, GEORGE FOOT – Judaism, 2 Vols.
STEINBERG, MILTON – Basic Judaism (A Brief Introduction To the Jewish Religion)

Confucius and the I-ching

by

Dr. WEI TAT, F. R. S. A.
Academician, The China Academy; Member of the Institute of Buddhist Philosophy; Professor of Philosophy, The College of Chinese Culture, Hong Kong

I wish, first of all, to extend to you the cordial greetings of the President and Members of the China Academy of the Republic of China, for it is as their delegate that I find myself among you here in Calcutta. I am going to present to you the important teachings of the remarkable Chinese classic, the I-Ching or Book of Changes, which constitute the less well known aspect of Confucianism and which may throw some light on the world situation to-day.

The I-Ching is perhaps the most ancient and venerated among the sacred books known as the five canonical classics of China. Its teachings constitute the essential basis of Taoism and Confucianism and have been an important source of inspiration and enlightenment to philosophers and scholars throughout the long history of China.

The importance of the I-Ching is clearly reflected in the fact that it was the subject of intensive study on the part of Confucius, in the evening of his life, after he had returned from his long and fearful wanderings among the feudal states and settled down in his native state of Lu. It was said of him, by the "grand historian" Ssu-ma Ch'ien, that he applied himself with such diligence to the study of the I-Ching that the leathern thongs which bound the bamboo tablets of his copy gave way three times from wear and tear. In the analects of Confucius, he is reported to have said on one occasion, when he was already advanced in age, that if a number of years were added to his life, he would complete his study of the I-Ching, and thus save himself from falling into grave errors.

Before I proceed to deal with the basic tenets of the Book, I should like to relate a few more facts about our Master, who came to be the greatest of our sages and teachers, and whose teaching led his people to the path of Man's well-being, the "Tao of Spirit and Earth."

According to Ssu-ma Ch'ien, Confucius was born in the year 551 B.C. in the state of Lu, somewhere near the present town of Chüfu in Shantung or the Province of the Eastern Mountains under the shadow of Tai Shan, the most sacred peak of China. He lost his father when he was three years old and was brought up by his mother. When he was nineteen he married, and about the same time took up an administrative post in Lu. After many experiences, he became, in 501 B.C., Prime Minister of his native state. So great was his success, that the rival state of Ch'i, fearing his growing influence, sent a company of female dancers and musicians to the Lu ruler, who thereupon neglected the affairs of state and closed his door to Confucius. Confucius forthwith resigned his position and, followed by many of his disciples, set out in 497 B.C. upon his travels, which were to last for thirteen years. He visited many of the feudal states of China, staying now in one and then in another, undergoing many hardships and dangers. When he returned to his native state, he spent the last years of his life in moral and historical studies, in editing the classics, and in teaching his disciples. He died in 479 B.C., and was buried in Chüfu, where his tomb is kept in good repair as a place of national pilgrimage.

The spread of Confucius's teaching began not long after his death. After mourning their Master's death, the disciples separated and each went his own way to carry on his teaching with their own expositions and comments. Thus there grew an ever-widening circle of scholars who took up the study of the old classics collated by Confucius; and as time went on these ancient writings took deep root in the minds of the people.

Ever since, Confucianism has inspired Chinese thought. It molded the national character; it touched every corner of the people's activities; it permeated their life in every aspect, moral, political and social. It vitalized a Chinese civilization which has survived to this day in its struggle against rival and foreign doctrines. In our everyday speech we often use his words to make a point, for they carry more weight than the passing slogans of our day.

In pronouncing his eulogy on Confucius, Ssu-ma Ch'ien writes:

Numerous are the princes and worthy men that the world has seen in its time; glorious in life, forgotten after death. But Confucius, though only a humble cotton-clothed member of the common people, remains among us after more than ten generations. He is the model for such as would be wise. By all, from the Son of Heaven down to the student of the Six Arts, the supremacy of his principles is fully and freely admitted. He may indeed be pronounced the greatest of our sages.

That the I-Ching is a main source of Confucius's ideas and ideals is testified by his disciple Tzu-kung. The latter said that his Master needed no teacher, or guru, since he learnt from King Wen and King Wu, the early Chou rulers who lived six centuries earlier. Now, King Wen was the author of the main text of the I-Ching. Therefore, to learn from King Wen was to learn from the I-Ching. While imprisoned at Yu-li by the last wicked sovereign of the Shang dynasty, King Wen studied the *hsiang* or symbols of the sixty-four hexagrams. These hexagrams were composed by Fu Hsi, the legendary founder of Chinese civilization in the third millennium B. C. King Wen explained the hexagrams, one after another, in short paragraphs giving indications of their significance in the various circumstances of life. These sixty-four terse essays are symbolical expressions of various important themes, mostly of a moral, social, or political character.

This exposition was continued by his son Tan, better known as the Duke of Chou, who by means of symbols or emblems expounded the significance of each line of each hexagram. He pointed out the good or bad fortune indicated by each line. The combined significance of the six lines as interpreted by the Duke of Chou corresponds, in general tenor, to his father King Wen's interpretation of the whole hexagram.

When Confucius, several centuries later, devoted himself to the study of the I-Ching, he wrote ten appendices, called the "Ten Wings", to elucidate the texts of King Wen and the Duke of Chou. In one of them he told how Fu Hsi had discovered the eight trigrams and given China her first numerology. In the other appendices, Confucius gave directions on the conformities of the human to the cosmic situations represented by the symbols, and explained the sequence of the hexagrams, and so forth.

Confucius's veneration for King Wen is borne out by the remarks he once made to his disciples when confronted with great danger. He said, "King Wen being dead, has not his message been passed on to me? If God had wished this message to vanish, then I, King Wen's successor, should never have received it; but if God has not yet wished this message to vanish what harm can the people of Huang do to me?"

This reference to the will of God by Confucius testifies to his belief in the existence of a Supreme Being or Divine Spirit indwelling the universe. The earliest symbolic representation of God in Chinese is a wedge pointing downwards, without any anthropomorphic significance whatsoever.

On another occasion, Confucius said, "God begat the power that is in me; what have I to fear from such a one as Huan T'ui?" Again, in reply to a disciple who asked him what he meant by saying that nobody understood him, Confucius said, "I do not murmur against God, nor do I grumble against man. My studies are pursued here below, but my penetration rises high; and there is God: He knows me."

Thus Confucius spoke of God whom he represented, as the Chinese still do, by the ideograph depicting the great vault of heaven called *T'ien*, the abode of God. During his long life with its many vicissitudes of fortune, he was sustained by a sense of the divine revelation first received by Fu Hsi, relayed by King Wen, and handed down to him. He sought assiduously the realization of sagehood whereby, as he said in his exposition of the *Ch'ien* Hexagram, he could, "in his moral attributes, harmonize with Spirit and Earth; in his brilliancy, harmonize with the sun and moon; in his even tenor of life, harmonize with the four seasons; and in his good and evil fortunes, harmonize with gods and demons."

Now, what are the esoteric tenets taught by the sage-authors of the I-Ching? As our time is limited, I can only set forth two or three of the essential doctrines. The Book teaches us that there exists one Boundless Immutable Principle, one Absolute Reality, which antecedes all manifested conditioned Being. It is called in the I-Ching the *T'ai Chi*, i.e., Supreme Ultimate. This Ultimate Reality is the One Life, the One Self-Existence, the Absolute All-in-All, Eternal and Infinite, the Causeless Cause of all things, to which all things eventually return. The phenomenal universe, with all things contained therein, is the outward manifestation of this Absolute Reality.

In Chinese the *T'ai Chi*, which is only by intuition, has two aspects called *Yin* and *Yang*, that is, the Receptive and the Creative. These two aspects or principles, being inseparable parts of unity, are always at work in space and time, interplaying and co-operating with each other, and it is the interplay and co-operation of these two cosmic forces that causes the ever-changing phenomena of our universe. In the world of relativity as we know it, these two polar opposites appear as spirit and matter, father and mother, day and night, light and darkness, life and form, good and evil, motion and rest, the positive and negative poles of electricity and magnetism, and many other dualities familiar to us in daily life. I am sure my Hindu friends here will agree with me that these two aspects of ultimate reality are in agreement with the Hindu teachings regarding the absolute or *Parabrahman* with its two aspects, *Purusha* and *Mulaprakriti*, and that this duality correspond to the Hindu duality of Manvantara and Pralaya. In the text of the I-Ching are many sayings expressing this truth. For instance, one of the Ten Appendices to the Book (The Great Treatise) says: "The creative rhythm of *Yin* and *Yang* constitutes what is called the *Tao*." Again: "In the I [Changes] there is the Supreme Ultimate which engenders the two primal forces [*Yin-Yang*]."

In Western literature, this principle of interaction of *Yin-Yang* is known as the Law of Polarity. It is interesting to note that this law has been expounded by RALPH WALDO EMERSON in his ESSAY ON COMPENSATION in the following manner:

Polarity, or action and reaction, we meet in every part of nature; in darkness and light; in heat and cold; in the ebb and flow of waters; in male and female; in the inspiration and expiration of plants and animals; in the systole and diastole of the heart; in the undulations of fluid and of sound; in the centrifugal and centripetal gravity; in electricity, galvanism, and chemical affinity. Superinduce magnetism at one end of a needle, the opposite magnetism takes place at the other end.

If the south attracts, the north repels. To empty here, you must condense there. An inevitable dualism bisects nature, so that each thing is a half, and suggests another thing to make it whole; as spirit, matter; man, woman; subjective, objective; in, out; upper, under; motion, rest; yea, nay.

Modern science furnishes some illustrations of this central doctrine of the I-Ching. Let us, for instance, take the case of the atom. As we all know, the solid atom, once considered the indivisible and unchangeable basis of the universe, can now be broken up into tiny granules of negative and positive electricity, respectively known as electrons and protons, the electrons revolving around the proton, or the nucleus, just as the planets revolve around the sun. If we had the faculty of being able to observe the atom of hydrogen, we would notice the dizzy circuits of a negative electron revolving round a positive nucleus at the rate of six thousand billion times per second. Recently, physicists have also discovered that the whirling electrons themselves are also both positive and negative, corresponding to the masculine and feminine aspects of the Absolute.

Another principle taught in the Book of Changes is the absolute universality of the law of periodicity, of flux and reflux, ebb and flow, which physical science has observed and recorded in all departments of nature. An alternation such as that of day and night, life and death, sleeping and waking, is a fact so perfectly universal that it can easily be recognized as one of the fundamental laws of the universe.

This law of periodicity is also known as the law of cycles and the law of growth and decay. Suffice it to note here that all things are subject to the law of growth and decay; there is hardly anything of which the outward expression, in the sense of possible development, is not limited. Even the culture of a nation must die, once the meaning it embodies has found full expression. The rise and fall of civilizations, the regular succession of the four seasons, the ebb and flow of the tides are all governed by this basic law. In accordance with this law, worlds, solar systems and universes, too, have their birth, growth, decay and death. OVID expressed this truth long ago in the following lines in his METAMORPHOSES: "There is nothing constant in the universe. All ebb and flow, and every shape that's born, bears in its womb the seeds of change."

In a unique fashion, the I-Ching also embodies and expounds the law of reversion in extremis, i.e., the reversion of one pole to its very opposite at the extreme point, similar to the change of night into day and day into night at a certain moment. In Western philosophical terminology this law is known as the law of Enantiodromia, a Greek word used by HERACLITUS to signify reversion to the opposite. The truth is that when the creative principle, Yang, has reached its extreme limit, the dark power of Yin is born within its depths and thus night begins; and when Yin has reached its extreme limit, the bright power of Yang appears and causes daybreak. Herein lies the explanation of the phenomena of cycles – cycles of creation which can be found in all things, in the rise and fall of civilizations, the regular succession of the four seasons, the ebb and flow of the tides, and so forth.

This principle may be perceived in the following diagram called the T'ai Chi T'u, i.e. the diagram, of the Supreme Ultimate with its two aspects Yin-Yang:

Here the *Yang* principle, indicated by the white portion, is born from the centre and gradually grows, expanding and increasing till it reaches its utmost limit of manifestation, as represented by the straight line at the upper part of the diagram. At this stage of fullness and maximum expression, its polar opposite, *Yin*, begins automatically to manifest itself. Likewise, *Yin*, indicated by the black portion, appears from the centre and gradually grows, expanding and increasing till it attains its utmost limit of manifestation, as represented by the straight line at the lower part of the diagram. Thereupon *Yang* is reborn and the cycle is repeated ad infinitum. This alternate growth and passing away of *Yin-Yang*, their successive influx and efflux, and their transformation at an extreme point are simultaneous manifestations of two basic laws taught in the I-Ching, namely, the law of cycles and the law of *Enantiodromia*.

Now, if it is true that this cyclic law of periodicity operates in all spheres of existence, then the old belief that the progress of mankind has an automatic character and proceeds in the form of a straight line does not hold. In fact, this belief which emerged in the West in the Nineteenth Century has been exploded by our two world wars. Furthermore, history has shown time and again that mankind rises to the heights only to fall again into the abysses. The progress of mankind does not take a linear form, but proceeds in waves rising and falling through various peoples and civilizations, rising to serve nature's purpose and falling after the purpose has been fulfilled. Even within a nation, such successive waves of regeneration and degeneration, of the rise and fall of the race, are clearly perceptible. This is the *Samsara* of Buddhism.

What we perceive in human life is also perceived in the starry vault of *T'ien*. Every astronomical revolution, every return of a wandering planet to the same point in the zodiac which it has touched and re-touched before, proves this truth of cyclic alternation as a universal law. Throughout nature we find this dual characteristic – construction on the one hand and destruction on the other. This is why the history of both the inferior and the superior kingdoms of nature moves through a series of well-defined epochs. In the I-Ching it is frequently pointed out that the end of each evolutionary wave is succeeded by the beginning of a new one. Owing to this overlapping of the two waves, both the decaying and the nascent phases of civilization co-exist. Their mutual play precipitates temporary confusion.

It seems that we are today moving through a transitional period which marks the decline and end of an outworn phase side by side with the commencement and growth of a new one. This epochal decline is brought about by an increasing manifestation of the evils of materialism which have been inherent in the passing phase. Thus materialism – with its belief that reality is solely contained within sensual objects, that the mind of a man is a mere lump of nervous matter in his head, with its denial of the existence of a super-mind in the universe, and with its setting up of a laissez-faire philosophy in the conduct of life – represents the essential culture and actual practice of mankind in the declining phase, whatever its pretended culture is supposed to be. The I-Ching teaches that during its early and intermediate phases the historic cycle proceeds slowly, but when it approaches its culmination, the momentum of change, disintegration and destruction increases with dramatic speed.

This process of development, acceleration, and transformation is indicated by the first line of the second hexagram, *Kun*, the symbol of Earth. This line shows its subject "treading on hoarfrost, leading to the formation of solid ice in due course." Commenting on this text, Confucius writes: "The dark power of *Yin* has begun to take form. Allow it to go on quietly according to its nature, and the hoarfrost will become solid ice." Commenting on it further, he writes: "The assassination of a ruler by his minister, or of a father by his son, is not the result of events of a single morning or a single evening. Its causes have gradually accumulated – through the absence of early discernment."

However, at the general turning-point when a new cycle is about to open, the disturbance of conditions becomes like a great avalanche, men and their methods going to devastating extremes. At the final stage, the movement of events becomes accelerated and leaps forward erratically like a horse out of control. In the Book of Changes this situation is symbolized by the sixth or topmost line of the *K'un* Hexagram which signifies "the fighting of a host of dragons in the wilderness causing injuries and bloodshed to all of them, the victorious as well as the defeated."

It seems that we are confronted today by such a terminal period, the closing of an entire cycle of world history. At the same time the ascending phase, i.e., the spiritual phase, has also started its course, so that we really stand in a transitional stage between the two. Hence the presence at one and the same time of two contradictory currents in our civilization as, for example, an insensate desire for sensuous pleasure occupying one group of human minds on the one hand and on the other an earnest desire for spiritual understanding and transformation of consciousness into transcendental wisdom occuppying a different group.

Throughout the Book of Changes emphasis is laid on the importance of harmonious co-operation between the various lines of a hexagram, for they are inseparable. In every symbol we are shown the auspicious results of harmonious co-operation and the inauspicious consequences of antagonistic relations. Thus the text of Line 2 of the *Lin* Hexagram, which is harmoniously related to Line 5, reads, "There will be good fortune; (advancing) will be in every way advantageous." On the other hand, Line 2 of the *Sui* Hexagram, which is "antagonistically related" to Line 5, shows "one who cleaves to the little boy, and lets go the man of age and experience." Furthermore, Line 4 of the *Kuan* Hexagram, which is harmoniously related to Line 5, shows "one contemplating the glory of the kingdom. It will be advantageous for him, being such as he is, to seek to be a guest of the king." Finally, the text of Line 4 of the *Li* Hexagram, which is antagonistically related to Line 5, reads, "How sudden its coming! Then (with) flamelike (swiftness) it is dead and cast away."

Co-operation is thus a vital need of the present age. It should prevail among classes within a nation, among the nations themselves, and even among the five continents. What has emerged for every thoughtful observer is the fact that no satisfactory solution of the practical problems which harass modern mankind can be found of any other basis than a broadly co-operative one. All other solutions will be partial at their best, ineffectual at their worst. This is true not only of the relations between the different classes, castes, or groups which compose a nation, but also in regard to those between the different nations. We are learning at last that we must share our lives on this planet together. World society must one day become a commonwealth. This is the ideal cherished and taught by the greatest of our sages, Confucius, both in the Record of Rites and in the Book of Changes. In his commentary on the latter, Confucius envisaged an ideal world state in which sages make their appearance in accordance with the spirit of the times, and all nations harmoniously co-operate with one another and enjoy the blessings of world peace.

Monastic Experience and the East-West Dialogue

by

The Rev. THOMAS MERTON (Brother LOUIS) (1915–1968)
Monk of the Abbey of Gethsemani, Trappist, Kentucky

EDITOR'S NOTE: As the reader will observe, this article consists in part of notes intended for further development. It is a working document, giving a singularly lucid picture of one of the clearest of contemporary poetic minds at work.

1. In all the great world religions there are a few individuals and communities who dedicate themselves in a special way to living out the full consequences and implications of what they believe. This dedication may take a variety of forms, some temporary, some permanent; some active and some intellectual; some ascetic, contemplative and mystical. In this paper the term "monastic" is applied in a broad way to those forms of special contemplative dedication which include:

(a) a certain distance or detachment from the "ordinary" and "secular" concerns of wordly life, a monastic solitude, whether partial or total, temporary or permanent;

(b) a preoccupation with the radical inner depth of one's religious and philosophical beliefs, the inner and experiential *ground* of those beliefs, and their outstanding spiritual implications;

(c) a special concern with inner transformation, a deepening of consciousness toward an eventual breakthrough and discovery of a transcendent dimension of life beyond that of the ordinary empirical self and of ethical and pious observance.

This monastic "work" or discipline is not merely an individual affair. It is at once personal and communal. Its orientation is in a certain sense supra-personal. It goes beyond a merely psychological fulfilment on the empirical level, and it goes beyond the limits of communicable cultural ideals (of one's own national, racial, etc. background). It attains to a certain universality and wholeness which have never yet been adequately described – and probably cannot be described – in terms of psychology. Transcending the limits that separate subject from object and self from not-self, this development achieves a wholeness which is described in various ways by the different religions; a self realization of *Atman*, of Void, of life in Christ, of *Fana* and *Baqa* (annihilation and reintegration according to Sufism) etc.

This is not necessarily a matter of personal charismata (special divine illuminations or prophetic tasks) but it is usually expected to follow from discipline and initiation into a *traditional religious "way"*, that is to say a special mode of life and of consciousness which meets certain unwritten, indeed inexpressible, conditions. The special formation required to meet these conditions is imparted by experienced persons, or judged by a community that has shared something of the traditional consciousness we may call mystical, contemplative, enlightened, or spiritually transformed.

2. At this point – a parenthesis on the problems of language. There are great difficulties inherent in words like "mystical". Lack of agreement on their meaning, etc. Without deciding all these problems here, what matters is to clarify the distinction between the "monastic" type of dedication, the "monastic" quest for a higher type of consciousness, from "active" types of dedication oriented to "good works" like education, care of the sick, etc. Jesuits are not monks (though in fact they include today scholars who have a more sympathetic understanding of monastic questions and problems than many monks have). Missionaries are generally not monks. Confusion on this point is nevertheless present in the Western Church, especially now, when the very notion of the "contemplative life" is under attack even in the (Catholic) monastic milieu. Having referred in a general way to these problems, one might emphasize two points:

(a) Even in the highly active "west" there is nevertheless a monastic tradition which is primarily contemplative and this tradition is being renewed even in the Protestant milieu which was originally hostile to it.

(b) There is a real possibility of contact on a deep level between this contemplative and monastic tradition in the West and the various contemplative traditions in the East – including the Islamic Sufis, the mystical lay-contemplative societies in Indonesia, etc. as well as the better known monastic groups in Hinduism and Buddhism.

3. A word on Orthodox as distinguished from Catholic (Western) mysticism. The emphasis on contemplation in Greece and Russia. The Hesychast tradition. Athos. Problems of Orthodox monasticism today.

Though Catholic monasticism is less frankly contemplative, it is in a better position for dialogue with Asia at the moment because of the climate of openness following Vatican II. Christian monasticism has a tradition of adaptation and comprehension with regard to Greek philosophy, and many Catholics realize that this could also apply very well to Hindu and Buddhist pilosophies, disciplines, experiences. An articulate minority exists. It is ready for free and productive communication. Encouragement has been offered by the Vatican Council.

4. To return to our main theme, we can easily see the special value of dialogue and exchange among those in the various religions who seek to penetrate the ultimate ground of their beliefs by a transformation of the religious consciousness. We can see the point of sharing in those disciplines which claim to prepare a way for "mystical" self-transcendence (with due reservations in the use of the term "mystical").

Without asserting that there is complete unity of all religions at the "top"‹ the transcendent or mystical level – that they all start from different dogmatic positions to "meet" at this summit – it is certainly true to say that even where there are irreconcilable differences in doctrine and in formu-lated belief, there may still be great similarities and analogies in the realm of religious experience. There is nothing new in the observation that holy men like St. Francis and Sri Ramakrishna (to mention only two) have attained to a level of spiritual fulfilment which is at once universally rec-ognizable and relevant to anyone interested in the religious dimension of existence. Cultural and doctrinal differences must remain, but they do not invalidate a very real quality of existential likeness.

5. The purpose of this paper is primarily to make clear that, on this existen-tial level of experience and of spiritual maturity, it is possible to achieve real and significant contacts and perhaps much more besides. We will consider in a moment what this "much more" may be. For the present, one thing above all needs to be emphasized. Such dialogue in depth, at the very ground of monastic and of human experience, is not just a matter of academic interest. It is not just something for which foundation money could be obtained. That is probably true, but this paper is not considering that particular aspect of it. This is not just a matter of "research" and of academic conferences, workshops, study groups, or even of new institu-tional structuring – producing results that may be fed in to the general accumulation of new facts about man, society, culture and religion.

I speak as a Western monk who is preeminently concerned with his own monastic calling and dedication. I have left my monastery to come here not just as a research scholar or even as an author (which I also happen to be). I come as a pilgrim who is anxious to obtain not just information, not just "facts" about other monastic traditions, but to drink from ancient sources of monastic vision and experience. I seek not only to learn more (quantitatively) about religion and about monastic life, but to become a better and more enlightened monk (qualitatively) myself.

I am convinced that communication in depth, across the lines that have hitherto divided religious and monastic traditions, is now not only possible and desirable, but most important for the destinies of Twentieth Century man.

I do not mean that we ought to expect visible results of earthshaking importance, or that any publicity at all is desirable. On the contrary, I am convinced that this exchange must take place under the true monastic conditions of quiet, tranquility, sobriety, leisureliness, reverence, meditation and cloistered peace. I am convinced that what one might call typically "Asian" conditions of non-hurrying and of patient waiting must prevail over the Western passion for immediate visible results. For this reason I think it is above all important for Westerners like myself to learn what little they can from Asia, *in* Asia. I think we must seek not merely to make superficial reports *about* the Asian traditions, but to live and share those traditions, as far as we can, by living them in their traditional milieu.

I need not add that I think we have now reached a stage of (long overdue) religious maturity at which it may be possible for someone to remain perfectly faithful to a Christian and Western monastic commitment, and yet to learn in depth from, say, a Buddhist or Hindu discipline and experience. I believe that some of us need to do this in order to improve the quality of our own monastic life and even to help in the task of monastic renewal which has been undertaken within the Western Church.

6. At this point – a parenthesis on the problems of "monastic renewal" – state of confusion resulting from a collapse of formal structures that were no longer properly understood – exterior and formal ritualism, etc., or external observance for its own sake – a traditionalism that was emptied of its truly living traditional content, repudiation of genuine tradition, discipline, contemplation – trivializing the monastic life. This has resulted in a true monastic crisis in the West. It is entirely possible that many hitherto flourishing monastic institutions, which preserved a genuine living continuity with the Middle Ages, may soon cease to exist. Both good and bad in this. Will Asian monasticism sooner or later face the same kind of crisis? Source of the problem: obsession with "relevance" to the new generation – but the problem is only half understood. In reality, the secular quasi-monastic movement of the hippies in America shows that the contemplative dimensions of life (which some monks and clergy are actively repudiating) is definitely relevant to modern youth.

7. In order not to prolong this paper overmuch, let us confine ourselves to two particularly important topics: that of *communication* between monastic traditions, and that of the more obvious *wrong-directions* we must avoid. Necessarily both topics will have to be treated more briefly than we might desire.

8. The question of *communication* is now no longer fraught with too great difficulties. The publication of classical Asian texts and of studies on them, especially in English and in German, has led to the formation of what one might call an inter-traditional vocabulary. We are well on our way to a workable inter-religious lexicon of key words – mostly rooted in Sanskrit –

which will permit intelligent discussion of all kinds of religious experience in all the religious traditions. This is in fact already being done to some extent, and one of the results of it is that psychologists and psychoanalysts, as well as anthropologists and students of comparative religion, are now able to talk a kind of lingua franca of religious experience. I think this "language" though sometimes pedantic, seems to be fairly reliable, and it is now at the disposition of theologians, philosophers, and plain monks like myself.

This is a first step only, but it is an important step – which will often have to be completed by the services of an interpreter. He in his turn will be more helpful if he knows the "common language," and is interested in the common pursuit of inner enlightenment. Incontestably, however, this kind of communication cannot get far unless it is carried on among people who share some degree of the same enlightenment.

Is it too optimistic to expect the monks themselves to make this contribution? I hope not. And here we come to the "something more" that I referred to above. True communication on the deepest level is more than a simple sharing of ideas, of conceptual knowledge, or formulated truth. The kind of communication that is necessary on this deep level must also be *communion* beyond the levels of words, a communion in authentic experience which is shared not only on a *pre-verbal* level but also on a *post-verbal* level.

The *pre-verbal* level is that of the unspoken and indefinable *preparation*, the *pre-disposition* of mind and heart, necessary for all "monastic" experience whatever. This demands among other things *a freedom from automatisms and routines*, a candid liberation from external social dictates, from conventions, limitations and mechanisms which restrict understanding and inhibit experience of the new, the unexpected. Monastic training must not form men in a rigid mold, but liberate them from habitual and routine mechanisms. The monk who is to communicate on the level that interests us here must be not merely a punctilious observer of external traditions, but a living example of traditional and interior realization. He must be wide open to life and to new experience because he has fully utilized his own tradition and gone beyond it. This will permit him to meet a disciple of another, apparently remote and alien tradition, and find a common ground of verbal understanding with him. The *post-verbal* level will then, at least ideally, be that on which they both meet beyond their own words and their own understanding in the silence of an ultimate experience which might conceivably not have occurred if they had not met and spoken...

This I would call "communion". I think it is something that the deepest ground of our being cries out for, and it is something for which a lifetime of striving would not be enough.

9. The wrong ways that are to be avoided ought to be fairly evident.

First of all, this striving for inter-monastic communion should not become just another way of adding to the *interminable empty talk*, the endlessly fruitless and trivial discussion of everything under the sun, the inexhaustible chatter with which modern man tries to convince himself that he is in touch with his fellow man and with reality. This contemplative dialogue must be reserved for those who have been seriously disciplined by years of silence and by a long habit of meditation. I would add that it must be reserved for those who have entered with full seriousness into their own monastic tradition and are in authentic contact with the past of their own religious community – besides being open to the tradition and to the heritage of experience belonging to other communities.

Second, there can be no question of a facile syncretism, a mish-mash of semi-religious verbiage and pieties, a devotionalism that admits everything and therefore takes nothing with full seriousness.

Third, there must be a scrupulous respect for important differences and where one no longer understands or agrees, this must be kept clear – without useless debate. There are differences that are not debatable, and it is a useless, silly temptation to try to argue them out. Let them be left intact until a moment of greater understanding.

Fourth, attention must be concentrated on what is really essential to the monastic quest: this, I think, is to be sought in the area of true self-transcendence and enlightenment. It is to be sought in the transformation of consciousness in its ultimate ground, as well as in the highest and most authentic devotional love of the *bhakti* type – but not in the acquisition of extraordinary powers, in miraculous activities, in special charismata, visions, levitation, etc. These must be seen as phenomena of a different order.

Fifth, questions of institutional structure, monastic rule, traditional forms of cult and observance must be seen as relatively secondary and are not to become the central focus of attention. They are to be understood in their relation to enlightenment itself. However, they are to be given the full respect due to them and the interests of dialogue and communication should not be allowed to subvert structures that may remain very important helps to interior development.

10. It is time to conclude. The point to be stressed is the importance of serious communication, and indeed of "communion", among contemplatives of different traditions, disciplines and religions. This can contribute much to the development of man at this critical point of his history. Indeed, we find ourselves in a crisis, a moment of crucial choice. We are in grave danger of losing a spiritual heritage that has been painfully accumulated by thousands of generations of saints and contemplatives. It is the peculiar office of the monk in the modern world to keep alive the

contemplative experience and to keep the way open for modern technological man to recover the integrity of his own inner depths.

Above all, it is important that this element of depth and integrity – this
element of inner transcendent freedom – be kept intact as we grow toward
the full maturity of universal man. We are witnessing the growth of a truly
universal consciousness in the modern world. This universal consciousness
may be a consciousness of transcendent freedom and vision, or it may
simply be a vast blur of mechanized triviality and ethical cliché.

The difference is, I think, important enough to be of concern to all
religions, as well as to humanistic philosophies with no religion at all.

Extemporaneous Remarks by Thomas Merton

EDITOR'S NOTE: During the morning of the second day of the conference (October 23, 1968) Father Merton spoke *ex tempore*, in what was a singularly effective and affecting presentation of a part of his personal philosophy. He spoke as a Christian monk who had found, in other monks of other religions gathered here in Calcutta, his spiritual brothers.

Thomas Merton's sudden death near Bangkok, little more than six weeks after the conference, was a tragedy not only to his friends but to all who cherish the spiritual in man, and all who value the poet's ability to penetrate to the truth with words that sing. Thomas Merton was the author of 28 books, the most famous of which, THE SEVEN STOREY MOUNTAIN, is an *apologia pro vita sua* ranking among the finest of spiritual auto-biographies. In recent years he had published several works relating to other religions, including a study of Zen Buddhism and a collection of Mahatma Gandhi's statements on non-violence.

He was only fifty-three when he died. What further wisdom might have come from his pen, as a result of his visit to Asia, we shall of course never know, but what he said that morning in Calcutta affords us at least a clue.

First, let me struggle with the contradiction that I have to live with, in appearing before you in what I really consider to be a disguise, because I never, never wear this.[1] What I ordinarily wear is blue jeans and an open shirt; which brings me to the question that people have been asking to a great extent: Whom do you represent? What religion do you represent? And that, too, is a rather difficult question to answer. I came with the notion of perhaps saying something for monks and to monks of all religions because I am supposed to be a monk.

In speaking for monks I am really speaking for a very strange kind of person, a marginal person, because the monk in the modern world is no longer an established person with an established place in society. We realize very keenly in America today that the monk is essentially outside of all establishments. He does not belong to an establishment. He is a marginal

---

[1] A clerical collar.

person who withdraws deliberately to the margin of society with a view to deepening fundamental human experience. Consequently, as one of these strange people, I speak to you as a representative of all marginal persons who have done this kind of thing deliberately.

Thus I find myself representing perhaps hippies among you, poets, people of this kind who are seeking in all sorts of ways and have absolutely no established status whatever. So I ask you to do me just this one favor of considering me not as a figure representing any institution, but as a statusless person and an insignificant person who comes to you asking your charity and patience while I say one or two things.

Are monks and hippies and poets relevant? No, we are deliberately irrelevant. We live with an ingrained irrelevance which is proper to every human being. The marginal man accepts the basic irrelevance of the human condition, an irrelevance which is manifested above all by the fact of death. The marginal person, the monk, the displaced person, the prisoner, all these people live in the presence of death, which calls into question the meaning of life. He struggles with the fact of death in himself, trying to seek something deeper than death; because there is something deeper than death, and the office of the monk or the marginal person, the meditative person or the poet is to go beyond death even in this life, to go beyond the dichotomy of life and death and to be, therefore, a witness to life.

This requires, of course, faith, but as soon as you say faith in terms of this monastic and marginal existence you run into another problem. Faith means doubt. Faith is not the suppression of doubt. It is the overcoming of doubt and you overcome doubt by going through it. The man of faith who has never experienced doubt is not a man of faith. Consequently, the monk is one who has to struggle in the depths of his being with the presence of doubt, and to go through what some religions call the Great Doubt, to break through beyond doubt into a servitude which is very, very deep because it is not his own personal servitude, it is the servitude of God himself, in us. The only ultimate reality is God. God lives and dwells in us. We are not justified by any action of our own, but we are called by the voice of God, by the voice of that ultimate Being, to pierce through the irrelevance of our life, while accepting and admitting that our life is totally irrelevant, in order to find relevance in Him. And this relevance in Him is not something we can grasp or possess. It is something that can only be received as a gift. Consequently, the kind of life that I represent is a life that is openness to gift. Gift from God and gift from others.

It is not that we go out into the world with a capacity to love others greatly. This too we know in ourselves, that our capacity for love is limited. And it has to be completed with the capacity to be loved, to accept love from others, to want to be loved by others, to admit our loneliness and to live with our loneliness because everybody is lonely. This is then another basis for the kind of experience that I am talking about which is a new approach, a different approach to the eternal experience of the monk. The monk in his solitude and in his meditation seeks this dimension of life.

But, we do have to admit also the value of traditional monastic ways. In the West there is now going on a great upheaval in monasticism, and much that is of undying value is being thrown away irresponsibly, foolishly, in favor of things that are superficial and showy, that have no ultimate value. I do not know how the situation is in the East, but I will say as a brother from the West to Eastern monks, be a little careful. The time is coming when you may face the same situation and your fidelity to your ancient traditions will stand you in good stead. Do not be afraid of that fidelity. I know I need not warn you of this.

Behind, then, all that I have said is the idea that significant contacts are certainly possible and easy on the level of this kind of monastic experience, this poetic level of experience – not necessarily institutional monasticism, but among people who are seeking. The basic condition for this is that each be faithful to his own search.

And so I stand among you as one who offers a small message of hope, that first, there are always people who dare to seek on the margin of society, who are not dependent on social acceptance, not dependent on social routine, and prefer a kind of free-floating existence under a state of risk. And among these people, if they are faithful to their own calling, to their own vocation, and to their own message from God, communication on the deepest level is possible.

And the deepest level of communication is not communication, but communion. It is wordless. It is beyond words, and it is beyond speech and it is beyond concept. Not that we discover a new unity. We discover an older unity. My dear brothers, we are already one. But we imagine that we are not. And what we have to recover is our original unity. What we have to be is what we are.

The Unity of Religions

by

SWAMI CHINMAYANANDA

Chinmaya Mission (Sandeepany Sadhanalaya, Tara Cultural Trust) Bombay[1]

Differences do exist. Distinctions can be recognized. Subtile variations of opinion can be pointed out. And yet all religions and religious masters have been giving out one single solitary message everywhere: that there is a greater reality behind the obvious pluralism that we are observing all around. The various forms and names and their different functions are each one of them as important as any other one.

In this respect the Upanishads of India give us a beautiful analogy or metaphor of the tree. The trunk is not like the branch; the branch is not like the twig; the twig is not like the leaf; the leaf is not like the flower. But together we call it *the tree.*

If the trunk's function and form are different from the branches' and the twigs', the leaves' function and form are different from the flowers'. Each of them has a distinct form and expression and function, and yet all of them together we call *the one tree.*

This is not because the trunk is exactly like the branch, nor that there is no distinction at all between the flower and the leaf, it is because deep inside there is a sap that flows, that nurses and nourishes and nurtures all branches, all buds, all leaves, all flowers, all fruits, and hence we say that *the tree is one.*

Similarly, for Vedantism, Christianity, Hinduism, Sikhism, Jainism: there are as many religions as there have been masters who have inspired man to live the nobler life, and until and unless we come to contact and recognize and understand the factors that breed these pluralistic phenomena, they are confusing indeed. And yet in and through them all there is a sap that runs continuously on. In this life, in the various religions, one person may call it God, another may call it Atman, another Buddha; others may call it by other names. But the one reality is that there is a great consciousness, a greater soul, a greater factor in each one of us. And we at this mo-

[1] Delivered extemporaneously at the Birla Academy, October 22, 1968.

ment, not recognizing the different steps in us, but identifying with the outer carcass of a physical body and a mind and perhaps some portion of our intellect, look at the world and recognize the world in different ways. I can come in contact with the world only when I relate myself to the world. In my relationship to the world the question arises of the relevance of religion in life. The relevance of religion in life is only to organize my relationships with the world around me. I relate myself to the world from different standpoints in myself. Physically, I am seeing you all as human beings. Emotionally, I may love you, or I may hate you. Intellectually, I may be able to appreciate you, or not appreciate you. But from each standpoint I get a new evaluation of all.

When I came into this hall, I met and talked with Father FALLON. All I knew was that he is a French professor here at the University. He speaks fluent Bengali and he is translating the Bible into Bengali. That is all. But after we have heard and listened to his beautiful paper, don't you think that you can look at him with a different eye altogether? I do. Before, I saw him only as a physical form, and I have seen many priests and padres, and I thought: This is one among them. But when you understand him, you feel that there is a deeper chord in you that is touched by him, because he could talk to us from a deeper level.

And still we go into these questionings of ourselves. Where can there be any solution or relevancy in life? Therefore, the movement for seeking the relevancy of religion to life is not merely a horizontal movement; it must be vertical. It must be a spiritual quest, an attempt by each individual to unfold himself to himself, away from the paltry passions of the flesh, the agitations of the mind, the endless questionings of the intellect. This can come only on the transcendence into a higher plane of consciousness; when masters and generations have been able to realize this unfoldment, to that extent those masters have been able to impart their hope, their peace, their tranquility to others around them. This doesn't mean that every one of us will be able to unfold spiritually immediately. And it is not necessary. Even in this scientific age, not everyone is going to become an EINSTEIN. There may be only one EINSTEIN, one JAMES JOYCE or one great scientist here or there, but they contribute their knowledge. Other scientific men, men of ordinary science, try to live up to it. Similarly, spiritual mastery and spiritual total unfoldment may not come to everybody. It is not necessary. But the moment we have this vision in ourselves, we must understand that it is not necessarily the Scriptures, the Bible, the Koran, the Upanishads that will bring about relevancy to life in religion.

In this context, I must especially say that in earlier sessions there was general bemoaning from the platform that, due to the tragedy at Darjeeling we could not go to the peaks of the Himalayas and climb the serene heights. Absurd! It is the divine plan that has brought us here. Because what *is* our problem? Our very question here is how to bring into religion its relevancy to life. To go back again to the Himalayas? No, it is how to bring religion from the Himalayas, from the churches, from the mosques, from the books, into the market place. That is eaxctly what we are trying to find out, and therefore there is a symbolic rightness that we could not do it in the Himalayas. We have to do it here, now.

Therefore, friends, here is the right atmosphere. In the time we will be spending here listening to and understanding the papers and discussions, we will be constantly trying to find out how we can bring this idea to the ordinary man: Continue your victory over the world around. What matter if it is through scientific understanding? Continue that. Through economy? Continue bringing forth more wealth into the world. Let all the politicians try to discover how it can be distributed beautifully and equally all around the world. All these efforts must go on, but they must go on *inspired* by a greater understanding of the ulterior and greater goal in which we are all one regardless of distinctions of caste or creed or race or color. And this ideology can come only when that spiritual dimension is taken at the religious level.

At the religious level there will be and there should be distinctions, but in the realm of the spiritual one must recognize the intellect itself. There you enter the realm of peace and tranquility. In that larger and ampler dimension of the greater consciousness, there is no distinction between man and man or even between man and matter. There is no distinction at all, whether among plants or animals or humans in that awakened mode of higher awareness. Politically we know that there is government of the people, by the people, for the people; but practically we know there is government of the people, by the people, for the people, *on* the people. We also know that if this ideal and understanding is once accepted, when we are living in this world, we must say at all levels let there be new orientation, a new vision, a new dimension altogether; that with this we can all solve our problems. Pour one ounce of love in the world, shake the world, and keep it there. All problems will precipitate and go down, the clear waters of peace can come to the top.

The entire problem is why should I love, what exactly is love, why should I identify with you? After all, you are so different. But once I understand that between you and me there is no eternal difference, that the higher planes of imagination are one and the same, with this understanding certainly these problems can be solved. To that extent, from that spiritual standpoint, there is relevancy of religion in the world.

At the religious level the church may not look like a mosque, the mosque may not look like a temple. Religious ritualism must be distinctly different. In the shape and form there will be distinctions, but the fundamental spiritual wakening makes use of all these instrumentations The mighty experience is indeed where there is calm, peace and tranquility. Towards this man is moving. Whether we like it or not the word is that we are being pushed ahead. You find even international political organizations join together in crying, peace, peace, peace. The world has to move ahead because essentially man is demanding it. This great effort we can put forth through all of our great institutions. Where the emphasis is ultimately for spiritual unfolding, rather than a mere bigotry or a mere political subscription to a faith or an institution: working through the institution, with the help of faith, in the grace of the Lord, we can reach an unfolding within ourselves and come to experience it. This seems to be the ultimate means, goal or solution of bringing religion to the relevancy of ordinary life. I am not here to talk of the problems that already exist. The various speakers have already pointed them out. For this, understanding is necessary.

The Temple of Understanding, the Viveka which is called Vedanta Viveka, has the power to analyze the problem that is facing us and to find out what exactly is the core of reality in and through the nature that is ever expressing itself around us, this Temple of Understanding which has organized this great function and under whose egis we shall be discussing understanding for the next three or four days. Let us come to a solution to the problem: at least we see the distant horizons of a brighter day, when there shall be *more* understanding in the world and we shall learn to embrace each other without various mental inhibitions, fanaticisms, or religious obstructions, political distinctions or racial differences. Let us learn to see, in and through them all, the core, the oneness that is shimmering at all times, trying to express itself and fulfil itself in and through man.

Zoroastrianism - "Thus Spoke Zarathustra"

by

Dastoor N. D. Minochehr Homji
High Priest of the Zoroastrians, Bombay

I am grateful to the Temple of Understanding for inviting me to participate in this inter-religious meeting, in which we shall seek to approach current problems not from the sociological viewpoint but from the religious one. I shall treat religion as "a system of ultimate values and norms of conduct ...as such it tends to constitute the supreme synthesis of the dominant values and norms of conduct" (Reconstruction of Humanity, page 141).

The same source observes that the leading religions have "failed in the cardinal point, in making the overt conduct of their followers conform to the Golden Rule, to the principle of love towards their fellows, to the ethical norms of the Sermon on the Mount".

Let me also observe what U Thant said, in his message on "Religion and Peace", on 7th March 1966: "It is wholly appropriate that devout men of goodwill should join in search for peace at the present time. This search transcends religious differences, for peace and brotherhood of man are among the basic tenets of religion..." And lastly, we quote President Lyndon B. Johnson, whose message on March 15 appears in the same book referred to above. "The billions we appropriate to conquer poverty will be worth little unless we vanquish the most crippling poverty – man's insufficiency of understanding, his meagreness of spirit. The dollars we spent to eradicate disease will be wasted unless we isolate and control the deadliest of microbes – man's capacity for hatred, his penchant for violence".

The world today suffers from PDM, i.e. Poverty & Prejudice, Discrimination among races and Disaffection in the family, and a belief that Might is Right, which means, in other words, Power without Morality, leading to violence in individuals and groups, and when it is organized by the state, to war.

Science seems to reveal today more the destructive side than the constructive one. So science on the destructive side stands for RIP! But on its constructive side, science also stands for RIP: Research with Restraint, i.e. consideration for humanity, Idealism and Industry, embodying its techno-

logical application, and Progress with Peace, so that ORDER may be established, where "O" stands for social organization for equal opportunities for the
self-development of individuals as well as of nations; "R" for Reason and
Rationality and Right, in place of rage and rancour and wrong: "D" for the
Dignity of the Human Being – Black or White or Yellow; "E" for Equity,
i.e. Moral Justice, the Spirit of Justice enabling us to interpret laws rightly
and apply them ethically; and, "R" for Right is Might, not its opposite.

Zarathustra's principle for establishing order in the Universe is given in
the five Gathas[1] or the Songs: Gatha Ahuna-vaiti inculcates in mankind
the threefold lesson of Truth, Wisdom and Love or Law, Light and Love.
It has seven chapters. The first chapter is the Prophet's pledge (Yasna 28.4)[1]
to remove darkness, selfishness and violence and to establish light, selflessness and love, called in Avesta, Asha, Vohu Mano and Kshathra respectively. In
the second chapter, we have the background of darkness, selfishness and
violence, (Yasna 29.1)[1] to remove which the Prophet is born. The same picture is drawn in Bhagvad Gita (Chapter IV. 7, 8). In the third chapter the
Prophet outlines his philosophy of the two Powers of Mainyoo: The
Principle of Subsistance and the Principle of Resistance. It has been generally but erroneously believed that Zoroastrianism believes in a God of Light
and a God of Darkness. Nothing can be further from the truth, because our
ancient faith is a monotheistic faith, believing only in One Wise Creator.

The fourth chapter enunciates the Philosophy of Life. The Prophet
stresses the need of reason over sentiment and He exhorts people (in YS.
31.17): "Let the man of wisdom speak to a man who is eager to know, let
not an ignorant man lead others astray".

He also exhorts each person to make the choice between the right and
the wrong for himself or herself and not to believe anything on mere
hearsay, so that selfish men may not spread untruth.

In the fifth chapter, the Prophet shows his grim, uncompromising
opposition to the teachers of false values, to all anti-social elements –
political or economic – called Grehma. Chapter six shows self-sacrifice as the
remedy for selfishness, which is the root of all wrongs in the world.
Zarathustra taught that selflessness is sweetness and selfishness is bitterness, as is borne out by our experience. Chapter seven points out the path
of the Liberation of the Spirit through action – through good deeds, so that
renovation can be achieved slowly but steadily.

The second Gatha, Ushta-vaiti, teaches man the life of altruism: Others
first, myself afterwards. This Gatha also embodies the Golden Rule: "Do as
you would be done by".

The third Gatha, Spenta Mainyu, embodies the all-pervasiveness of the
spirit of God. Man should recognize the presence of the good spirit in
every man and in every sentient being too. This teaches one to be loving
and considerate to others and avoid misunderstanding and violence.

1 See the Appendix on pag 89.

> In every bosom is a Christ concealed,
> To be helped or hindered, to be hurt or healed.

The fourth Gatha, Vohu-Kshathra, means moral power. Power and morality should go together. Today's science, when it becomes the hand-maid of political power, is bane and antidote, i.e. creating poison or de-struction first, and then finding its remedy. Research without restraint will lead man to destruction. Power on the path of Spenta Mainyu is the destructiveness, which we witness all around us. To develop beneficent power is the discipline of life, whereas destructive power is an untamed animal let loose. Good deeds of service and sacrifice are the best prayers, says Zarathustra.

The fifth and last Gatha, Vahishta-Ishti, means the crown of fulfillment. In the first chapter of the first Gatha, Zarathustra gives his pledge: "As long as I am physically capable and have the will power, I *will* teach man-kind to yearn for truth". After grim opposition and struggle, the Teacher of Truth succeeds in establishing order and harmony in the world, and hence He sings in the final song his satisfaction on the fulfillment of his white dream.

> Truth from his lips prevailed with double sway,
> And fools who came to scoff, remained to pray. (p. 22, no. 67).

To sum up we shall have general observations on our topic. To begin with, one cannot say that religion has been tried in the past and found wanting. But it is true to say that religion has been found difficult and left untried. By religion, I mean the fundamental principles which are identical in all the religions. When children are taught these identical fundamental principles in their impressionable age, the phrase, "the man of a foreign country" is itself foreign to their minds. One meaning of the term "foreign" as given in Chambers' Dictionary is "alien, repugnant", – and this in mid-century of the 20th Century!

Such a definition and concept can only lead to violence, because the children are brought up, by practice and precept, according to the dictum, "this person is my own, and the other fellow is a foreigner". If science and technology advance without reference to and a consideration for huma-nity, civilization and culture will be a dream of the past.

We can get some idea of the destructiveness of violence and war by con-sidering the monetary cost of a modern heavy bomber: equal to that of constructing thirty school buildings or two power plants or two hospitals. One fighter plane costs as much as half a million bushels of wheat; and a destroyer as much as decent homes for 8,000 people! (from the *American Reporter* of 1953).

The world suffers, says an apostle of Zoroastrianism (Yasht XIII, 135–183: SACRED BOOKS OF THE EAST, vol. XXIII, pages 223–24), from four types of wrongs – social, economic, political and moral. The first is the person who is dead in his conscience, the Daeva, oblivious to the social good; the second is the grafter called the Gadha in Avesta, meaning literally the brigand; the third is the tyrant, misappropriating power and authority, for as LORD ACTON puts it, "Power corrupts and absolute power corrupts absolutely", and he is called Sastar in Avesta; and the fourth and the last is the person ruled by Aeshma or passion, greed and violence.

As a man of religion, i.e. as a man of sympathy and fellow feeling for man and even of all sentient beings, I can only interpret ICBM (the Intercontinental Ballistics Missile) as "I see the Bankruptcy of Man, Mind and Morals" in which man has ceased to be an individual and become a machine, having no knowing and feeling." (Please refer to C. J. JUNG in his THE UNDISCOVERED SELF).

Let me end on the note of the universal man, as TAGORE puts it in his RELIGION OF MAN. Another apostle of Zoroastrianism prays in that hoary past (Yasna 68.15:S. B. E. XXXI, pages 323–24): "I bless (or pray for) him who is truthful with Goodness (that is, with all the values of good life), whosoever he may be, between Heaven and the Earth, with (or for) a thousand healing remedies and for ten thousand of the same." RABINDRANATH TAGORE had, as the motto of his world-famous educational institution, Shanti-Niketan, "Yastra Vishwam bhavati eka Needam", i.e. "where the whole world becomes (under the influence of true education) one happy home".

APPENDIX

Comprising references from the Avestan Scriptures, of which most are from the Holy Gatha of Zarathustra himself, *bearing directly on and supporting the various concepts of our subject.*

Ashem Vohu

> *Righteousness is best of all* that's good,
> The *Radiant Goal* it is of life on earth;
> This Light's attained when one lives righteously
> For sake of Highest Righteousness alone. (Yasna 27.14)

Yenghe Hatam

> Those men and women both do we adore,
> Whose *every act of worship is alive*
> *With* Asha, the *Eternal Law of Life;*
> Who are in sight of Mazda Ahura
> As best and noblest mortals recognized: – – –
> These are *the truest Leaders of Mankind.* (Yasna 27.15)

> . . .
> As long as I have will and wield the pow'r
> *I'll teach mankind to love and strive for Truth.*

> To You the Soul of Mother-Earth complained:
> "Wherefore Ye gave me birth? Who fashioned me?

"Passion and *rapine, outrage everywhere*
"And violence enmesh me all around;
(*To Ahura Mazda, the Supreme Being).
"No other help than Yours I see, Ye lord;
"Reveal to me a Strong One, who can save." (Ys. 29.1)

Hear with your ears the *Highest Truths* I preach,
 And with illumined minds weigh them with care,
Before you *choose* which of two Paths to tread, – – –
 Deciding man by man, each one for each; – – –
Before *the great New Age* is ushered in
 Wake up, alert to spread Ahura's Word. (Ys. 30.2)

If ye will only *know and learn these Laws,*
 Which Mazda hath ordained for ye, O, men, – – –
 The Laws *of Happiness,* the Laws *of Pain,* – – –
That Falsehood brings on "punishment" overdue,
 That *Truth leads on to fuller, higher, Life,* – – –
 Upon all such the Light Divine shall dawn. (Ys. 30.11)

Whatever *words* and *deeds* are *noblest,* best,
 Teach me, O Mazda, *make my life express,*
Through Love of Fellow-man, through *Search for Truth,*
 The yearnings and the prayers of my heart;
Renew, Ahura, *through the Strength to Serve,*
 My Life, and *make it* as Thou wishest – – – TRUE. (Ys. 34.15)

This do I enquire of Thee, vouchsafe unto me the Truth thereof:
How *dedicate my whole Self* unto Thee
In Holy Service done with all my Strength? – – –
This the Religion, Wisdom taught to me. . . . (Ys. 44.9)

This do I enquire of Thee, vouchsafe unto me the Truth
On what side shall I stand, the True or False?
Shall I confer with False Ones, who do ill,
Or with their victims, suffering for Truth?
 The False, who ever spurn Thy precious gifts,
 Does not *Untruth pervade their Mind and Heart?* (Ys. 44.12)

This do I enquire of Thee, vouchsafe unto me the Truth thereof:
Our only Foes, *the False Ones, how will I*
Deliver into Asha's Holy Hands?
 Then *through Thy Holy Words I'll make them clean;*
 And through frustration of their evil hopes,
 Through suffering and pain redeem their lives. (Ys. 44.14)

This do I enquire of Thee, vouchsafe unto me the Truth thereof:
How shall I, Mazda, guided by Thee, reach
The Goal ecstatic, and be one with Thee?
 With voice convincing would I lead mankind
 To Perfect Life Eternal, through Thy Truth – – –
 Our best and only Guide – – – Thy Holy Word. (Ys. 44.7)

Whom Shalt Thou send, O Mazda, to protect
Us all, when *Untruth threatens us with hate,*
Other than Thine own Light* and Thy Love?
    When both these are aroused within our hearts,
    Asha shall be *fulfilled,* O ahura, – – –
    May my Soul realize this Sacred Truth. (Ys. 46.7)
(*Shining Being)

Both parties, True and False, *are put to test,*
    O Mazda, by Thy blazing Fire Divine:
This Fiery *Test lays bare their Inmost Souls,*
    As Thy award to each one indicates; – – –
Complete frustration shall the False One find,
    Thy blessings full the Truthful One shall reap. (Ys. 51.9)

That man, indeed, *who makes his every act*
    An act of worship, led by Asha's Law,
    Is *deemed as best* by Mazda Ahura;
Each one of these, who have been and who are,
    With reverence will I recall by name,
    And *strive to emulate his holy deeds.* (Ys. 51. 22)*
(*This is the original Gatha verse of which
    Yenghe Hatam is a paraphrase) (cp. p. 6, no. 2 sug)

. . . . . Those who opposed Him, even they have learnt
    To reverence the Teachings of His Faith,
    And *follow this Good Creed in every act.* (Ys. 53.1)

May Brotherhood Man, for which we yearn,
Come down amongst us and rejoice the hearts
Of men and maidens of Zar'thustra's Faith.
Bringing fulfillment unto Vohu Man* . . . . . (Ys. 54.1)
(*The Life of Law – Light-of-Love)

(The above quotations are from THE RELIGION OF ZARATHUSTRA
by Dr. I. J. S. TARAPOREWALA, Ph. D., Bombay.)

Buddhism and the Other World Religions

by

TRIPITAKA VAGISVARACARYA, PANDITA, MAHATHERA D. PIYANANDA
President, Buddhist Vihara Society, Inc., Washington, D.C.

Religion, in general, has been the most powerful guide and protection as well as the greatest consolation of humanity. It is the father of all the cultures and civilizations, the literatures and fine arts of mankind. It was through religion that we human beings learned to control our animal instincts and to aspire to higher and nobler goals. No religion in the world teaches man to do evil. On the contrary every religion supplies man with spiritual nourishment and helps to elevate his mind above mundane affairs. All religions seek to temper human emotions, and in theory at least, should help to reduce tensions and conflicts among individuals, races and nations. Despite glaring examples of failure in this respect, the religions of the world have brought about more consolation and peace of mind than any other power on earth. It is on this basis that we say there is a great deal in common in the main aims and objectives of all religions, despite differences in their beliefs and rituals.

WHAT IS BUDDHISM?

What the Buddha taught and spoke to his followers is popularly known as Buddhism. Some call it a religion, others consider it a philosophy, still others think of it as both religion and philosophy. It can also be called a way of life. The Buddha's teachings are guidelines for man's spiritual and intellectual uplift which are helpful not only in man's present life but also in the lives to come, and ultimately for the attainment of the "summum bonum" of Buddhism, called *nibbana*. The Buddha Himself called His teaching *Dhammayinaya*, the Doctrine and Discipline.

As a philosophy Buddhism is not merely the love of wisdom or a search for wisdom. It is the encouragement of a practical application of the Buddha's teachings for the cultivation of a better and more useful life until one attains enlightenment and becomes the master over all the forces of evil that keep him bound to the world and its cycle of birth, suffering and death.

Buddhism also advocates the search for truth and purity of mind. It is neither speculative reasoning nor theoretical dogma; nor is it mere acquisition and storage of knowledge. It is the application of knowledge to life; looking into life and not merely at it. It is neither a pessimistic nor an optimistic approach to life even though one can, to some extent, see the qualities of both in it.

THE CONCEPT OF GOD

Various branches of Christianity, as well as Judaism, Islam and Hinduism, teach hatred of the devil and love of God. Buddhism teaches the fear of evil and love of good. Evil is personified in Buddhism as "Mara", roughly equivalent to Satan in Christianity. While other religions are founded on the worship of God, Buddhism is based on the worship of "good". In a way, the purpose of the worship of God and the worship of good is the same, both having as their objective the betterment of man's character. The former prays to God for happiness, salvation and protection while the latter seeks to achieve the same goals through belief in "good" and loving kindness. It is quite certain that neither God nor good would ever be with the wicked. The main purpose of all religions is therefore to teach man to have good thoughts and to do good actions so that he can rise above the wickedness that has been with him from time immemorial.

IS BUDDHISM ONLY FOR LIFE HEREAFTER AND NIBBANA?

Not, it is certainly not. *Nibbana* is the ultimate and is far away, just like the heavenly life with the Creator in a religion that believes in God. According to Indian religions, lives in the hereafter are the natural result of actions in present and past lives.

All the Indian religions such as Jainism, Hinduism and Buddhism speak of a recurring rebirth. According to Buddhism and Jainism every being has an unending past and an unending future life. *Moksha* in Hinduism, *kaivalya* in Jainism and *nibbana* in Buddhism are final goals that are to be achieved through effort and understanding.

The past is beyond our control, the future is only in thought. We therefore have only the present to build up the future. Thus Buddhism as a doctrine of action depends only on the present. "*Atitam nanusocanti, Nappajappamana, atam: Paccuppannena yapenti*".

The Buddha said that his real followers "do not repent the past, do not depend on the future, but live and act in the present." On another occasion He said: "One's duties and work should be done today itself. Who knows whether death comes tomorrow".

To clarify this further he said: "Well expounded is the doctrine by the Blessed One: to be self-realized with immediate fruit, to be but approached to be seen; capable: capable of being entered upon; to be attained by the wise, each for himself".

In the Dhammapada he says: "Here he rejoices, hereafter he rejoices, in both worlds the well-doer rejoices. He rejoices, he exceedingly rejoices, seeing his own good deeds."

In another verse he says: "Health is the highest gain, contentment is the greatest wealth, confidence is the best kinsman".

On leading an economic life his advice was: "One portion of the income should be spent on living, two portions of it should go for the business that brings the income and the fourth portion should be preserved, thinking that it would be useful in bad times in the future."

Such sayings of the Buddha abound in the 31 books of the Tripitaka. The whole Parabhava Sutta, the discourse on Ruin, gives a long list of evil actions that causes man's ruin in this life. In the Sigalovada Sutta, – the discourse on advice to the householder, Sigala gives instructions on how to live happily with wealth and prosperity in this present life. Even though there may not appear to be the same teachings in the same words in other religions, there can be no doubt that none of them has anything to say contrary to these teachings of the Buddha. It is fair to say that those are applicable to followers of all religions.

The teaching of the Buddha can be divided broadly into two parts. The first part is for the individual who sees this life as a span of misery and longs to put an end to it. Fortunately such individuals are few. A major part of his teaching is devoted to these individuals because it is they who require the most help.

The second is for the individual as well as for the society in which he lives. It teaches how to live a progressive, useful, well-balanced and happy life through righteousness which is well depicted in the five precepts of Buddhism, namely: To refrain from killing, stealing, committing adultery, telling lies, and taking intoxicating drinks which cause infatuation and heedlessness.

As in Buddhism, eternal happiness is the ultimate goal of every religion. Whether it be the Buddhist *nibbana*, the Christian and Islamic Heaven, the Hindu *moksha* or the Jaina *kaivalya*, it is an expression of eternal happiness.

THE CONCEPT OF UNIVERSAL BROTHERHOOD

This is a teaching common to all religions. Those who have faith in a Creator inevitably have to accept what is meant by "Universal Brotherhood". In Buddhism and Jainism this concept is explained in the doctrine of *metta* (Universal Love) and in Hinduism in the world *maitri*. The Buddha's Mettanisamsa Sutta, the discourse on the happy results of *metta*, enumerates eleven results. The Buddha said in the Karaniya Metta Sutta – the discourse on Duties and Universal Love: "Just as a mother would protect her only child even at the risk of her own life, even so let one cultivate a boundless heart towards all beings". The Bible says, "Love thy neighbor as thyself".

With so much in common between the religions of the world, it is unfortunate that there exist even today such wide gaps of misunderstanding and such ignorance of the true meaning of the teachings of the different religions. If the followers of the different religions of the world would think less about the infallibility of their own faiths and a little more about the good in other religions, there would be greater understanding among the peoples of the world. This is the only basis upon which lasting peace between races and nations can be built. I have attempted to show the relevance of Buddhism to other world religions. Now let us take a look at ourselves and the great problems that confront us today.

OUR MODERN WORLD

We have great religions which speak eloquently about the lofty ideals of man. We have science developed to great heights in every field of human need. We have schools and universities in thousands to disseminate knowledge in abundance. The modern world with its modern, maximum efficiency buildings, television sets and jet planes, with its sputniks and satellites encircling the globe, is subject to unprecedented anxieties. We are witnessing both a psychological and a moral breakdown. Mankind is losing respect for law and order. Crime and violence are increasing and youth is in revolt against the established social order, parental control and discipline. In spite of the great increase in knowledge which is now available to most people and the material progress that has been achieved in the past few decades, there is a sharp rise in crime and in mental imbalance. We are also faced with the ever graver danger today of an atomic holocaust which would result in the total annihilation of the human race. Is this the world we are building with all our spiritual and scientific knowledge? What then is the reason for this gloomy prospect? Where have we gone wrong? With all our intellectual advancement we are still children of emotion, and the question which we must ask ourselves is, Have we regressed? Where can we now look for guidance and direction?

SOLUTION

The one and only solution to this dilemma is religion. Politics was never the answer to it and never will be. But religion is losing its sways over the people of the modern world. Religion has failed to lift human thought above the mundane. It has preached "Love thy neighbour", and has conspicuously not done so. It has praised poverty and deplored the excessive pursuit of wealth, but men of religion have sought wealth and power. It is not surprising therefore that religion is losing ground. It is time that each religion turned to its basic sources and preached what its founders really had in mind. But the chief need today is a united voice of all religions raised against evil and hatred, a voice that will convince mankind that love and compassion must prevail if the human race is to survive.

ASOKA'S APPEAL

Some 2,500 years ago the Buddha said, "*Sukha Samghassa Samaggi-Samagganam Tapo Sukho*" ("Pleasant is concord among the many, but more pleasant is concord in those who have self-control".) The great Indian Emperor Asoka (269–232 B. C.), who is said to have learnt Buddhism under the Venerable Saint Moggaliputta Tissa, found truth in the teachings of the Buddha and made it the ideological base of a peaceful and prosperous empire. He united many diverse elements; racial, social and religious. His monumental edicts pronounce a noble example of tolerance and understanding. One of them (Edict XII) declares:

One should not only honour one's religion and not condemn the religions of others, but should indeed honour others' religions for one reason or another. So doing, one helps one's own religion to grow and renders a service to the religions of others. In acting otherwise, even through devotion to one's own religion, one digs the grave of one's own and also does harm to another's. Concord is good. Let all therefore, be willing to listen to the doctrines professed by others.

These words that Asoka promulgated, some 2,250 years ago, remain as good, fresh and pertinent as ever.

In the land of the Buddha and Asoka let us decide and hope for unity of religions, at least to help to solve the great problems of today. To me that is the best way for the world's religions to demonstrate their relevance in the Twentieth Century.

May all beings be happy and peaceful.

Jainism- A Way of Thinking and Living

by

MUNISHRI CHITRABHANU
Divine Knowledge Society, Bombay[1]

It is customary with us to commence our day and work with a brief prayer and I will do so now.

मैत्री प्रमा।द्फ ा रूप्यम। द्वस्थयानि
सत्वगुना धिक वित्रश्यमाना विजेयेबु ।।

The prayer just recited is a prayer offered by the Jains. I have prayed that our conduct in life be guided by 4 principles – *maitri* (amity) *pramoda* (appreciation), *karunya* (compassion) and *madhyasthya* (equanimity).

I shall endeavour to explain these at a later stage in my discourse.

Today man lives in a world which is full of strife and frustration. Commercial values keep gaining precedence. Men seem to be full of greed, envy and pride. Not only do we try to keep up with the Joneses but we try to reach out for their throats. There is a sense of isolation within human beings and hate-spinning ideologies keep gaining more ground. Our different faiths have a common aim, "to make us realize the essential brotherhood of man". In practice they make us more aware of the divisions among us.

Why have we all met here today from the four corners of the earth? Not to argue dogmatically over differences, but to break the barriers of racialism and sectarianism – to learn something from each other, to see the same object from one another's point of view so that we can understand each other the better and help each other the better in solving our problems. The goal for each of us is the same, though the approach may be different. Argument will not take us any nearer the goal. I am here reminded of an incident which will bear out my point.

At an eye clinic where many patients were waiting for treatment, there were four who were blind. One of them inadvertently touched a window

---

pane and importantly announced to the others, "This is a window-pane – it is red, my son told me so."

Another cut him short, with the assertion that it was green and cited with equal emphasis, the authority of a brother. The other two contradicted them, each with a different color and different authority, but with the same querulousness and the same conviction. The storm in the tea cup was quelled by another patient who explained to them that the panes were multi-colored, much to the amusement of everybody.

A trivial quarrel, no doubt, and perhaps a trivial incident to be related here. But I ask you, have not men of different religions argued with the same triviality, the same intolerance and the same vehemence, over the centuries? Each has the conviction that what he was told by someone who could see clearly must be true. One cannot blame him for his absolute faith in his mentor, but surely there was room for others to be true? And what is the result of this dogmatism? Chaos and conflict, discord and disillusion. You will all share my feelings when I say with the poet:

> And much it grieves my heart to think
> What man has made of man.

Jainism is not a sect nor just one more conflicting ideology – it is a way of thinking and living.

The greatness of Jain philosophy lies in the fact that its teachings assure the greatest happiness of the greatest number, not only of men, but of all living beings, under all circumstances.

Its philosophy is not essentially founded on any particular writing or external revelation, but on the unfolding of spiritual consciousness which is the birthright of every soul. Mere words cannot give full expression to the truths of Jainism which must be felt and realized within.

The Jains are advocates of the development theory, hence their ideal is the development of man in all aspects – physical, mental and spiritual. Through knowledge and endeavour, the individual develops and unfolds the potential within him.

The word Jain is derived from the generic term "Jina". A person who conquers his lower nature i.e. passion, hatred and the like and brings into prominence the highest and achieves the state of the supreme being is called a Jina. There have been several Jinas and there can be many more in the future. A Jina who is a guiding force to his followers, reviews principles of religions and regenerates the community is called a "Tirthankara".

According to Jain tradition, Adinath, who dates back to the beginning of the world, was the first Tirthankara, and founder of the Jain religion. Today, we live in the era of Bhagwan Mahavir the 24th and last Tirthankara. Bhagwan Mahavir was born in 598 B. C. in modern Bihar, lived to the age of 72 years and attained *moksha* i.e. salvation, in 526 B. C. He revived the Jain philosophy 2500 years ago. Since that time Bhagwan Mahavir has been the spiritual guide of the Jains.

Even now about 4 million Jains of India practice the preachings of Bhagwan Mahavir and it is the duty of their mentors to guide them in practising it in its spirit in this rapidly changing world. "What then, is the essence – the spirit of Jainism?" – you may ask.

Jainism, viewed as a whole rests on the four pillars which are *ahimsa* (non-violence), *anekantwad* (theory of relativity), *aparigraha* (non-acquisition) and *karma* (deeds or action).

NON-VIOLENCE, THEORY OF RELATIVITY, NON-ACQUISITION AND DEEDS OR ACTION

Of *ahimsa*, Bhagwan Mahavir has said:

सव्वे जीवा वि इच्छन्ति जीविहं
न मरिज्जिहं ।

The instinct of self-preservation is universal. Every animate being clings to life and fears death.

The universe is not for man alone, it is a field of evolution for all living beings. Live and let live is the motto of Jainism. Life is sacred, not only irrespective of caste, color, creed or nationality, but it is sacred to all living beings – at all levels – right down to the tiny ant or the humble worm.

There is not an inch of space in the Universe where there are not innumerable minute living beings. The entire Universe is full of living beings.

A man cannot even sit quietly and breathe without killing and harming life around him.

Then the question will arise, How can a man live in this world without taking life and thereby committing violence? Life at this rate will become impossible.

An answer is given in the Dasavaikalika Sutra as follows:

जयं चरे जयं चिट्ठे

Perform all your activities but with great care. It demands constant wakefulness. Where an action is done with due care not to hurt anyone no violence is committed. The emphasis has been laid on the word "care".

As long as man lives as a member of society, besides what he owes to himself for his spiritual betterment, he owes a great deal to the society in which he has to live.

Man in his desire to continue his life, so that he may do the highest good while living here, is obliged to destroy life, but the fewer and the lower the forms of life he destroys, the less harmful the *karmas* or deeds he generates. This leads to strict vegetarianism.

The doctrine of *ahimsa* is not merely a matter of profession, but of constant, scrupulous practice to every Jain.

The practice of *ahisma* is both an individual and a collective virtue. The principle of *ahimsa* has great potential significance, because it is basic in concept and universal in its moral principles.

Ahimsa, though a negative term, is full of positive meaning, from an act of simple kindness to a comprehensive outlook of universal fraternity.

A great Jain scholar of the 10th Century, Acharya Hemchandra, said in Yogashastra:

आत्मवत् सर्वभूतेषु सु:खदु:खे प्रियाप्रिये ।
चिंतयन्नात्मनो निष्टां हिंसामन्यस्य नाचरेत् ॥

"In happiness or suffering, in joy or grief, we should regard all creatures as we regard our own self. We should, therefore, refrain from inflicting upon others such injury as would appear undesirable to us, if inflicted upon ourselves."

Ahimsa in Jainism is not only physical non-violence, but it is also non-violence of speech and thought.

One can harm others by harsh speech or even by uncharitable thoughts and this form of violence must also be abjured.

The practice of non-violence does not stop with the devotee, himself following the principles of non-violence. It goes further, inasmuch as no violence shall be commissioned or consented to by an honest devotee of non-violence.

We now turn to *anekantwad* (theory of relativity). Gunratna Suri, the commentator of a Jain work on "Comparative Philosophy" says: "Although the various schools of philosophy, through sectarian bigotry, differ from and contradict one another, still there are certain aspects of truth in them which would harmonize if they were joined into an organic whole".

The age-old saying of "a coin having two sides" is well known to this gathering. Jainism, however, makes this one of its basic principles. It requires that any object, situation or controversy be looked at from all aspects.

An individual who allows his vision to be narrowed by turning a deaf ear to the opinions of others, or a community or nation that does this, is heading for self-destruction.

Jainism promises to reconcile all the conflicting schools, not by inducing any of them necessarily to abandon their favorite standpoints but by proving to them that the standpoints of all others are tenable. They may be representative of some aspects of truth which can, with some modification, be represented. The integrity or truth consists in this very variety of all its aspects,

This philosophy makes the Jain catholic in his outlook and ever ready to understand the nature of other systems of theology.

This brings us to the third pillar of Jainism, *aparigraha* (non-acquisition).

Has it not been said: "It is easy to free oneself from iron chains but not from the attachments of the heart?"

What are these "attachments of the heart?" Things that you desire so much that you spend all your energy in acquiring them and when you have acquired them, you get so attached to them that their loss would render your life most unhappy. The principle of non-acquisition teaches us not to give too much importance to acquiring worldly things – a house, a car, comforts of various kinds, and not to value them so much that their loss would mean the end of the world for us. Every man needs things to make life comfortable. Jainism does not enjoin a layman to renounce everything: that is only for the Sadhu – the ascetic. But Jainism does enjoin that even a layman should set a certain limit to his desires, his wants, so that he does not keep on acquiring and accumulating and in the process deny others what they need.

The ideal is to cut his requirements to the bare minimum.

This non-acquisition or non-possession should extend even to attachments to human beings – to our dear ones. It would be unnatural for a parent not to love his or her child, but there should be no possessiveness about this love. It is this possessiveness that is called attachment, and one should try not to be bound by it.

How strange is the mind of man! It does not appreciate what it has and hankers after what it has not. Neglecting the light of the soul that burns within it, how long will it grope in the darkness of the world without chasing shadows that ever elude it?

Let me cite here how a Muni was given a practical lesson in this matter by a number of stray dogs. The Muni, engrossed in his philosophical thoughts of acquisition and renunciation, was passing through a street. Suddenly he was disturbed by the savage barking of dogs.

He saw that a dozen dogs were chasing one dog who was running away with a bone in his mouth. Soon they caught up with him and mauled him. Bleeding from the wounds, the dog dropped the bone and was left in peace. No sooner had he dropped the bone than another picked it up and he too met with the same fate; and so the chase for the bone and the consequent punishment went on.

Reflecting on this ugly incident the Muni realized the truth. So long as the dog clung to the bone, he had to bleed for it; the moment he gave it up he was left in peace.

Did not man bleed mentally and spiritually to gratify his lust for acquisition, and would he not attain serenity if he renounced it? thought the Muni.

It is only human desire, but the noblest desire for man should be to attain a state of "desirelessness" – when he can accept things as they come to him, and can look on indifferently when they leave him.

This ancient principle of limited possession is extremely significant and valuable in the context of the economic conditions prevailing in the world today. The object is to secure equitable distribution and economic stability for society. A social order based upon this principle of limited possession will certainly prevent unnecessary accumulation of wealth and its inseparable counterpart, poverty and wretchedness. It will lay the foundation of a welfare society – a modern term.

The principle of *aparigraha* can guide every individual, society, or nation in its positive efforts to enhance the happiness of mankind in general.

After having dealt with non-violence, the theory of relativity, and non-acquisition, we come to the last pillar on which Jainism rests, the law of *karma* (deeds or action).

Destiny is shaped by deeds done during the previous incarnation as well as deeds done during this life. We enjoy the fruits of those good deeds now, during our present life. But we should be careful not to fritter away or misuse these fruits – rather we should think of moulding our destiny for the next incarnation, ever progressing in our spiritual evolution. It is easy to waste these fruits; much more difficult to utilize them in shaping our future destiny.

Jainism explains joy and sorrow, prosperity and adversity, and differentiation in physical, mental and spiritual abilities through the theory of *karma*. It explains the problem of inequality and apparent injustice in the world.

Karma denotes that substance which we continuously absorb as the result of our bodily and mental activity. We produce *karma* through all our daily activities. Different kinds of activity produce different kinds of *karma* which may ripen either immediately or after some time, or even in one or another of our subsequent existences.

And yet, Jain philosophy does not view the soul as hopelessly condemned to act and react upon the consequences of its earlier deeds, as if it were an automatic machine, and beyond all responsibility for its moral attitude and action. On the contrary it clearly states that the individual is gifted with a certain amount of freedom of will. It emphatically declares that the soul is invested with the freedom to exercise its own resolution.

Acting under its own free will, it can break the heaviest fetters of this *karma*. It implies that, to a considerable extent, by positive application of one's own free will, the soul is indeed the lord of its own fate.

Good deeds that spring from love, compassion, charity, hospitality and selfless service secure the basis of happiness, whereas bad or undesirable deeds will sow the seeds of future sorrow.

Life existed before this birth and will continue to do so after death. It is here on this shore and will be there on the opposite shore, too. In between is the flow of birth and death. Because of *karma* and attachments the soul has to revolve in the cycle of birth and death.

Bhagwan Mahavir while explaining the true nature of the soul said:

The nature of the soul is like that of a hollow gourd, i.e. it keeps afloat. But when this hollow gourd is given several coats of clay, then, even though its inherent capacity is to keep afloat, it will sink.

Similarly a soul coated with violence, falsehood, dishonesty, intemperance, anger, pride, hypocrisy and greed becomes heavy; despite its original virtue to keep afloat, it sinks to the bottom.

But when the layers on the gourd peel off one after another, it will gradually recover its tendency to keep afloat. So, too the soul. Were it to get rid of the eight vices by acquiring eight corresponding virtues – non-violence, truth, honesty, temperance, forgiveness, modesty, simplicity and generosity it could unburden itself and regain its natural virtues of lightness and volatility.

Having explained the four pillars of Jain philosophy, let me get back to the prayer in which I have asked our conduct to be guided by amity, appreciation, compassion and equanimity.

By amity we mean the attainment of a mentality which would want to be friendly with, and bear goodwill towards, one and all.

Just as the dry bed of a lake is criss-crossed with a myriad cracks, because it is devoid of fresh water, similarly a religion that is not sweetened with the milk of human kindness is soon weakened by the cracks of internal dissensions.

Mere austerity may shrivel up a man's nature. Even as he does penance and practices renunciation, his heart must be full of love.

What supports this on a wide-world basis? Surely not the much – trumpeted deeds of the blustering heroes but the silent sacrifice of the humble servers of humanity: little deeds of amity such as the one you will hear presently.

A young Brahmin trudging along was startled by a scream of terror. A Harijan girl – an outcaste – had been bitten by a cobra. Failing to get anything to check the venom from spreading through the blood stream, he snapped his holy thread with his pen-knife, tied it tightly round the foot and saved her life.

A cry of sacrilege was raised by the orthodox. Could anything be more sacrilegious than the holy thread being tied around the foot of an untouchable?

The answer given by the youth was very brief, but to the point. What could be more humane than the saving of a human life with a holy thread?

A humanitarian approach to life is holier than the mere wearing of a holy thread. Religion has to be practical and not theoretical. It should pulsate with life.

The aim of religion is to establish peace and harmony both at home and in society. Love and tolerance alone can promote concord at home and elsewhere.

The spirit of amity if understood well can bridge the gulf between one religion and another as between one nation and another.

Appreciation and compassion are in a way two other aspects of amity.

Appreciation: In this world we come across those who are better than we are in many different ways. Too often we see the sad spectacle of men filled with envy for those who are more fortunate than themselves. Our prayer teaches us that we should learn to appreciate those who are better, admire them if they are worthier than we are, whether or not they are of the same religion, race or country. If this is practised much of the envy and jealousy we find in this world will be removed.

Compassion: Compassion should govern our attitude towards those who are less fortunate than we are. It should extend even to the erring and the criminal.

After all, when Jainism believes that living beings often suffer because of their past misdeeds, does it not behoove a true Jain to extend compassion rather than criticism to one who pays for his misdeeds of the past?

Equanimity: Equanimity is more of an introspective virtue. It governs our attitude towards ourselves, irrespective of the world around us. We achieve a certain balance of the mind that remains unruffled in spite of the vicissitudes of life. Whether the world treats us well or ill, whether we reap a reward for our good deeds or not, we should maintain that serenity of mind that brings contentment in its wake.

When a tiny pebble is dropped into the still waters of a pool, the pool is soon covered with ripples. It is in the very nature of water to break into ripples. But when the pool is frozen, even if you drop a stone in it there is hardly any disturbance in its smooth, hard surface.

The mind reacts to circumstances by breaking into ripples of disturbance. One would say that this is but natural. Perhaps – but is it inevitable? When the mind is trained to resist stoically all outward disturbances it will acquire a calm that nothing can ruffle.

I hope I have succeeded in making it clear that these four principles, when put into action, guarantee the highest amount of happiness and peace within the brotherhood of all living beings. I wish them to be universally adopted and followed for the benefit of all living beings.

This then is the basis of Jain philosophy in a nutshell.

It is a philosophy which can be practised by a follower of any religion.

It is indeed very difficult to distill the elusive essence of religion so as to use it in one's daily life, but he alone is truly religious who carries out the precepts of his religion in all his dealings with the world.

We have spoken at some length to explain, to each other, the fundamental principles of our religions and how the essential elements in all are very similar.

Coming to the problems that face us, they, too, are essentially the same:

the menace of destructive weapons of war, the malaise of racialism, the problem of economic imbalance, the unrest among our youth.

After having discussed *ahimsa* what is left for me to add about missiles or bombs? If the killing of a worm is an act of cruelty to a Jain, it would be superfluous to talk about the atrocity of wiping out the human race! So, too, we have already covered the ground for the malaise of racialism. If we recognize the fact that the soul is the same, whatever outward form it may be given, where then is the reason for racial prejudices? In *aparigraha* (non-acquisition) lies the solution for the unequal distribution of wealth. There need not be any "ism" about it. Jainism is not like any of the modern "isms". 2,500 years ago Bhagwan Mahavir gave us the antidote to unequal distribution of wealth – in his doctrine of *aparigraha*.

The last problem – youthful unrest – calls for a more detailed analysis. I will endeavour to show how we may deal with it.

WHAT IS THE RELEVANCE OF RELIGION TO MODERN YOUTH?

Is not modern youth justified in demanding why so many crimes have been committed in the name of religion? He has read in his history books lurid accounts of persecution and atrocities by religious fanatics in all parts of the world. He is fully conscious that it is might, and not right, that rules the world. He sees the truthful and the just belabored by the selfish and the unscrupulous, and no gods rush down to the rescue in their heavenly chariots as one is told in legends. How can he then believe that "God's in His heaven – all's right with the world?" He sees for himself that all's wrong with the world, and he doubts whether there is a God in heaven or anywhere, and if He exists, whether He is as omnipotent as they make Him out to be.

Jain philosophy, with its theory of *karma* can explain to him that sufferings – of an individual or a nation or a race – are the result of misdeeds of the past, that there is a causal relationship between the woes of this life and the evil done during an earlier incarnation, and so he cannot maintain that there is not justice in the world. As for religious persecutions that fill him with revulsion, the tolerance and broad-mindedness that Jain philosophy emphasizes might persuade him to modify his outlook on religion. Amity and appreciation would not be incomprehensible to him, for youth is not wicked. If approached with sympathy and understanding, he will respond. Think of the stress and strain of modern life. The speed, the noise, the hectic bustle of today has robbed the young man of the opportunity to move in life with measured strides. The machine has taken the place of hands. The bubbling creative energy of youth was formerly channeled into constructive crafts, be it spinning, weaving, pottery, metal-work, wood-work, carving or whatever. Today that energy is turned into destructive channels.

In what way can religion help to divert this flow of energy once again into constructive channels? The simplifying of religion may do it. Stripped of rituals, prejudices, superstitions, even separated from the noble but complicated philosophy that is the bed-rock of religion, the simple essence of religion – friendliness, sympathy, tolerance, justice – this the youth will understand, and will not reject summarily as humbug or trickery, or as something beyond his mental powers.

If homes and teaching institutions would sow the seeds of religion as here suggested, emphasizing particularly the oneness of all religions, we could be reasonably optimistic that this early initiation to religion would bear fruit in good time.

The aim of all religions and philosophies is to seek the freedom of man from the bonds of ignorance and blind faith, from the meshes of prejudice, superstition and ritual. Religion means freedom. Only when man rids himself of his mundane bonds does he free himself from the bonds of *karma*. Just as gold attains its pristine purity only when the dross is separated from it, so, too, the soul, only after it has shed all desire and *karma* will attain a state of blissful tranquillity and immortality.

Sikhism and the Sikhs

by

SARDAR SHER SINGH "SHER"
Principal, Shaheed Sikh Missionary College, Amritsar

It is a matter of great privilege to us that this ecumenical religious conference is being held in India. The credit of the initiative and organization of this Summit assembly of representatives of the world religions goes to the Temple of Understanding.

I shall begin by discussing the main principles of the Sikh religion. In this, I shall use the term, *Sikhology* instead of Sikh theology. The term Sikhology is being employed here for the first time. Although the literal meaning of Sikh is disciple or learner yet *kes* (unshorn hair) is a basic requisite of the existence and identity of the Sikhs. So much so that we say in our Ardas or prayer, "*Waheguru, Sasa Sikhi Sidg, swawan sang nibhae*" ("O wonderful God, sustain us to maintain our faith in Sikhism, with unshorn hair, till our last breath"). Although the suffix or title of "Singh" is an essential part of every Sikh's name, yet Sikhologically it is conferred on him, and is the reward of his regular baptism, administered to him by the five baptised Singhs of high character, called "Penj Piyaras". Attributively, the God of the Sikhs is described in the Mool Mantar as:

> There is only, and only one God
> Whose Name is True
> Who is Omnipotent or All-Doer, Fearless, Enmityless, Timeless
> Unborn, Parthenogenetic
> And who is realized by the Grace of a true Precepter.

His existence is taken for granted and no ontological and teleological intricacies and controversies are entertained by Sikhism.

The practical morals of Sikhism, as enshrined in two Trinities, are essential ingredients of Sikhology, the code of conduct or morals of life for the followers of the Sikh religion: the belief in eschatology, providence, soteriology, the fatherhood of God (though Sikhism has also treated God as a husband and the human soul as a wife, always yearning for union with Him), metempsychosis, the existence of heaven and hell, (though they are

not described in detail), the merits of married life and the efficacy and
sanctity of prayer, are accepted by the Sikh religion. The Sikh prayer Ardas
is unique among prayers in the world religions in that it contains the
history of the Sikhs, their Gurus and their martyrs, their struggles, sacrifices,
sacred places and shrines.

Sikhism is a universal religion. So, the Ardas ends with the words:
"*Nanak Nam charhdi kala, Terey bhaney sarbat da bhalla*" ("O Nanak, the power
of God is ever-increasing and by the grace of His Will, all may be blessed").
The word "all" includes all animate beings. The gratis and voluntary
service of one's fellow-beings, confession of one's imperfection or sins,
amrit' wele da jagna (rising early in the morning for meditation), and
humility, are considered especially meritorious in Sikhism.

The sacred scriptures of the Sikhs basically comprise the Guru Granth
Sahib and the Composition of Guru Gobind Singh contained in the Dasam
Granth, though the writings of Bhai Gurdas are also revered by the Sikhs
like Gurbani (the Word of the Guru). The followers of Sikhism have received their scriptures direct from the hands of their Gurus from Guru
Nanak, the founder of the faith, to Guru Gobind Singh who concluded
its tenets and founded the *Khalsa Panth*.

Secondly, its scriptures have been written in the language of the people,
the script for which was invented by Guru Nanak and that is why they are
called *Gurmukhi* (from the mouth of the Guru).

The Sikh scriptures are written and set to the classical notations of Indian
music, and being catholic in nature have honored and recorded the hymns
of the saints of the lowest and humblest origin. The present spiritual Guru
or guide of the Sikhs is the Guru Granth Sahib, to a volume of which they
bow and give respect as the people do to their living prophets or founders
of religions. Therefore, being present in the volume by Guru Granth Sahib,
the saints of different castes and parts of India are respected as much by the
Sikhs as their gurus.

The Sikh concept of evolution needs a small note. Sikhism believes in
creation and, being aware of evolution, professed scientific vision long before the birth of exact science as we now know it. In recent times many of
the old religious beliefs about the age of the universe and the nature of
the earth have been repudiated by the new discoveries of evolutionists,
archeologists, geologists, paleontologists, astronomers and physicists. But
Guru Nanak said in the Fifteenth Century, "There are countless heavens
and earths and all the departments of knowledge have exhausted their
resources to determine them exactly, and confess their inability with one
voice." He says about the age of the earth, "No sage knows the time and
day of its origin. Only its Creator knows it." Guru Gobind Singh has written,
"all describe the universe according to their knowledge but O God, none
knows how you created it." Guru Nanak was aware of microbes or micro-
organisms and while admonishing the Brahman for his concept of human

impurity or *sootak* he says to him, "If you believe in it then there are living beings in dung, wood, grains of food and water which gives life to all. Only knowledge can dispel the superstition of *sootak*."

Religion and politics are not divorced in Sikhism. The ethical doctrines of religion must be maintained in putting political principles into practice. That is why a Sikh is called "sant-sipahi" (saint-soldier). This is why he invokes in his Arda, the victory of the sword and the cooking-kettle (*deg-teg-fateh*). This is why the sixth Guru wore the swords of *Meeri* and *Peeri*. The existence of *Harmandar* (The Temple of God) and *Akal Takht* (The Throne of God) are the greatest proofs of the symbiosis of religion and politics like the combination of soul and body so that the political life of the Sikhs may be directed by the moral truths of their religion.

The Sikhs have two types of trinities – the spiritual trinity and the temporal trinity, both of which are essential and interdependent. The spiritual trinity comprises *Guru* (preceptor), *Granth* (holy Bible of the Sikhs), and *Panth* (The Sikh community). A Sikh has to remain under the guidance of the decision of his community. His willing surrender to the decision of the *Khalsa Panth* is the proof of his spirit of democracy, infused in him by the Sikh *gurus*, especially by Guru Gobind Singh. The temporal trinity of Sikhism consists of *kirt karni* (earning an honest livelihood by his work), *wand chhakna* (helping the needy) and *nam japna* (meditation for the realization of God). The practice of the balanced combination of these trinities makes one an ideal Sikh. But the actions of life are always below the mark of the ideals. This is the purpose for which all of us have assembled here – to bridge the gulf between religious ideals and practical life. The concept of grace is one of the most important features of Sikhism. A Sikh believes that his qualities without the grace of God have no value.

None can question anybody's ethnic origin or ideology while sitting in *pangat* (the row of the persons being served with food in the Sikh refectory, *landgar*), *sangat* (the Sikh congregations) and while bathing in a *sarowar* (a tank at a holy place of the Sikhs). As a matter of fact the Sikh gurus founded these institutions to eradicate caste and the practice of untouchability. These institutions are not only religious in nature but also have a very great sociological importance. Most of the employees and priests of the major religious shrines of the Sikhs belong to the *shudar* communities and the present Head Granti of the Golden Temple, Amritsar, the Mecca of the Sikhs and the president of the supreme religious body of the Sikhs, are originally scions of the *shudar* communities. But Sikh baptism abolishes man's former caste and makes him *sardar* or chief.

At present, three problems are taxing, or rather torturing, the conscience of the well-wishers of humanity – the dangers of racial discrimination, poverty in plenty and the future of religion in the modern materialistic, warring and scientific age.

First of all I take up the problem of racial discrimination. Broadly speaking, race connotes the physical and inheritable characters of a human group which differ from those of other groups of *Homo Sapiens*. Yet it has no standing as a scientific term. It has a very checkered history but in this paper, we cannot go into its details. The fact is that many people believe themselves to be racially superior to other sections of mankind and think that this gives them the right of domination over them. "Racist" has become the trigger-term to emit emotionally conditioned contempt against certain groups of human society.

The concept of this unscientific and mythical term, race, is rejected by every legitimate thinker, and replaced with the term "ethnic group". The greatest dissent against the race concept and racialism is given by the greatest anthropologists and other scientists of different fields of enquiry like CALMAN, KALMUS, CARTER, PENROSE, HOUSEMAN, HUXLEY, HADDON, RUTH, PARKERS, HANKINS and FRANZ. Besides these, anti-race scientific research papers of COMAS, KLINEBERG, LEIRIS, LEVY-STRAUSS, LITTLE, ROSE, DUNN, MOURANT and SHAPIRO, have been published by UNESCO, to reject scientifically the increasing and perilous concept of racialism. UNESCO also published the statements of social scientists and physical anthropologists and geneticists against racialism on July 18th, 1950, and July 15th, 1952.

What is the result, 15 or 16 years after the publication of these statements? Has racialism faded? Not at all. It teaches us that science cannot inculcate the spirit of the basic Biblical belief, "Love thy neighbor as thyself" – the neighbors may be the human beings of any country and color; not necessarily men of one's own class. The Sikhs, as taught by their religion, have never done any wrong to anybody on the basis of racial discrimination. As Guru Gobind Singh has said: "*Manas Ki jaat sabhey ekey paihchanbo*" ("Recognize the whole of the human race as a unitary brotherhood"). Guru Arjan Dev says as follows: "*Bisar gai sabh taat prai Jab te sadh Sangat mohey pai Na ke bairi nahi begana Sagal sang ham ko ban aai.*" ("Our otherness of descent has been ended, since our company with the congregation of the Spiritual comrades, none is stranger or enemy to us. We are in tune with all.")

Can the inferences culled from scientific laboratories teach these lessons to us? Not at all, because fraternity is the offspring, not of science, but of religious faith.

Now comes the problem of poverty amidst plenty. Poverty amidst scarcity sounds natural but poverty amidst plenty is a paradoxical statement. It shows that the materials for the needs of man are plentiful but their distribution is defective. Selfishness has overcome the spirit of common welfare. The legislation of old age, industrial and public service pensions, care by relatives, alms-houses, national and international financial aids, have not been able to destroy the demon of poverty in general and the monster of misery of orphans, the aged, the diseased, the disabled and the unemployed, in particular. Too many selfish persons, exploiters, withhold and control too much of the wealth. The world needs better distribution of its wealth.

Before this can become a reality, we must have a revival of sympathy, honesty, fellow-feelings, and a realization of the wealth and greatness of simplicity which are the concepts of religious faith, conscience and ethics. Religion teaches man to earn his bread with his hard labor and by the sweat of his brow. On seeing the poor groaning under the weight of want, but selfish people enjoying great luxuries, Guru Nanak said: "The enjoyment of illegitimate wealth is pork to a Mohammedan and beef to a Hindu."

Legislative measures to banish poverty, to bring equality by equitable distribution of wealth, cannot be effective unless all earn their livelihood with honesty and hard work, and help the needy as their moral duty; the motivating force from within, as Guru Nanak says: *"Badha chatti jo bharey na gun na upkar"* ("One's forced charity is neither quality nor generosity".) The concept of poverty does not lie in the amount of one's wealth. It lies in the opulence or poverty of one's possession of contentment. The greatness of a man is not shown by the largeness of his wealth; it is shown by the smallness of his wants. This rare wealth is called contentment which is the source of wealth, wisdom and peace. Guru Arjan Dev has rightly said: *"Bina santokh nahin ko-oo rajaiy"* ("None could be satisfied without contentment"). Hence religion is indispensable to divide equitably plenty as well as poverty.

The problem of this modern, materialistic and warring age is baffling and appalling. Man has crossed the stage of low-energy and high-energy production and has arrived at the stage of atomic energy. The achievements at this stage have dazed him and he is running towards his own destruction at break-neck speed. Power and booty were the causes that incited man to wage war for the annihilation of his own species and its hard-developed civilization. The modern warring concept of "nation" has replaced the primitive belligerent concept of "tribe". Man's materialistic views of life have strangulated his humanity. The first World War was fought with weapons, the second World War was fought with machines, but now man will wage war with missiles, supersonic air-fighters, poisonous gases, atom bombs, hydrogen bombs and rockets. In the second World War, the Germans called this type of conflagration "Blitzkrieg". Space travel and interplanetary discoveries have inflated man's vanity still more. Medical science is promising him security and longevity by many wonderful discoveries and extraordinary operations, the transplantation of hearts being the latest. These prodigal achievements are weakening his faith in God. Formerly war used to be local or limited in effect but now being universal in its destructiveness, the whole of humanity suffers from regimentation, conscription, destruction of the biological quality of the race (the best men and the youth being killed), destruction of cultural heritage and the creation of an ever-increasing compulsion of the defeated party towards waging another war and then another. Even the scientists who are among those who have eminently contributed to the inventions of atomic energy are vague about and afraid of its use in the future. Once President EISENHOWER sent a message to the United Nations Atomic Conference at Geneva and said, "The phenomenon of nuclear fission having been revealed to man, it is still left to him to determine the use to which it should be put."

A scholar who has done extensive research work on the economics of war, says, "Putting it another way, the money costs of each battle-death rose from 75 cents in Caesar's Rome to $ 3,000 in Napoleon's time, the cost was about $ 21,000 in the First World War and exceeded $ 50,000 in the Second World War." This shows that war is not only the enemy of our life but also a main cause of the poverty of the world because so much of the productive resources and so many of the productive agencies are engaged militarisation and armament. Toynbee says, "Warfare is the commonest cause of the breakdown of civilization during four or five millennia." International conferences to achieve limitation of armament have been held since 1899 when the first of its type was convened by Nicholas II of Russia. Since then the League of Nations and the United Nations have been trying to restrict armament and the use of atomic energy in war, but with small effect. A crisis of moral character is rampant amidst material advancement. Hence the reformation of moral character is badly needed. Sihkism says: "*Sachonh orey sabh ko uper sach aachar*" ("Everything is below truth but high character is higher than truth").

The scientists have revealed that one pound of pure, fissionable uranium 235 has the energy potential of about two and a half million pounds of coal. The electric power generated from the new sources of atomic energy can supplement coal, oil, gasoline, gas and water power and can do an incalculable good to mankind in the fields of agriculture, industry and medicine. But who is to do it? The atom bomb, the hydrogen bomb, many other scientific inventions and their mother, atomic energy, are neither moral nor immoral. They are helpless inanimate products of the intellect and diligence of man, but if they are triggered once, they can bring about his genocide quicker than I can speak or write these words.

Again religion comes to save the intellect-intoxicated, science-stupefied and suicidal modern, materialistic and scientific world. The urge to and accomplishment of right action takes birth from religion, as religion is the voice of God. Guru Nanak has said: "*Dharam karai karm dhuron farmaiya*" ("Religion, being the voice of God, guides us to accomplish right actions").

But how is religion going to survive to do its duty, uninhibited, when it is beseiged by materialism, pragmatism, voluntarism, individualism, naturalism, rationalism, positivism, scepticism, syllogistic cynicism and criticism of all sorts?

The success of religion depends on the extent to which it can scramble out of the ditch of dogmatism, to refute the arguments of critics and especially to stop the increasing irreligiosity of challenging youth, to meet the modern trend of society and to satisfy the scientific and inquisitive attitude of the people, because after all science is also a systematic study of the works of God, scientifically called Nature, by rigorous observations and inferences. Its success also depends on the extent to which different faiths can agree to serve all human beings equally and alike without any discrimination of creed and country (in spite of having doctrinal differences) so that the world at large may be humanized, spiritualized and immunized against the onslaughts of the blind and destructive forces of materialism.

CONCLUSION

Sikhism is a monotheistic religion and has no dogmatic conflict with the modern science of cosmology, the age and chronology of earth and the discovery of new planets, about which Guru Nanak forestalled the scientists in the 15th Century. It has no concept of "The Chosen People" because it basically believes in panhumanism and brotherhood. It rejects human discrimination of all categories – racial, social, cultural, religious and economic. It believes that the energy and efforts of men are graceful gifts of God and so their results also belong to the Lord Almighty. This concept purges egoism and egotism. That is why Guru Gobind Singh has enjoined on the Sikhs the greeting, "*Wahiguru ji kakhalsa; Wahiguru ji ki fateh*" ("The Khalsa belong to God and so their victory also belongs to Him"). Sikhism believes that in the Kingdom of God the pure will rule and the Sikhs sing every day in their prayer, "*Raj kareyga Khalsa; aaki rahey na koey*" ("The pure will rule and no rebel will be left unsurrendered"). Its scriptures are non-denominational and universal. The militancy and spirituality of the followers of Guru Gobind Singh are melded together in a sacred symbiosis. It has courage to crush the tyrant but uphold the righteous. Its baptism, *pangat, sangat, langar* and *sarovars* are the ideals of democracy and human equality. It places more emphasis on the merits of a noble deed than on mere theories of creed. It is a practical way of life and is not confounded with the hodge-podge of astounding intellectual exercises. It is a religious synthesis having the noble ideas of other faiths. It believes in the earning of one's livelihood with one's hard labour, *kirt karni*, which is its first fundamental because it condemns idleness and exploitation, and believes that work is worship. Humility to serve and the spirit to face sufferings and sacrifices for humanity are its essentials. It is the youngest of all the major religions of the world. Therefore, being the youngest faith, it can easily make adjustment with young times and younger generations.

The Relevance of the Protestant Branch of Christianity to the World Today

by

The Rev. Dr. LOWELL RUSSELL DITZEN
Director of the National Presbyterian Center, Washington, D. C.

I am pleased to be with you at this Spiritual Summit Conference, not alone as a member of the Board of The Temple of Understanding, but as informally representing the National Council of Churches of the United States of America. However, I do not speak for the National Council, nor can I expect to speak for the many Protestant branches of Christianity, or even my own, which is the Presbyterian-Reformed tradition which has churches in more than seventy countries of the world. Rather, I speak as one individual.

First, I would mention some aspects of Protestantism that I think *are irrelevant* to the new world that is emerging where we need to understand each other and communicate with each other as never before in human history.

It must be understood that we Protestants are fragmented into diverse groups with differing emphases in theology and various convictions as to what is of priority in faith and life. According to the WORLD ALMANAC (1968 edition) there are 229, 290,000 Protestants. The Eastern Orthodox branch of Christianity represents 144,820,000, and the Roman Catholic are listed with 595,472,000 adherents.

It will be seen from these statistics that Protestants, though not a majority group, do have a sizable number of individuals within the total Christian community. However, we are broken up into approximately three hundred different denominations and sects.

In my judgment divisiveness and sectarianism are not relevant in the world in which we live. We cannot live in isolation from each other. The forces of technological and scientific advance, together with the increased speed of communication and transportation, are making us live in a "global village." To be rigidly sectarian in such a world can be a hindrance rather than a help to constructive progress.

We Protestants are trying to come closer together. In this great land of India where we are now meeting, one of the most exciting Christian advances in church union was accomplished with the formation of the United Church of South India. Other such unions as that of the United Church of Canada, the formation of a National Council of Churches of Christ in the United States of America, and in 1948, the institution of the World Council of Churches, are steps toward togetherness rather than increased fragmentation. Though this is a trend, we have a long way yet to go.

Secondly, I do not like the argumentation that has at times occurred in the family of Protestantism. We write long papers and we engage in endless debates about what is the mission of the Church, what are the needs of mankind, and the role we ought to try to play in the drama of life. Within our ranks we have called each other bad names. We have engaged in painful conflicts of ideology and concerns as to our mission. I am convinced that this kind of interaction is destructive to the exalted influences needed to guide mankind into higher levels of intelligence, harmony, and peace.

Thirdly, we have often been poor missionaries. I know that for some of the other world religions the missionary zeal of the Christian community has been a source of irritation. All here will understand the motive, when I tell you that the majority of the Protestant peoples of the world believe deeply in Jesus Christ. We, at our best, love Him, worship Him as God's Son, and try to do His will. In the New Testament, which tells of His life and teaching, there is the admonition, "Go into all the world and preach the gospel to all creation."

Within the variegated churches that make up Protestantism, leaders in our various sects have interpreted those words in different ways. Some have come to your lands and been insufferably arrogant in trying to impose the religion of Christianity on your people. Many Christian missionaries have had inexcusably bad manners. There can be no place for chestpounding nor for any attempt to impose one set of beliefs on anyone else in the kind of world in which we live. We need, as never before in human history, to communicate with each other, to listen to each other, to have respectful regard for each other, and then, as world religionists, to inspire leaders in government to form the organizational structure needed to carry the human race forward toward peace.

Fourth, another aspect of Protestantism that I would call irrelevant has been our failure to appreciate other world religions. All branches of Christianity have been so devoted to their faith, have been so convinced that they had "the light and the truth" that they not alone have been offensive to some other faiths, but blinders have been over our eyes, keeping us from seeing the rich merits, the noble dedications, the high ideals of other world religions. I am sure you know, as I do, that there have been dedicated and devoted Christian servants who have done much good throughout the world in education, medical care, and agriculture, and they continue to do so. The missionary movement was prompted by the most idealistic of motives. But often there was lacking the sensitive appreciation that is needed to live and work together today.

Fifth, there is another item which has been emphasized by Protestant Christians and often has been pushed beyond the point of wisdom, namely the rights of the individual. I believe deeply in the doctrine that God alone is Lord of man's conscience. Its emphasis had led to some of our most creative thinking and to the development of constructive ferments that have caused mankind to think and to move forward.

But in some instances, within the Protestant community, that great thesis has been misapplied. It has permitted individuals and groups to become arrogant, to condemn others who do not share their convictions. It has made for altercation where there ought to be reconciliation. It has created confusion where there ought to be harmony. It has allowed self-willed, and at times mentally and emotionally unbalanced, individuals to preach their strange doctrines under the banner of the eternal spirit of wisdom and of truth, namely God Himself.

Sixth, in some instances Protestantism has appeared to support economic, political and military forces that have been seeking their own ends rather than the ends of the ultimate good of the human race. We are all at home with our own cultures. We all love our countries. It would be strange if it were not so. But those of us devoted to the high world of religion, who are dedicated to furthering the ultimate well-being of the human race, cannot approve of such an attitude and such a spirit as I have mentioned above, nor accept it as relevant today.

So I stand before you in confession. I repeat, I do so as one individual. But I think I reflect the spirit of a wide segment of the many groups that make up Protestant Christianity.

But now, having confessed some faults – and there are many, many more – let me speak of some aspects of the Protestant heritage and convictions that I think are worthy of being reaffirmed as we think of our several world religions.

First of all, one matter that I listed as among our faults may, properly applied, be a source for some of the greatest helpfulness and service to the human family, namely, the right of the individual conscience. The longer I study history, the longer I live, the more widely I travel, and the more friends throughout the world I listen to, I am convinced that we go forward through strong individuals more than by any other force. Who can measure the power engendered in the world by Gandhi? Or Buddha? Or Jesus? And the endless circle of great souls that have been inspired by their genius, their wisdom, their love.

The problems of the world cannot be solved alone by conclaves of committees or commissions, however great their military, political, or economic power. These often are thought to be the hinges on which the doors of history are swung. It is not so. *It is individuals* who, in freedom of conscience, have come to point the way out of immediate dilemmas, who bring the light that is needed for man's next thrust forward on the road of human progress.

We Protestants believe in this. God speaks "in a still small voice" to individuals of receptiveness. It was so in the life of Moses and Mohammed, and in hundreds of others in all religions who have blest their fellow men.

Out of this conviction of personal freedom will come many strange and individualistic voices. But because we all are "stamped within with the image of the Divine" mankind will know which is the voice that speaks the new truth that needs to be heard. This is relevant.

Secondly, Protestantism is relevant, in my judgment, in that it is constantly seeking to keep in balance belief and action. Our Bible has the phrase, "Faith without works is dead." This means that we are not alone to engage in prayer, in reciting our creeds, in liturgy and in worship, but we are also to engage in works and service for the good of mankind. Loving service to our fellow men gives evidence of the depth of our faith.

I grant you this leads to much shifting of the balances between these two kinds of religious observance. We Protestants are constantly pricked in mind and conscience as to what to do now and how to do it.

But I say to you that this tension deserves to be included in the assets that mankind has won by thinking and praying and living across the centuries.

In my work in Washington, D.C., we have a wide variety of conferences. A recent one brought together young Protestant clergymen from across our country. Their emphasis, as it came forth at that conference, shocks some older and more conservative Protestants. These younger men of the church say "Forget about rhetoric! Stop preaching! Listen to man's needs! The structures of society must be changed! The Gospel is preached – not in words but in acts that seek justice, equity and prosperity for all of God's children." Holding these views, they create tension. They may at times push the pendulum too far, and then others must pull it back, but the tension is there, and it is healthy.

For a time I served as pastor of one of our churches that is a part of the Reformed denomination in the United States. Occasionally I would get a letter addressed to me at "The Reforming Church." I felt a certain excitement on these occasions. Protestantism *is a reforming body*, seeking to find out how God's truth and light and wisdom and judgment apply to the changing scenes of our society. I say to you that this spirit and point of view is worthy and relevant.

As we work together and pray and move forward together, this sense of "reforming" – reforming our relationships individually, and then our groups, nationally, racially, religiously – can be a force for great good.

"One is our Father. All we are brethren." How do we make this truth and vision a reality without constantly being engaged in finding ways of reforming, of reformation?

Again, the majority of Protestants believe that the person and the teaching of Jesus Christ have been, are, and always will be a redemptive force in personal life and in history. Friends, I put this before you as a relevant fact for our modern world. You cannot understand the majority of Christians without understanding that we believe this deeply.

We do not contend we are worthy of Jesus Christ, but we honor and worship Him and seek to follow in His Path. And we feel that path will lead us to God's Kingdom and to the brotherhood of man.

Before I close this paper I must share with you some thoughts of colleagues and old friends in the Protestant ministry to whom I wrote telling them of my assignment to prepare these words for you.

All of them spoke warmly of the validity of our meeting together. The voices were one in declaring that our world religions must face each other, talk to each other, learn from each other, so that together they may be a more effective instrument for the service of God and man. However, as I have tried to indicate to you in speaking of the nature of Protestants, their ideas differed as to what is relevant about our religion. One emphasized that although we are institutionalized, in our freedom we are not dominated by the institution. In freedom the Spirit of God can lead men to change the institution.

Another said Protestantism's relevance was in its sensitivity to the individual, its emphasis on personal confrontation of man to man, the attempt to express Christ's divine love in human love.

Yet another mentioned the constant effort in Protestant Christianity to find "reconciliation" between freedom and order, and also between God's grace and man's sinfulness.

I cite these only to underline how diverse we Protestants are, and how individualistic in our emphases.

But the spirit of each of my colleagues bespeaks a concern, a commitment and a lovingness which is the spirit that graces our meeting here.

Iqbal, the poet of India's Punjab, wrote "– the true end of the men of the earth is to love each other."

We Protestant Christians believe that. And behind our outward noise and diversity, that longing "to love each other" is in our hearts. I have found it in the hearts of all who are at this conference. Letting that spirit be present in all our gatherings here, a shining step forward will be made.

Religion as a World Force: A Jewish View

by

Dr. Ezra Spicehandler

Professor, Hebrew Union College, School of Archaeology and
Biblical Studies, Jerusalem, Israel

This conference could only have held in the Twentieth Century. We are
able to gather from all parts of the world because of technical advances
which have occurred in this century. Rapid and mass communications
systems now enable us to cover distances of space and language. But the
same forces which have made for the technical and scientific conditions
which have brought us together, have also created a new ethical situation
for man. Science which has conquered space has also produced Hiroshima.
Man has the capacity to eradicate malaria but also to annihilate his neighbor. The blessing and the curse of progress hang over us all. United by the
promise and the threat as never before, we who take our respective theolo-
gies with some seriousness have become a little more humble about our
religious certitudes, a little more conscious of the fact that perhaps our
truth is not necessarily the truth of others. Slowly we are opening our
minds to modes of thought and faith of which we have been hitherto
innocently ignorant or which we deliberately ignored. This conference will
fail if we come here to press our truth against the truth of those who do
not worship as we do. It will not succeed if we merely learn to tolerate one
another. It will achieve its purpose only if we try to grasp for the truth that
underlies all systems which strive for the redemption of man.

What I have to say about Judaism and its relevance for Twentieth Century
man is presented in the spirit of these introductory remarks. According
to Jewish tradition, Hillel, a great Rabbi who lived in the Land of Israel in
the 1st century, B. C., when asked to define Judaism in a brief sentence
replied: Do not do unto your neighbor what is hateful unto you – this is
the Torah (teaching); the rest is commentary. Having neither the talents
nor the piety of Hillel, I shall require more time and doubtless say far less
than he. Allowances must therefore be made for my own limitations.

Judaism like Hinduism, Buddhism, and Zoroastrianism is one of the
several older religions of mankind which have continued to be meaningful
to contemporary men. Like them it developed in the first millenium B.C.

just as men were first discovering the ethical dimension of deity. Like them it modified, corrected, and changed its doctrines to meet the challenges of different cultures and civilizations.

As an historic religion Judaism has a beginning, a middle, and an antici- pated ending. It begins its history with the creation of the world by God, it continues with the description of the discovery of God by Abraham, Isaac and Jacob, and it reaches its midpoint when, through Moses, the God discovered by individuals becomes the God of a nation – that is the God of a society of men operating within the framework of historical time. During the age of the prophets (until approximately 350 B.C.) and the Talmudic period which followed it (ended 600 A.D.), Jews discovered that just as knowledge of God could not be confined to particular individuals, so it must ultimately not be confined to particular nations. In the end all nations are destined to recognize God: all men will become Israel. The ultimate purpose of Jewish history is therefore to reach the end of Jewish history – for to say that all men will become Jews means the same as saying all men will become non-Jews. National distinctiveness will disappear. "On that day the Lord shall be one and his name will be 'One'" – says the prophet Zachariah and indicates that all mankind shall also be one.

To begin then with the beginning: *What is the significance of the story of Genesis for modern man?*

The idea of creation posits a view of a cosmos which is open-ended and dynamic. Other cosmogonies insisted that there was no creation and that the world was eternal, that is a static and closed system. The Bible is not a philosophical work, but it nevertheless implies a world of becoming. It is not a scientific work in biology but its account of the creation indicates an evolutionary progression from simpler to more complicated forms of life. Man created in the image of God is placed at the pinnacle of the creative process. He becomes an imitation of God on earth and is promised that he shall ultimately rule the world by means of his will and his intellect. According to a Talmudic legend God gave man the Torah but denied it to the angels. The history of man is the history of becoming. Man, God's agent on earth, is driven from paradise on earth with right knowledge. All through the prophetic literature this knowledge of God is consistently defined as ethical knowledge. "It hath been told thee O man what is good and what the Lord doth require of thee, only to do justice and love mercy and walk humbly before thy God." (Micah 6:8).

Maintaining an ambivalent view as to the nature of man the Bible portrays him neither as an incorrigible sinner nor as a blameless saint. He is rather viewed as a free agent who is given an ethical option: 'I have put before thee life and death – the blessing and the curse. Choose life." (Deu- teronomy 30:18). Judaism is neither pessimistic nor optimistic about the future of man. Man can be a sinner or a prophet or both, or neither. God affords man the possibility of choice.

Judaism's idea of *teshuvah* (returning) which we loosely translate as repentance best defines the nature of this ethical option given to man. The Jerusalem Talmud contains a difficult passage which deals with the doctrine of returning. It reads: "They asked wisdom. What is the punishment for a sinner? She said to them, 'Evil shall pursue the sinners' (Proverbs 13:21). They asked prophecy: What is the punishment for the sinner? She said to them: 'The soul that sinneth, it shall die' (Ezekiel 18:4). They asked God: What is the punishment for the sinner? He said to them: 'Let him repent (lit., make a return) and he shall be forgiven'. Thus it is written, He shall show the sinners the way (Proverbs 26), meaning, He will show the sinner the way of repentance." (Jerusalem Talmud, Makket 2:6).

Professor SAMUEL ATLAS, my teacher and colleague, has brilliantly interpreted this passage and with your indulgence I shall quote him at length:

"In the first stage as expressed by the answer of wisdom, namely that sin consists in being pursued by evil, is implied the conception of sin as a natural phenomenon which has its effects like any other natural phenomenon... The effects resulting from sin are not confined to the person committing them. It is a remnant of the mythological concept of sin as an offense against nature...Sin has inevitable effects like any other natural phenomenon, just as putting one's hand in fire will result in a burn whether it is done knowingly or inadvertently. In Biblical legislation, however, sin was bound up by consciousness and choice. Only a sinful act committed knowingly ... could be considered a crime. Thus, the mythological-natural concept of sin was abolished and replaced by the prophetic conception of sin...connected...with the concept of man as the being who has an idea of an 'ought to be', a goal. Sin is an offense not against nature as it is, but against an 'ought'. It makes no difference whether this 'ought to be' is given in the form of a law or is granted in the ethical consciousness of man... 'The soul that sinneth will die.'

"But in the prophetic view there is yet no mention of man's creative ability to transcend sin. In the third or latest stage...is expressed the capacity for creativity as an essential characteristic of human personality...By attributing...repentance to God, the impossibility of deriving it from nature is suggested. Only a God who transcends nature can be the ground of a creative, self-transcending act. In a naturalistic conception of the world the phenomenon of Repentance is a paradox. Repentance implies the possibility that the wicked become righteous. The sinner who is the repenting subject and the object into which he has transformed himself are one and the same person. The act of repentance involves...an act of jumping out of one's skin. Spinoza had good cause to deprecate repentance. In his conception of the world as a completely closed system regret and remorse would serve no purpose...man can neither undo the past nor undo himself.

"In our passage God grants the possibility of repentance; it is a creative act that is possible only in an open universe. The idea of God as the one who creates out of nothing adumbrates the possibility of creativity. Repentance...is an act of *creatio ex nihilo* and the idea of man as created in the image of God implies man's capacity for creativity."

The relevance of such a view of man in our own age is of course quite clear. This view rejects the mythological fatalism of all closed systems, be they Marxist or behaviorist. The divine ideal has placed before man the vision of what ought to be and the man who strives to live must overcome what he is, a creature of dust, a product of the animal world and become what he ought to be: "A little lower than the angels."

This he can do through Torah – the teaching – through knowledge of himself and the natural world, not a knowledge which leads to a fatalistic acceptance of what is but a knowledge which would assist him to arrive at what ought to be.

The discovery of personality, of the self, however, can be debased to an internalizing egocentrism at the expense of the society of men – a kind of spiritual onanism. At the mid-point of its history Judaism discovered society, the people of Israel. God makes a covenant not with individuals alone but with a society of men. If we examine the Ten Commandments we will find that except for the first commandment against idolatry, all are ethical in nature, i.e., they involve not only the self but the self in relation to others. Man can transcend himself only through mankind.

We all know the dangers of nationalism which in the West has led to the forgetting of the individual's ethical responsibility for the alleged good of the nation. The prophets also indicate when Judah sinned – he did so in the name of the nation. But prophetic Judaism maintained the razor's edge between the self and society. Note that the Ten Commandments, although they form the covenant between God and the nation, are styled in the second person singular, they are addressed to "Thou". In the Nineteenth Century a Jewish saint, concerned that the, bustle and clatter at public worship might distract him from concentrating upon the meaning of his prayers, removed himself to a private room which adjoined the synagogue hall, but he left the door between the room and the synagogue open, as if to indicate that God can be approached by the individual but only if that individual is also part of mankind.

Today all over the Western world youth is in revolt against the excesses of a highly impersonal industrial society which have turned government agencies and universities into unfeeling machines. But in their attempt to rediscover their own humanity – young men and women tend to reject all society and seek salvation only in cultivation of the self. The discovery of the self, however, has meaning only if it liberates the individual from the shackles of personal passions and avarices so that he can rejoin mankind and form a society of redeemed men. Mass society must not be allowed to destroy the integrity of the individual. (The Talmud teaches that he who destroys one soul, destroys a universe), but the individual cannot escape his responsibility to God and man by luxuriating in the contemplation of the self alone.

We are told that when the children of Israel stood on Mt. Sinai, they proclaimed their faith in the revelation by declaring: We shall do and we shall hear – which in the Hebrew also means understand and observe.

Ultimately the test of any religious ethic is the deed. In the famous passage of Deuteronomy which I quoted, in which God gives man the choice between good and evil, life and death, Moses proclaims: "The word is very right unto thee, that thou mayest do it."

Most religions have been eloquent with the word but evasive with their doing. Contemporary young people have come to question the grandiose utterances of man. They are instead demanding committed action in place of words. Some have even suggested that only through the act does man discover the program of redemption and that ideologies shall not precede the ethical act but follow it. "*We shall do and then understand.*"

As the sainted Rabbi LEO BAECK put it: "Judaism has its word ... to do. The deed becomes the proof of conviction. Judaism too has its doctrine but it is a doctrine of behavior which must be explored in action that it may be fulfilled."

Never has there been so wide a gap between the professed views on social issues of our several faiths and the deeds which need be done in order to fulfill these views. There is great virtue in expressing what "ought to be" but the ultimate proof of conviction is the creative act of fulfillment. Perhaps here is an area which transcends theological diversity. Men of the spirit of all nations, races, and religions can join a unified and uniting program of social action. Our several faiths engage in programs of relief and education, work for peace, fight hunger and disease. Could we not at least integrate these programs into some more coherent plan if only by exchanging ideas and information and opening our resources of communication to all parties striving for peace and plenty in the name of God?

Religion if it has any relevance to man must never make its peace with what is, but must strive for what ought to be. It must move from the discovery of man to the redemption of humankind – from the liberation of the self to the salvation of society.

Buddhism in the Present Age

by

Dr. REIMON YUKI
President, Kyoto Women's College, Kyoto, Japan

Never before in the history of mankind has the validity of religion been questioned as it is today. The situation is such that many in the present generation seem to feel that religion has very little – some would even say nothing – to do with the ever-increasing problems of mankind. Many scholars and critics of modern civilization have pointed out our poverty of spirit, in contrast to the abundance of our scientific and technological achievements. Drunk with his material prosperity and the triumph of his intellect in mastering nature, man has seemingly become utterly indifferent to the pursuit of virtue. Everyone seems to know how to live, but not what to live for. Ours is a life of such deep dilemma that our own splendid civilization becomes the major cause of spiritual chaos. The extent to which the dangerous situation in which man finds himself has been talked about, might lead one to say that the deepest problems are of a religious nature; the present generation, however, remains skeptical about the possibility of finding a solution there.

What has been happening in the religious situation since the advent of the modern age is that man has become increasingly unwilling to accept the validity of the supernatural. There are many who hold that religion must go, on the theory that psychological science has proven that man's belief in the supernatural is derived from childhood experiences. I suspect that the mass of mankind would readily agree with Sigmund Freud's analysis of religion. The mood of discrediting the supernatural is well illustrated in FREUD's book entitled THE FUTURE OF AN ILLUSION. According to FREUD, the idea of God is conceived by man in order to cope with the threatening forces surrounding him, which he feels are beyond the control of his reason. FREUD tried to prove, by means of psychoanalysis, that religion is an illusion, and a hindrance in realizing maturity. As ERICH FROMM excellently summarizes it:

Religion, according to FREUD, is a repetition of the experience of the child. Man copes with threatening forces in the same manner in which, as a child, he learned to cope with his own insecurity by relying on and admiring his father. FREUD compares religion with the obsessional neuroses we find in children.

One remarkable change which has taken place in the modern age is that man has seized on the notion of the "strong man" freed from subordination to the supernatural. Man has affirmed (out of his faith in reason) that he had better develop his own power of reason as well as his capacity to love, rather than relying on supernatural help. Although there has not been even the slightest sign of man's achieving this goal, the present majority seem to believe that this spirit of "rationalism" must be retained.

Confronting this trend, religionists have concluded that this is an age of "pride of intellect", a man-centered rather than a theocentric age. Accordingly, theological or philosophical studies have been focused on a reinterpretation of the supernatural, which would combat the prevalent skepticism. But no matter how earnestly they advance the notion of the supernatural the situation remains the same. Moreover, being so preoccupied with this purpose, the religionists themselves have failed to remain aware of what are the primary religious concerns. The primary concern for most religionists, if not for all, must be belief in the supernatural. With the exception of Buddhism, a non-theistic religion, if I am not mistaken, religion has traditionally been allied with the idea of a supernatural Truth and Power. However, what I would like to point out here is that mere philosophical or theoretical speculation on the supernatural is not necessarily religious. As KIERKEGAARD remarked, the religionists may be regarded as a group of people who are caught by utterly unhuman curiosity. It is time for all religionists to give their thoughtful attention to this criticism.

The majority of Japanese Buddhist scholars should also feel guilty in the light of this criticism of KIERKEGAARD. In the atmosphere of modern rationalism most, if not all, of us have emphasized that Buddhism is "a rational religion," while criticizing the weakness of current rationalism. The term "rational religion" is a very curious, almost unintelligible expression. However awkward it may sound, the studies of Buddhism in Japan have gone along with this line in the belief that the more we make explicit the unique rational principle of Buddhism, the more we are able to meet with and give solutions to the problems embodied in modern rationalism. However, in this climate, the concern of Buddhist study has been focused on the "logic" of "oneness" ,"suchness" or "naturalness" which is certainly neither formal nor dialectic. "Logic," no matter what sort of logic it may be, is certainly not the primary concern in Buddhism.

This confrontation between religion (belief in the supernatural) and the so-called "logic" of the contemporary denial of the concept, has cast the present generation all over the world into intolerable doubt as to man's potential to develop his power of reason and love. This doubt is intolerable, because modern man believes there is no way to build a better world, if man fails to develop his power of reason.

Today people see a dark cloud beginning to form. People are continually witnessing such horrifying incidents as the assassinations of great figures who were men determined to achieve peace and brotherhood, the senseless killing of the war in Vietnam, and the violent struggles of students against the existing system of our society. Witnessing these, people begin to doubt if men will ever improve understanding. We have gradually become aware that we have learned to fly like birds through the sky, but we have not yet learned to live together as brothers. The Nobel-Prize-winning nuclear physicist, Dr. TOMONAGA, expressed his serious concern about this situation of man's soul. He said that he was himself determined to search for a fire unknown to man on a vast wild plain, and when he found a new fire he was satisfied. However, he said, when he saw this new fire spreading on the vast plain, he thought man had serious problems within himself.

Thus one might say that man has become a stray sheep who is unable to find, either in religion or within his own mind, the lamp to guide him through the horrifying darkness. The only thing he has in his hand is an improved means of exploring the physical world. In short, modern rationalism's once cherished belief in man's reason is facing its total collapse. This was impressively shown when a natural scientist concluded his commentary on the success of Apollo 7 by saying that he hoped this would make people on earth aware of the senselessness of war. What disbelief in man's power of reason! No one believes anything anymore. And yet people are longing to find a world where we may live together as brothers.

If we look carefully at the present world, we may notice a little lamp of hope in the midst of darkness. We can hear a voice which says something of a very religious nature. I met a man who expressed his feelings as follows: "I am sick and tired of hearing so many people arguing in terms of good and bad, right and wrong". The feeling he expressed is of cardinal importance. It expresses a keen doubt about the justice of judging others in terms of good and bad. As long as man throws doubt on judging others in terms of this dualism, there is always a path to the heart of religion.

What Buddhism regards as the essential problem for every man is the realization of wisdom and compassion within himself. In the pamphlet of the Temple of Understanding, we read the words of the Buddha as follows: "Hurt not others in ways that you yourself would find hurtful." As they are quoted in the same pamphlet, Confucianism, Christianity, Hinduism, Islam and Judaism have very similar words. These explicitly express the ultimate goal for man to realize.

However, as we have seen before, man is living in a world where he feels like a fool if he acts in accordance with this teaching. People say that to follow this principle is impossible in this society. Since the present majority has lost a sincere religious concern, it is natural that the words of religion are not received seriously. As FROMM points out, "People go to churches and listen to sermons in which the principle of love and charity are preached, and the very same people would consider themselves fools or worse if they hesitated to sell a commodity which they knew the customer could not afford."

But to my mind there is still a wonderful thing in man's mind, no matter how irreligious people appear to be. It is true that as long as we are alive it is impossible to be free of self-centeredness.

Deep-rooted selfishness is the basic nature of man. And yet it is also a fact that man is impressed when he sees someone putting a rock aside on the road to clear the way for others. Here we see the contradictive nature in man. The deeper our awareness of this contradiction becomes, the more we are able to listen to the teaching of compassion.

The more aware of compassion we become, the more we are aware of the sin of selfishness. This awareness that man's self-centeredness is truly sinful is the essential basis for the virtues of understanding, love and justice. The words of MARTIN LUTHER KING, Jr., in his address on the occasion of his receiving the Nobel Prize are impressive. He said:

The movement does not seek to liberate Negroes at the expense of the humiliation and enslavement of whites. It seeks no victory over anyone. It seeks to liberate American society and share in the self-liberation of all the people.

What makes this impressive is that it so explicitly expresses the unselfish determination embodied in the struggle for freedom and justice. There have been many struggles for freedom, justice, liberation and peace, but one can scarcely find a struggle like his. Almost all other struggles all over the world today are more or less selfish. This is the reason why people cannot help but regard those struggles as dangerous. But, by contrast, the struggle that was led by MARTIN LUTHER KING, Jr., is certainly a bright torch of hope in the midst of darkness. And here is something very important for every religionist to consider if he intends to reassess the role and validity of his religion.

People are of two minds, divided into two camps. Each has its own standard of justice. Each regards justice as that which serves its own interests. If this is the case, and I believe it is, the term "justice" no longer means what it is supposed to mean. In the minds of people now the word "justice" is regarded as one which effectively evokes the fighting spirit in men's minds. People of the present should realize that justice rests only in the realm of non-self. The word justice does not stand for the justification of a particular interest.

To seek the realization of justice in this world is to seek a way to free man from his self-centeredness. This is of cardinal importance if man is to achieve his goal of becoming a truly compassionate and enlightened person. As long as Buddhism is able to lead man to this goal, the words of Buddha will reach into men's minds.

Difference and Similarity Among Religions

by

SWAMI LOKESHWARANANDA
Ramakrishna Mission, Narendrapur[1]

Long ago one of our Vedas declared "Truth is one. Scholars described it variously." This is something fundamental to Hinduism. Again and again saints and seers have reaffirmed this. Today we heard a Sikh friend spell out how Guru Nanak reaffirmed this. Later, in Bengal, the Brahma Samaj again reaffirmed this, as did Ramakrishna at about the same time.

But he did it in a way which was entirely different from the way others had. He was born a Hindu. Naturally he practiced his own religion, but he was not content with Hinduism alone. He said, "Let me practice Islam, and let me practice Christianity also." He practiced them with the help of experts. What made him do this I don't know. But he did it.

And finally he declared, from his own experience, not as a matter of intellectual assent, not merely acquiescence in something which was already widely accepted in Hindu society, but as a matter of his own personal experience, that: "Religions are like so many paths, leading to the same place." He lived at a place not too far from here, a place called Dakshaneshwar, in the northern suburbs of Calcutta. He used to say: "If you come here by the Ganges River, you hire a boat. But if you are coming by road you walk or you hire a carriage, and come here. It is a matter of choice or a matter of means, but you come to the same place. It doesn't matter what is your mode of travel, you come to the same place." Some of you may have read what the Gita says in this connection: "It doesn't matter what path you choose, you all come to me." Me. The Guru. It makes no difference how we travel. Similarly, in our great Sanskrit text you find this idea described with a little imagery. It says: "Look at the rivers. They start from different places. They start, some in the Himalayas, for instance, some elsewhere. Their travels cover hundreds of miles. They are different; some are straight, some are crooked. But their ultimate goal is the same. It is the sea. All of them finally flow into the sea."

That is what we are. We are different from each other. We have to be dif-

1 Delivered extemporaneously at the Birla Academy, October 23, 1968.

ferent from each other, if we are going to be ourselves. I can't be your prototype, just as you cannot be my prototype. You and I differ in many ways. Our food habits are different. The kind of clothing we wear is different. We have to be different. It is God's wish that we differ. It is natural that we should differ also in our religious beliefs. But, what is important is that we recognize that, underlying the different religious faiths, there is much that they have in common. They are the same truths, only they have been spelled out differently, in different paths. The language has to be different, the manner of presentation also has to be different. We have different backgrounds, we have been brought up in different traditions. But our goal is the same. It is wrong to stress the differences that mark different religious beliefs, for there is also much that they have in common. Or, to be more precise, there is a common ground which exists between the different religious points of view. Why therefore, emphasize only the differences?

But if you think – one might almost say, if you recognize – that there is one common truth, to which all of us are slowly wending our ways, it will be a mistake. It is not that easy. We forget that religion is not just an intellectual exercise. It is being and becoming. It is the realization of this. You fill your hearts with God-consciousness. Merely talking about the unity of religions will not take us anywhere. We may be nice to each other, we may pat each other on the back and say, "Yes, friend, I believe you are a good man. You have a very fine religious tradition. I have every sympathy for you." That is not going to take our hearts anywhere. Only if we get close to God, if we really care for God, if we really love God, then only will it be possible for us to love our fellow man.

You praise us here in India for religious tolerance. Lots of people like to stop at religious tolerance. And yet the same people make it plain to us, in their individual behavior with the man living next door, that they are most intolerant. An intellectual assent is not enough. It is being and becoming. Your love for God should be such that you cannot but love your fellow men also, because you realize they are also the children of the same God whom you worship.

So, it is with God that we should fill our hearts, if we are going to achieve the purpose of this conference. Let each of us be a simple but sincere Temple of Understanding. It is not a matter of constructing something with bricks and mortar, this Temple of Understanding. It is something that you and I are, individually, or collectively. It is a question of how we treat each other, how we love each other. That is what the Temple orUnderstanding is going to be. It is not merely creating a physical symbol to help solve the problem of religious discord. It is something that we are able to achieve through a process of growth and development in our religious life, something that will broaden our hearts, which will embrace everybody, which will not emphasize the difference that exists between one man and another. That is what the Temple of Understanding is going to be.

The Pertinence of Islam to the Modern World

by

Dr. Seyyed Hossein Nasr
Vice-Chancellor, University of Tehran[1]

One speaks so often today of this or that idea or element being no longer pertinent to the modern world that one forgets both the essential reality of the doctrines and ideas which are of permanent significance and the real needs of the modern world. Whatever is not fashionable in this whirling pace of superficial change is suddenly declared outmoded and irrelevant, whereas in actuality what is trivial and irrelevant is precisely that world or climate of thought which rejects and ignores the perennial and permanent truths, the truths which have always had meaning for men because they have appealed to something permanent in man. If a whole segment of modern humanity no longer finds meaningful the perennial truths of religion and the wisdom that has been cultivated and followed by sages throughout the ages, it is most of all because the very existence of this segment of humanity has itself ceased to have any meaning. And taking itself and its imperfect perception of things which it calls the "existential predicament of modern man" too seriously, this type of man is not able to turn the sharp edge of its criticism toward itself and so does no more than criticize the objective, revealed truth contained in all orthodox and authentic religions, which in reality are themselves the only possible judge and criterion of man's worth and value. The pertinence of Islam to the modern world, as the pertinence of any other authentic religion, must be discussed in the light of the ontological priority of the one to the other; that is, religion issues from the absolutely Real and is the message of Heaven, whereas the world is always relative and whether it be modern or ancient remains the "world". The modern world is no less "the world" than "the world" to which traditional religious imagery refers. In fact, quite on the contrary, it is more removed from the Immutable and the Permanent than any other "world" of which we have historical knowledge, and is therefore even more in need of the message of the Immutable[2].

1 Presented in absentia.
2 See F. Schuon, Light on the Ancient Worlds, translated by Lord Northbourne, London, 1965, Chapter I and II.

Islam is precisely such a message. It is the direct call of the Absolute to man, inviting him to return to the Absolute and the One, and it appeals to what is most permanent and immutable in man.[1] And because it is such a message it is of pertinence to all "worlds" and generations as long as man remains man. Today, even in academic circles in the West, so long dominated by the evolutionism of the Nineteenth Century, certain scholars and scientists are beginning to discover and confirm the permanent nature of man and his needs, and to focus their attention on the permanent elements to which the Islamic message most of all addresses itself.[2] Men are born, live and die and are always in quest of meaning, both for the alpha and the omega of their life and the period in between. This quest for meaning, which is as essential as the need for food and shelter, is in reality the quest for the Ultimate, for the Absolute, and it is as permanent a need of man as his need for food. Religion provides precisely this meaning and in a sense is the shelter in the indefinity of cosmic manifestation and the uncertainties of temporal and terrestial existence. It is not accidental that the Islamic prayers have been considered by certain Muslim sages as a refuge in the storm of daily life. The message of Islam is as enduring as the need of man for this spiritual "shelter" and for meaning in human existence.

From a more specific point of view Islam remedies one of the particular maladies of the modern world, which is over-secularization, a process which is nothing else than depleting things of their spiritual significance. It was first the temporal domain having to do with government and rule that was considered as secular in the West, although in the Middle Ages and even later periods, as long as traditional political institutions survived even the temporal possessed a religious significance.[3] Then "thought" became secularized in the form of a secular philosophy and science, then art in all its branches and now finally religion itself. The rebellion of the Renaissance made this process appear as a gradual movement toward the attainment of freedom, but now that the process has reached such dangerous proportions many realize that it was only the freedom to lose the

---

1 "Islam is the meeting between God as such and man as such. God as such: that is to say God envisaged, not as He manifested Himself in a particular way but inasmuch as He is what is and also by His nature He creates and reveals.

"Man as such: that is to say man envisaged, not as a fallen being needing a miracle to save him, but as man, a theomorphic being endowed with an intelligence capable of conceiving of the Absolute and with a will capable of choosing what leads to the Absolute." F. SCHUON, UNDERSTANDING ISLAM, translated by D. M. MATHESON, London, 1963 p. 13. See also S. H. NASR, IDEALS AND REALITIES OF ISLAM, London, 1966, Chapter I.

2 See for example J. SERVIER, HOMME ET l'INVISIBLE, Paris, 1965, which brings so much ethnological and anthropological evidence in favor of the essentially permanent nature of man throughout the ages. It is significant that only this year the Institute Accademico di Roma under the direction of ELEMIRE ZOLLA, organized for the first time in recent years a full symposium on the question of permanent values in historical process.

3 See S. H. NASR, "Spiritual and Temporal Authority in Islam" in ISLAMIC STUDIES, Beirut, 1966, pp. 6–13.

possibility of the only real freedom open to man, the freedom of spiritual deliverance. Every other apparent freedom is no more than slavery to either outward natural forces or inner passions.

Against this malady of over-secularization and the negative freedom which now verges upon anarchy, Islam presents a view of life which is completely sacred and a freedom which begins with submission to the Divine Will and which therefore opens upward towards the Infinite. In fact in the languages of the Islamic peoples, there is no distinction between the secular and the profane or temporal; terms do not even exist to translate such concepts.[1] Through the Divine Law or *Sharī'ah*, which encompasses all human life, every human activity is given a transcendent dimension; it is made sacred and thereby meaningful. Of course this implies that one has accepted the *Sharī'ah* and is applying it, and therefore making a sacrifice from the point of view of human nature. But then one cannot make anything sacred without some form of sacrifice, for what does sacrifice mean but literally to make sacred, *sacer facere*? And it is surprising for a non-Muslim to observe to what extent Islamic society has been able to apply the *Sharī'ah* and how even in those regions where its hold has weakened among certain classes of Muslims, the attitudes which it has cultivated still endure.[2]

At the heart of the *Sharī'ah* lies the daily Muslim rite or *salāt* (*namāz* in Persian and Urdu), which according to prophetic tradition is the support and pillar of religion. Now, one of the remarkable characteristics of this rite, which corresponds not to the individual prayers of other religions such as Christianity but to a rite such as the Mass, is that it can be performed anywhere and by any Muslim. The sacerdotal function, which in certain religions is relegated to a particular class of men, is divided in Islam among all members of the community, giving the possibility to members of the Islamic faith to remain a part of the community of believers, the *ummah*, without needing to be geographically attached to it. Thus, in an age such as the present, when men travel often and where distance from a particular land or people may make the practice of certain religions difficult, Islam possesses this relative advantage of being possible to practice anywhere.

In fact Islam possesses to an eminent degree, this power of adaption, of being able to live and be followed anywhere, but this does not of course mean that it should conform to the modern world and all the errors that comprise it. Islam, like every other revealed truth, comes from God. Therefore, it is the world that must be made to conform to this truth, not vice-versa. But with this provision in mind it can be said that in whatever situation he is placed, the man desirous of practicing Islam can do so with-

1 See S. H. NASR, "Religion and Secularism, their Meaning and Manifestation in Islamic History" in ISLAMIC STUDIES, pp. 7–14.
2 Concerning the significance of the *Sharī'ah* in Islam see S. H. NASR, IDEALS AND REALITIES OF ISLAM, Chapter IV,

out the outward difficulties which beset certain religions based on continuous daily rituals.

The daily Muslim rites also bestow the great advantage upon man of being able to carry his center with him. The great malady of modern man can be reduced to his loss of center, a loss which is so clearly depicted in the chaotic so-called literature and art of modern times. Islam offers the direct remedy to this illness. In general, prayer places man in the axial and vertical dimension which points to the Center. In particular, the Islamic rites make possible the "carrying" of this Center wherever one goes. The fact that wherever one may be on earth, the daily prayers are directed toward Mecca, the supreme center of Islam, indicates clearly this reflection of the Center whenever and wherever one happens to be praying. By virtue of the power of these prayers man continues to possess the Center which coordinates and harmonizes his activity and his life.

The cardinal Islamic doctrine of Unity (al-tawhid) itself emphasizes this need and the necessity for integration. God is One and so man, who is created in "His Form", must become integrated and unified. The goal of the religious and spiritual life must be the complete and total integration of man in all his depth and amplitude.[1] Modern man suffers from excessive compartmentalization in his science and education as well as in his social life, which through the very pressure of technology tends to disintegrate social bonds and even the human personality. The Islamic ideal of Unity stands in stark opposition to this multiplicity and division, reversing the centrifugal tendencies of man which make him ever more prone to dissipate his soul and energy toward the periphery, and returning the soul to the Center.

Today everyone cries for peace but peace is never achieved, precisely because it is metaphysically absurd to expect a civilization that has forgotten God to possess peace. Peace in the human order results from peace with God and also with nature.[2] It is the result of the equilibrium and harmony which can come into being only through the integration made possible by tawhid. Islam has quite unjustly been depicted as the religion of the sword and of war, whereas it is a religion which seeks to bring about peace through submission to the Will of God, as the name Islam, in Arabic meaning both peace and submission, indicates. And this is made possible by giving each thing its due. Islam preserves a remarkable equilibrium between the needs of the body and those of the spirit, between this world and the next. No peace is possible in a civilization which has reduced all human welfare to animal needs and refuses to consider the needs of man beyond his earthly existence. Moreover, having reduced man to a purely terrestial being, such a civilization is not able to provide for the spiritual needs which

1 See S. H. NASR, "Sufism and the Integration of Man", ISLAMIC REVIEW & ARAB AFFAIRS, Sept. 1967, pp. 11–14.
2 See S. H. NASR, THE ENCOUNTER OF MAN AND NATURE, London, 1968, Chapter IV,

nevertheless continue to exist, with the result that there is created a combination of crass materialism and an even more dangerous pseudo-spiritu-
alism, whose opposition to materialism is more imaginary than real.[1] And
thus we are faced with the endangering of even the terrestial life which has
come to be cherished as the final end in itself. One of the basic messages of
Islam to the modern world is its emphasis on the importance of giving
each thing its due, of preserving each element in its place, of guarding the
proportion between things and discriminating between the snake and the
rope. The peace that men seek is only possible if the total needs of man, not
only as an animal but also as a being born for immortality, are considered.
To be concerned only with the physical needs of men is to reduce men to
slavery and to produce problems even on the physical plane whose solution is impossible. It is not religion but modern medicine that has created
the problem of over-population, which religion is now asked to solve,
by taking away the sacred meaning of human life itself, if not totally, at
least in part.

Likewise of vital concern today is peace between religions. In this domain
also Islam has a particular message for modern man. Islam considers the
acceptance of anterior prophets as a necessary article of faith in Islam itself
and asserts quite vigorously the universality of revelation.[2] No other sacred
text speaks as much of the universality of religion as the Quran. Islam, the
last of the religions of the present humanity, joins in this domain Hinduism,
the first and most primordial of existing religions, in envisaging religion in
its universal manifestation throughout the cycles of human history. In
the metaphysics and theology of comparative religion, Islam has a great
deal to teach to those who wish to study comparative religion on a more
serious plane than just collecting historical and philological facts. The
reason, in fact, why Muslims have been less interested than followers of
other religions in comparative religion in modern times is mostly that they
have not found any discomforting theological challenges to Islam by
discovering the existence of other authentic and valid spiritual traditions.

Finally in discussing this theme of peace, something must be said of the
inner peace which men seek today desperately, desperately enough to have
caused a whole army of pseudo-yogis and spiritual healers to establish
themselves in the West. Men now feel instinctively the importance of
meditation and contemplation but alas only too few are willing to undergo
the discipline in the matrix of an authentic tradition which can guarantee

1 On the stages of revolt against true spirituality leading through materialism to pseudo-
spiritualism see R. GUENON, THE REIGN OF QUANTITY AND THE SIGNS OF THE TIMES,
translated by LORD NORTHBOURNE, London, 1951, pp. 229 ff.
2 See S. H. NASR, "Islam and the Encounter of Religions," XITH INTERNATIONAL CONGRESS
OF THE INTERNATIONAL ASSOCIATION FOR THE HISTORY OF RELIGIONS, Vol. VII, Leiden, 1968,
pp. 23–27. For a more general discussion of this question see F. SCHUON, THE TRANSCEN-
DENT UNITY OF RELIGIONS, translated by P. TOWNSEND, London, 1948.

them access to the joy which only the contemplation of the celestial realities makes possible. Thus they turn to drugs or self-realization centers or the thousand and one "pseudo-masters" from the East who are taking a veritable revenge upon the West for all the West did to Oriental traditions in the colonial period.

Islam possesses all the means necessary for spiritual realization in Sufism, which is its inner and esoteric dimension. Sufism cannot be practiced without Islam; but Islam can lead those who have the necessary aptitude to this inner court of joy and peace that is Sufism and which is the foretaste of the "gardens of paradise". Here again the characteristic of the contemplative way of Islam, or Sufism, is that it can be practiced anywhere and in nearly every walk of life. Sufism is not based on outer withdrawal from the world but on inner detachment. As a contemporary Sufi has said, "It is not I who have left the world, it is the world that has left me." The inner attachment may be combined with intense outward activity. Sufism achieves the wedding of the active and contemplative lives again in character with the unifying nature of Islam. The spiritual force of Islam creates, through intense activity, a climate in the outer world which naturally induces man toward meditation and contemplation, as is seen so clearly in Islamic art.[1] The outward opposition with which, by definition, the world of activity is concerned is resolved into an inner peace which is a characteristic of the One, of the Center.

Islam, like all other authentic religions, bears a message from the eternal directed to that which is immutable and permanent in man. As such it knows no temporality. But in addition it possesses certain characteristics, placed there providentially, to enable men in any circumstances and in any "world" to be able to follow it and to benefit from its teachings. Were there ever to be a world for which religion in general and Islam in particular were to have no meaning at all, that world itself would cease to possess any meaning. It would become sheer illusion. As long as there is any element of reality to *the* world, or to *a* world, Islam continues to possess a valid message for that world, for this message comes from the Truth, and as Islamic metaphysical doctrines teach us, Truth and Reality are ultimately one.

[1] On the spiritual principles of Islamic art see T. BURCKHARDT "Perennial Values of Islamic Art", STUDIES IN COMPARATIVE RELIGION, Summer 1967, pp. 132–141. See also T. BURCKHARDT. SACRED ART IN EAST AND WEST, London, 1967. Chapter IV.

The Significance of Religion to Human Issues in the Light of the Universal Norms of Mystical Experience

by

Pir VILAYAT INAYAT KHAN
École Internationale de la Méditation, Paris

Beloved Ones of God:

Towards the One, the perfection of love, harmony, and beauty, the only Being, united with all the illuminated souls who form the embodiment of the Master, the spirit of guidance...

We are meeting on this historical occasion, made possible by the Temple of Understanding, in order to seek together a way of cooperation between the present-day leaders of the great world religions, with a view towards building a better world. We hope that in the prevailing atmosphere of communion with the spiritual preceptors and contemplatives of all religions, custodians of their predecessors, teaching in all epochs of history, we may be enabled to scrutinize human affairs of our times. We are aware not only of being the heirs of various religious traditions, but of echoing a deep aspiration, felt dimly by some and more poignantly by those who have an intuition of the azimuth towards which the thought of the planet is progressing – the point of convergence of human consciousness attuned to its highest pitch in our time – to discover the contribution of religion to the solution of human problems. We are overwhelmed by the magnitude of the forces that are being brought to bear the human issues that are being raised here, as the great dialogue of the world religions is about to be woven among those to whom so many involved in life look for guidance, and who may be considered as the ambassadors of the great traditions of the contemplatives who themselves have wandered across the outposts of the soul in the pursuit of that to which each one of us aspires in rapt moments of silence. People look to us desperately, urgently, to do something concrete. How can we communicate the vision of unity at a conference of this kind to the masses, so that it may have an influence on the way people think, which will in turn affect the way they live. It is a matter of communicating vision. Perhaps the most wonderful and sacred moments of our life are those when we respond to something we had not yet realized or gleaned in our perspective. One feels like exclaiming: well of course, so it is.

We are living in a highly significant era in the history of our planet, in which the mind of the planet, taken globally, is undergoing a shattering revolution. Mental frontiers and collective "isms" are giving way to higher loyalties. The planet is in the throes of welding itself at the cost of over-coming frustrating resistances, into a whole not only in the domain of politics, science, technology, and art, but also in that of religion. We are tackling something so fundamental that I think it true to say we are living not in the atomic age, nor in the electronic age, but in the age of inter-religious ecumenicity, including all members of the human family, which is of course the original meaning of the word. The present meeting is a landmark in a very slow process that has been unfolding itself for a long time and which, until recently, remained confined to those on the prow of human progress. Only now is it beginning to have an influence upon at least the most progressive strata of the masses.

The Sufis have played a pioneering role here. As you probably know, Emperor Akbar, himself a Sufi, convened a Congress on Religion, the first in history to my knowledge. This took place at Fatehpur Sikri, near Agra, in the 17th Century. Cyrus (Emperor Khusro), the Mazdean Magi-King, who freed the Jews from Babylon and was regarded by them as the "anointed one" (Christos), promoted religious understanding 25 centuries earlier. In-terestingly enough, the Sufis carried the heritage of the tradition of the Magi, as Shihabuddin Suhrawardi has shown. In 1910, HAZRAT INAYAT KHAN, my father, was sent to the West by his Pir of the lineage of the Chishti Sufis to bring a message of religious unity. He instituted the Universal Worship in which the holy scriptures of the world religions are read from the same altar. And on the last day that he was among his disciples in Suresnes, near Paris, on 13th September, 1926, he laid the foundation stone of the "Univer-sal" temple, church or mosque of all religions. The Master had designed it in the form of a fourfold human being sitting in meditation and turned towards the four cardinal points. It was to serve as a center for all religions. Since man is the real temple of God, the temple should have the form of man, yet cosmicized. I am sure that he would be pleased that this scheme of world importance will now be carried out by the Temple of Understand-ing, under Mrs. HOLLISTER's leadership. No sooner had we met her, than we understood why she had been earmarked from above for this great venture. It is important for the present stage of the evolution of the planet Earth that a temple should be built in our time as a point of convergence. MAHATMA GHANDI set the example by including the holy scriptures of several of the great religions in his daily prayer meetings. And today many organizations are working to foster religious rapprochement; here we might mention the Baha'i faith, the Ramakrishna Mission, the World Congress of Faiths, The World Spiritual Council, the World Fellowship of Re-ligions, the Geestelijke Reveil in Holland, and the Congrès International In-terreligieux which I convene every year in Paris and which I also held last year in Rome and will hold in London. The end of this Congress is always a joint service of worship where Hindu swamis, Buddhist bikkhus, Zoroastrian dastours, Jewish rabbis, Catholic and Orthodox priests, Protestant ministers, and Muslim imams pray side by side at the same altar

We wish these world congresses and conferences to have an effective impact upon the religious masses of the world, but we will be defeating our purpose if we present the various dogmas of each religion in a *"dialogue de sourds"*, a dialogue of deaf but courteous and amiable well-wishers, at most reciprocally tolerant, each one propounding the virtues of his creed. The dumb have an advantage over the deaf in that generally they try to listen. But when we seek, beyond the formal differences, the underlying human experience of the divine, then something happens which may have a snowball effect, for it is moved by the power of conviction. Where men leavened by their highest ideal come shoulder to shoulder together at the round table of the real chivalry which is the service of the spiritual government of the world, and seek to understand one another across the abyss of religious particularisms, in the exchange and sharing of their ideals, the common denominator of spiritual experience becomes evident of itself.

We do not advocate syncretism or any new form of proselytism, for syncretism is a jumbled juxtaposition of exogenous dogmas. We affirm the fundamental unity of human norms faced with actual experience. Tolerance means that we should tolerate the intolerant. And as the overall mind of the planet matures from superstition to realization, it is important for men and women in our time to examine objectively how they stand in the religious landscape. Many are Muslim, or Hindu, or Buddhist, or Christian, or Zoroastrian, or Jewish, or Sikh because they were born in a family, community or country where that particular denomination prevails. Sometimes, out of a feeling of loyalty, the adherents to a faith tend to neglect studying the religion of others and, in certain cases, assume *a priori* the superiority of their own creed. We think the child who says "My mother is the most beautiful woman in the world," is most touching, but we know that when he is grown up he will realize that other women are also beautiful. There are those exceptional few who, having deeply and thoroughly studied all religions, have made a definite choice of one to which they are drawn by temperament.

We rejoice in the wealth of the different forms and beliefs and, of course, respect those who say, "For my part, this is the religion that corresponds most to my temperament or aspirations," and we hope that, as a result of this confrontation of points of view, an intuition may arise in us leading us to the discovery and appreciation of aspects of our own religion unknown heretofore. But do we ever ask ourselves to which religion God belongs?

Where human thought, lifted to its apogee, meets itself in the thought of another in reverential communion, then new perspectives open up by the miracle of the interfusion of souls. In the friendship of those who have shared bread at the same table a new loyalty is born so that some come to see the prophetic chain of religious revelation as a total sweep instead of considering its phases separately. HAZRAT INAYAT KHAN taught his disciples to open the windows of their consciousness to the wider perspectives of the procession of human destinies progressing towards a fulfillment that cannot be assessed by an individual consciousness; and to grasp divine guidance beyond the various media through which it manifests itself.

Think of the strength that would be generated if the religious powers of the world were to join forces. There is a growing minority which has abandoned outer forms and allegiances, or anything but the most formal membership in churches or religious institutions, but wishes very sincerely to delve into the real subject matter of religious experience and draw out the essence. It is not good enough to say that we believe that all religions are one, but we should be able to show where the parallels are to be found and point this out. Times have changed. We cannot limit the march of progress by allowing ourselves to be trammelled by hackneyed formal observances, when there is a fresh breeze of spiritual freedom blowing in the fields of religion. For this fast-growing elite, the study of comparative mystical experience is important, and they are setting a trend pointing to where the future lies. In fact, it is in the realm of mystical experience that religions meet although in dogmas they diverge. There is a coming subject-head of science called the science of religion. Here religion is studied from the vantage-point of experience rather than dogma. It may be considered as a science adjacent to psychology; the psychology of the higher strata of the thinking process. The actual application of the art of this science is the practice of meditation.

The role of religions in our society can be assessed by the fact that it was the innate striving of the creature for communication with an ultimate reality that triggered the fateful leap, in the course of evolution, from the animal to man. If man has been able to lift himself to the point of devising the intricate system of thought-forms and material amenities that form the mainstay of civilization, it is because, at some time in the course of the evolution of his ancestors, he took the step that brought him into a new dimension of thought, namely the awareness that he was part of a great reality beyond his existence considered individually, for evolution is spurred by the rising of consciousness becoming more and more effulgent and cosmic at each point of forward progress. Intelligence becomes awareness by the reflex act whereby it cognizes itself as being the one that cognizes, as described by Aristotle. According to TEILHARD DE CHARDIN, that which catapulted the leap forward from the state of the animal to the state of man was that change of focus from the animal's knowing to the human being's knowing that he knows. Granted that the cells of the body are endowed individually with a measure of consciousness – a consciousness of their individuality – from the vantage point of the cell all that exists is cells; the body as a whole is unthinkable. But let us imagine that an individual cell should arise to the consciousness of the thought of the body, this cell would raise itself to a higher sensitivity and consequently a further degree of evolution. This may, incidentally, actually happen by instilling cosmic awareness into the very flesh and is called, esoterically, the transfiguration of matter by spirit. Therefore, it is the intuition of a reality enfolding our individual existence that has permitted the animal to gain the new dimension of awareness that makes for the status of man. And religion is the system devised by man to foster the experience of a relationship with a reality viewed on a super-individual scale, and an analagous leap forward is promoted esoteric schools, at yet higher levels, into yet higher dimensions of transcendent thought.

A comparative study of the religious or mystical experiences of the adepts of the great world religions points to certain fundamental steps in the relationship, or the awareness of the relationship, of the human being with a reality contemplated at the scale of a higher order of being. The ultimate reality may appear differently according to the level of consciousness of the contemplative, or the strata of mind of God in order to indicate specifically the type of experience referred to. The first stage is one in which the contemplative becomes aware of being part of a whole; the ultimate reality here is conceived of as a totality of being. This is called by the Sufis, *Wahdat al-Wujud*, losing oneself in the outlook which conceives the totality of physical being in its oneness instead of its diversity. This can be placed in parallel with the point of view held in the Chandogya Upanishad: All is Brahman. This happens when the consciousness of the individual ceases to limit itself to awareness at the scale of individuality and begins to experience, or perhaps vaguely to sense, a total consciousness of physical being, of which his own individual awareness of being is but a part. Imagine the consciousness of the coral reef as a whole instead of that of each coral individually. Buddha shows, in the Anqutta Nikaya, that when the act of consciousness is no longer bound by the scale of the individual, it identifies itself with all physical being, extending horizontally indefinitely and also vertically into orders of reality other than the physical. The method of promoting this experience consists in shattering the acquired notion of the individual self. This dispersion of consciousness from the focal point of individual awareness may result in a diminution of mental acuity, unless consciousness is trained to survive the abolition of its reference points.

This experience is defined by the term of pantheism or panentheism (to use the word coined by Professor NICHOLSON). Typical of this point of view is the famous expression in the Chandogya Upanishad: *Tat Twam Asi*. IBN ARABI, suspended precariously at the edge of Islamic Orthodoxy, ventured the sentence: "God is the created Creator and creating creature." The belief in divine immanence butts itself against the difficulty that if God is all this he is subject to change, dissolution, imperfection, a devil. This is why the Upanishads move in their historical sequence towards the concept of the ultimate reality as being other than the physical or mental strata of being or even the strata of being corresponding to the levels of the soul. One may find oneself at a stage in which one is bewildered by the manifestation of His beauty, by the forms of the world, called *ayat* (signs) by the Sufis, and which, according to them, espouse the profile of His countenance. Again these forms might appear to one as illusory, *nada*, when one passes through the "night of the senses" depicted psychologically by St. John of the Cross, and further on the road one may meet yet another state wherein are revealed the subtle signs of God's Being, called *sifat* by the Sufis, the divine attributes or the archetypes of qualities latent in all human personalities. The Persian Sufi poet, Jalaluddin Rumi, declared, "Sometimes He Abolishes our intuition of His transcendence in order to reveal to the contemplative the image of His immanence, and sometimes He shatters the veil of His immanence before the eyes of those lost in its contemplation in order to lift them into the mysteries of His transcendence."

It is the immanent aspect of reality that is called, monistically speaking, *prakriti*, and theistically it is referred to as Brahman, according to the Chandogya Upanishad. Yet it is referred to in more transcendental terms in the Mundaka Upanishad as *brahman yoni*, the matrix of all created being. In Islam or Judaism, emphasis is placed on the "otherness", that is the transcendence of God. However, references to this aspect of God in His immanence are to be found amongst the mystics. An Iranian Dervish, Baba Quli, says: "All I see is Him". Another Sufi challenger of the generally accepted norm, ABDUL JABBAR-AL-NEFARI, an Egyptian Dervish, once cried out in his ecstasy: "Seek Him not 'there' where He is only a potential, for 'here' He is a reality." The Sufis have developed in their practices the art of provoking the switchover into the higher levels of awareness by seeking, through the veil of outer forms, signs of the Divine Countenance. This is particularly in the glance of a mystic who has been shattered by the discovery of the divine in His physical manifestation, for the glance reflects a vision that he has grasped in a flash of extreme lucidity – the magic of the reflection of the divine countenance passing from one contemplative to another, the secret and transforming power of the dervish.

It is divine immanence which is the hallmark of Christianity. That man should have existed latently as an archetype of the divine image before the beginning of the world is a poignant realization. But it is still more overwhelming to discover that this archetype manifests itself in the course of time. This is the key to the theology of the trans-historicity of Christ. For the Ebionites, Christ is an event in the realm of the soul and this gives Him His trans-historical character. However, that a cosmic law cognized by the soul should become an event inscribed in space and time and subject to the control of the senses is the miracle of life, and it is this miracle that is feted in Christianity. Incarnation, the passage from transcendence to immanence, the infusion of the Self into the ego, is the great challenge to reason, the "impossible possibility." As in the cry of the poet: "How can the eternal accomplish itself in a temporal act and infinity in a finite act?", the Mundaka Upanishad launches the question: "In what object can this all be known?"

For Islam, incarnation, *hulul*, is untenable and, indeed blasphemous. Mansur al-Hallaj was crucified for asserting the incarnation of spirit in matter. On this point we engage deeply the most painful phase of the dialogue between Christianity and Islam. At our Paris Congress, the Christian answered: only faith has the force to glean the trans-historic beyond the historic for it does not, as reason does, reduce cosmic events to the phenomena of the senses. It calls upon the use of higher strata of thinking in the transformation of the notion of selfhood. If the epiphany is that which appears in the historical framework, the resurrection is that which transpires beyond the historical plane. When Christianity used the historical Christ as a springboard to the resurrected Christ, it was a way of expressing a metaphysical truth according to which the personal aspect of God may serve as a springboard to the transcendental at the dawn of awareness. Yet by limiting incarnation to one person, the Christians made it difficult to account for the experience of the baffling encounter with the Holy Spirit whereby it penetrates and infuses the soul with a fresh lease on a life greater than life. Of this experience, called "transforming union" in the LIVING FLAME OF LOVE, St. John of the Cross says: "The Holy Spirit celebrates joyous festivities in my soul." The Hesychites, the early Christian hermits who abandoned the philosophical squabbles of the Orthodox Church of the 4th century to follow the example of Jesus, in the solitude of the desert, bear witness to the experience of the incarnation of the spirit in the flesh which Gregory of Nicea called "Theosis."

The "otherness" of God in the aspect of transcendence wards off the danger besetting all mystics, of confusing their experience of their own act of existence, which MARTIN BUBER calls their prebiographical individuality, with the foundation of all existence. It is to guard against this dangerous aggrandisement of the ego that the Jews respect the vertiginous distance, the immensity of the interval, between man, shattered by the divine tremendum, and God in His absoluteness as the "One That Is". This is why the Jews have little room for incarnation or the testimony of an identity with any form whatsoever of God. The only bridge thrown over this abyss between the divine and the personal is the adage: "Man is made in the image of God". Thus, it is the mirroring of the divine visage which transfigures the faces of the Khasidim, causing them to tend more and more to resemble the perfect image, Adam Kadmon. And does not Metatron (the nearest to God's throne), the mysterious personage seated on the Mercaba, the Divine Chariot, in the vision of Ezekiel, correspond to a descent of God into His immanence? And did not Rabbi Ezra say: "God limited Himself in order to make creation possible."

We could place in a second category those mystical experiences which do not refer any more to incarnation or immanence. Here the contemplative adjusts his awareness to a feeling of being part of the total soul of the universe, *anima mundi*, the psycho-sphere, *purusha*. Theistically, this order of reality refers to an aspect of God known by the Hindus as *Atman*, which functions, in Sufi terminology, in the realm of *Lahut*. This awareness lifts one not only to a higher dimension of vision but indeed to a higher level of being, corresponding to a higher level of thinking, and as such, it is the moving power of religion. It involves areas of meditation other than those concerned with perception and imagination. The *samprajnata samadhi* of the Yoga Sutras of Patanjali is an experience of identification with the ground of one's soul, *atman tattva*, and it is only in the later Upanishads that *Atman* is anthropomorphized as "the Lord of all this", obviously beyond soulness. At any rate, the experience of soulness requires the annihilation of identification with the physical universe and, therefore, isolation. A Sufi, Junaid, said that the path to union passed through the station of isolation, *tajrid*, a return to the state in which one was in pre-eternity, according to the Quran, before one was involved in the process of becoming. This means, of course, a switchover from identification with the physical to awareness of being, qua soul, an integral part of soulness. Al-Hallaj stressed the utterly different nature of this level by qualifying it as uncreated. Therefore, the aspect of God related to this level is other than that of God as the Creator; one stands at this level in a different relationship to God than that of the creative aspect which implies "otherness". In fact, the relationship here is in the discovery of identity, and it was for asserting the identity between that which says "I" at the level of the soul and a reality, called *haqq* meaning Truth, that is considered to be God as it is uncreated (as opposed to *khalq*, that is, created) that al-Hallaj was suspended on the cross. Meister Eckhart had been equally arraigned before the Pope of Avignon for having asserted that the soul is *"increatus et increabile"*.

However, al-Hallaj was no monist and well aware that where love is the leaven of contemplation there is the "other", until the merging has been completed in utter oneness. For love, the essence of all attributes, according to al-Hallaj, to free itself from its pristine condition as a pure latency and become a reality, there must be the "face to face" encounter with an "other", an encounter between two wills, for love can only be a reality when it becomes objectified in a being. God the subject becomes the object out of sacrifice so that love may pass from the stage of latency to that of reality. When God transforms Himself in His descent from the Self to the ego, then the creature may rise towards Him; the ego discovers itself to be the Self. Therefore, the musings of the mystics are most often a dialogue between the ego and the Self: "How could I have ventured to address Thee if Thou

hadst not already whispered, "It is I", said al-Hallaj. The notion of the personal I undergoes transformation; it is first seen as the vehicle of the Supreme I, then completely vanquished: "O take away my 'it is I' from between You and me," cries al-Hallaj. In Islamic metaphysics the contemplative uses the word *hu* when addressing God in his impersonal and
transcendent aspect. Referring to God in his immanent, and therefore,
personal aspect, they use the word *ana* the eminently present person yet
more interior than oneself. The Quran says: "Closer than your jugular
vein..." These two facets of the same reality are linked in the famous
interjection of the Dervishes: *ana huwa!*

As soon as the notion of self undergoes a transformation whereby it
identifies itself with individual soulness, new dimensions of cognizance open
up: non-dualistic cognizance. This stage is depicted in the Hadith of the
Prophet: "He is the eyes through which I see, the ears through which I
hear..." The same state is described in the Brihad Arayaka Upanishad: "He
is the unseen seer, the unheard hearer..." The nondualistic form of cognizance can be outlined as follows: Where there is duality one sees another,
one hears another, one thinks of another; but where all has become one,
how can the one who sees see himself, by what knowledge can the knower
know himself?" This form of cognisance is often called intuition. In
perception there is a subject perceiving and an object perceived, but in intuition, the notion of the perceiver and that of the perceived are both
obliterated. And consciousness, when freed from the channels through
which it ordinarily functions, intuits a higher order of reality. When all
notion of an ego, or a self-functioning through an ego, has been obliterated,
all that remains is the Absolute, the "non-created, the non-become", as
Buddha calls it; the stage where there is a cessation of the created. This may
be experienced when one descends into the deep strata of the psyche
corresponding to transcendental levels beyond the threshold at which the
non-manifested passes into the realm of manifestation, into those far
reaches where the seeds of all beings are latent and from which they bloss-
om forth by dint of the eternal play of the forces of light in their process of
perpetual self-renewal.

It is through an expanded awareness of this sort that the personality of
man may knit into his being non-physical, one might say, sidereal components. Here, once more, the role of religion is evidenced as a catalyst in the
formative process of the personality. If as HAZRAT INAYAT KHAN has said:
"The fruit of life is our personality," and if, as TEILHARD DE CHARDIN
suggests: "The worth of human work is the establishment in each of us
of an absolutely original center in which the universe is reflected each time
in an inimitable way," then surely our purpose in life is to incorporate in
our being ever wider fields of reality. At the start our personality carries a
heritage from all levels of the universe, and as it unfolds it enriches itself
through communication with all orders of reality. It gathers impressions

from the angelic spheres and also impressions from the levels of the archetypes of pure beauty. A thought, ensouled by an emotion of glorification, can transfigure a face, and if it becomes permanent it may leave an indelible mark on the personality and even on the actual flesh. That the entire universe, including all the planes of existence and those of the non-manifested, should become ourselves is the great miracle of man; and it is only in striving to realize this that man can integrate himself in the total purpose for which he was created. Therefore, human problems can only make sense in the perspective of spiritual awareness.

The relevance of religion becomes yet more intensely evident when one realizes that the attitude of glorification forces consciousness to adjust itself to a finer setting: the focal point of consciousness at the deeper levels of the psyche takes precedence over the activity of consciousness at the periphery where the notion of individuality has its roots. It is only from this vantage point at the summit of our being that we are able to contemplate the great human issues in their totality and avoid losing ourselves in the particular. In this light then, meditation can be seen as the art that enables one to meet the challenging question: what is the purpose that one must achieve during this brief sojourn on the planet? If man fulfills his purpose in life by accomplishment, that is by applying his creativity in order to materialize his ideal of perfection, he limits himself to his true attainment, that is by the illumination of consciousness when it rises above the limitations of the vehicle in which it functions. If creativity is the way of materializing an ideal, then it is a form of glorification, for the features of all created beings are the works of art through which the angels express their glorification of God. Glorification is the fountainhead of all beauty. Our religious ceremonies are but the shadows of that great universal worship celebrated in the heavens by the legions of heavenly beings on all planes, and our prayers drill a channel across the mist separating our earth-bound plane from the celestial ones through which a communication may be established with the powers that be. Therefore, there are great rejoicings in the heavens today as leaders of the world religions meet in a spirit of communion.

There is a divine guidance piloting the forward march of human destinies and the sacred task of all those human beings to whom others look for guidance, whether they occupy official positions in religious institutions or not, is to stand on earth amidst all strife as the custodians and also the vassals of divine sovereignty, so as to ensure that the divine plan may be carried out. Maybe some of us are aware, at those rare moments when we feel most intensely the heartbeat of creation pulsing through ourselves, and indeed beyond ourselves, of the innate longing of all created forms for perfection, or rather, for the objectification as a living reality of the vision of perfection which our Maker has trusted us to materialize. By such awareness, we grasp a purposefulness and may watch this purpose fulfilling itself in all beings. It is in this purpose that lies the divine plan, but since creatures are endowed with that greatest of all divine gifts which is free will, the divine will remains an intention, *ma'ana* in Sufi terminology, until individual wills will the same in all freedom. This is why HAZRAT INAYAT KHAN completes the adage: "Let Thy will be done," by the words "Let Thy wish become my desire," Inasmuch as we desire and pursue the very same thing that is desired and intended above, we are called upon to serve in the hierarchy of the Spiritual Government of the World. This is the tradition of the kings, the magi, the dervish, the hierophant. It is the spirit of service which confers upon man his real nobility. HAZRAT INAYAT KHAN said: "The service of God demands that all should work for all," and "Each creature is placed in life in the position to which he belongs so that the divine plan may be carried out."

> Thy light is in all forms, Thy love in all being;
> In a loving mother, in a kind father, in an innocent child,
> In a helpful friend, in an inspiring teacher.
> Let us know Thee in all Thy holy names and forms:
> As Rama, as Krishna, as Shiva, as Buddha;
> Let us know Thee as Abraham, as Solomon, as Zarathustra,
> As Moses, as Jesus, as Mohammed,
> And in many other names and forms, known and unknown to the World.
> May the Message of God spread far and wide
> Illuminating and making the whole of humanity
> One single brotherhood in the Fatherhood of God.

Zoroastrianism Today

by

HOMI B. DHALLA, M. A.
Bombay

Today, the human race is passing through a new stage of its history. Profound and rapid changes are spreading by degrees around the whole world. Triggered by the creative intelligence of man, the changes recoil upon him, and upon his decisions and desires, both individual and collective. Hence we can speak of a social and cultural transformation, one which has repercussions on man's religious life as well. This transformation has brought serious difficulties in its wake, as happens in any crisis of growth. Thus while man has extended his power in every direction, he has not succeeded in subjecting it to his own welfare. Striving to penetrate further into the deeper recesses of his own mind, he frequently appears unsure of himself. Gradually he lays bare the laws of society, only to be paralyzed by uncertainty about the direction to give them.

Modern man, however, has little belief in the meaningfulness of the world and its interpenetration by transcendence. Minds are spiritually disinherited and without certainties. How can we account for the uncontrollable upsurges of psychic energy in the contemporary era, the seizures of whole peoples, the general destructiveness?

CARL JUNG detected in modern man a vast spiritual need which each individual's religion had the capacity to supply. Moreover, he held that the revealed scriptures would heal man's psychic illness and help him to overcome his distress.[1] TILLICH argued that religion supplies the feeling of purposefulness upon which man's courage and vitality, and hence his civilization, ultimately depend. Conversely, the loss of a religious center to life leads to acute anxiety, and hence to reduced courage and even to despair. The contemporary age is the age of anxiety par excellence. It suffers from what TILLICH calls "the anxiety of emptiness and meaninglessness". In consequence of the decay of religious belief in modern times, there is no answer to the meaning of existence, no meaning to participate

---

[1] C. JUNG, MODERN MAN IN SEARCH OF A SOUL. (1934), pp. 277–78.

in.[1] C. E. N. JOAD ascribed the troubles of modern civilization to what he called "the dropping of the object". By "the object" he meant absolutes, objective values (truth, beauty, goodness, God) which are located in an order of reality not subject to time and space. "The dropping of the object", therefore, means the denial of absolutes which now appear to be subjective only, the inventions of men rather than of the gods. When this occurs in history, as in the present age, the human ego swells up and proudly imagines that it creates everything, and that nothing is impossible to it. At the same time, however, it necessarily turns in on itself, and becomes morbidly subjective in its lack of objective standards, "creeds and codes", by which to be guided.[2]

In this present state of indecision, we need a direction, a hope and a philosophy to save us from sheer chaos. In the volume on the Universal Churches, ARNOLD TOYNBEE expressly rejects the theory formulated by GIBBON and Sir JAMES G. FRAZER, of the churches as "cancers" which eat away the tissues of civilization. On the contrary, "in seeking God", says TOYNBEE, "man is performing a social act", and indeed, without the fruits which religions supply, civilizations cannot long endure. Among these fruits are a belief in human fellowship, and hence power to overcome discord in human society; a solution to the problem of the meaning of history, and the means of exorcising the peril inherent in the worship of man-made "isms". He holds that it is religion that shapes civilization.

Religion, however, should be dynamic and penetrate all forms of human life besides influencing every type of human activity. In modern times, the central axis of religious concern has shifted from matters of ultimate salvation, and of heaven and hell, to questions pertaining to the meaning, necessity or usefulness of religion for this life.

An endeavour has been made in this paper to scrutinize the fundamental principles on which Zoroastrianism rests, and to determine whether a contemporary Zoroastrian is able to derive from his faith inspiration and inner strength to face the challenges of the modern world. Each of four principles will be discussed in its wider connotation. These principles appear in Yasna 12.9:

Fraspayokhedram: One should endeavour to promote unity amidst diversity, and be tolerant of the views of others. Significant differences crop up between races and various kinds of social orders; between wealthy nations and those which are less influential. What results is mutual distrust, enmity, conflict and hardships. Man is at once the cause and the victim.

God did not create man for life in isolation, but for the formation of social unity. For, in his innermost nature, man is a social being, and unless he relates himself to others, he can neither live nor develop his poten-

1 P. TILLICH, THE COURAGE TO BE. (1952).
2 C. JOAD, DECADENCE. (1947), pp. 108 ff.

tial. One of the salient features of the modern world is the growing interdependence of men, a development very largely promoted by modern
technical advances. Nevertheless, brotherly dialogue among men does not
reach its perfection on the level of technical progress, but on the deeper
level of interpersonal relationships. These demand a mutual respect for the
full spiritual dignity of the person.

Barriers do exist between individuals and nations but a sympathetic
understanding of other relations acts as a social cement.

This attitude of tolerance helps to promote unity among nations,[1] and
also stimulates inter-religious friendship. ALBERT SCHWEITZER holds the
view that Western and Indian philosophies should aim at the common
good of mankind, instead of each attempting to prove itself right in opposition to the other.[2]

Moreover, for the propagation of one's faith, the employment of force
can never be justified, as cruelty and oppression are the very negation of
spiritual wisdom and sublimity.

We are all searchers for the truth, and we ought not to be intolerant
and assert that ours is the only religion that possesses the truth. Each
individual has been endowed with a free will and has the right of making
his own choice, after hearing the truth.[3] An intolerant or false teacher
distorts God's message,[4] brings about misery,[5] and leads one astray.[6]

Tolerance towards others is imperative where a pluralistic society prevails, so that all mankind should live as one family.[7] Universality of thought
and catholicity of outlook is demonstrated in the *Fravartin Yasht* where the
fravashis of holy men of all nations, including Turan, known in history to
have been the enemy of Iran, are reverentially invoked.[8] Moreover, respect
is paid to all spiritual masters,[9] and the highest stage of existence to all holy
men of the past, present or future.[10]

Nidhasnaithishem: Non-violence or, positively put, love for all creation, is
fundamental to Zoroastrianism.

While religions have exalted non-violence as the supreme virtue, some
men have held the view that wars are means to good ends. MUSSOLINI
declared that violence is perfectly moral, and in fact even more moral than
compromise; moreover, war is as natural to man as motherhood is to wo-

1 *Yasht* 10.29.
2 G. SEAVER, ALBERT SCHWEITZER. (1947), p. 276.
3 *Yasna* 30.2.
4 *Ibid,* 32.9.
5 *Ibid.,* 31.18.
6 *Ibid.,* 45.1.
7 *Quran* 11.209.
8 *Yasht* 13.143.
9 *Havan Gah* 4.
10 *Visparat* 18.2.

man.[1] RUSKIN writes that war is the foundation of the faculties of man, and of his high virtues.[2] Sir ARTHUR KEITH in his Rectoral Address delivered to the students of Aberdeen University in 1931, said that nature by pruning her human orchard keeps it healthy, and it is war which is her pruning-hook. Men of all nations have praised war as the eliminator of weakness and the promoter of survival.

But there was one man who said that he who enjoyed marching in line and file to the strains of music, fell below his contempt; he had received his great brain by mistake – the spinal cord would have been amply sufficient.

That man was ALBERT EINSTEIN. He saw, not the chivalry and the pageantry of war, but its hideousness and rapacity.

Predatory passion has masqueraded as patriotism, and men have sung the glories of victory. The weak have always lived in fear of the strong and the innocent have been exterminated by insane cruelty. So it has been from the beginning of time; will it be so to the end of the world?

We are deeply concerned over the continuing nuclear arms race and the proliferation and testing of nuclear weapons. While extravagant sums are being spent on the production of weapons, an adequate remedy cannot be provided for the multiple miseries afflicting the modern world. The arms race is an utterly treacherous trap for humanity, and one which ensnares the poor to an intolerable degree. It is much to be feared that if this race persists, it will eventually produce all the lethal ruin it is now making ready.

The world is split into factions – political, social, economic, racial, ideological. Over them all lurks the menacing atom.

With all the powers we have developed, with all the resources at our command, we are unable to live in peace and safety. We have grown in knowledge, but not in wisdom and virtue.

Peace nurtures cultures and civilizations. It is an integral belief of Zoroastrians that if we are to save our civilization from destruction, we ought to esteem friendship,[3] root out discord from our homes,[4] and work for peace in our countries.[5] The social order ought to be founded on truth, built on justice and animated by love. We should love our fellow men,[6] and overcome hatred through the joy of inner life.[7] Evil can be conquered through love.[8] Our minds should not be tempted by violence.[9]

1 Quote in C. JOAD's DECADENCE. (1947), p. 82.
2 Quote in C. JOAD's DECADENCE. (1947), p. 98.
3 Yasht 6.5.
4 Yasna 60.5.
5 Yasht 16.19.
6 Yasna 34.15.
7 Ibid., 28.6.
8 Ibid., 49.1.
9 Ibid., 54.1.

If we are to save our children from future wars, we ought to assert our faith in basic human rights. Article 56 of the Charter of Human Rights of the United Nations lays down an obligation on the member states to co-operate with the Organization in promoting universal respect for human rights and freedoms and universal observance of them. A firm determination to respect other men and their dignity, as well as the studied practice of brotherhood, are absolutely necessary for the establishment of peace. We should yearn for universal brotherhood [1] – a universal brotherhood under which a wrong to the humblest is an affront to all – so that there may be good will among men [2] and tribulations may vanish evermore.[3]

Love in Zoroastrianism also embraces the animal kingdom. Man should afford animals protection from oppression.[4] In later Zoroastrian theology, *Bhaman* is the special guardian angel of animals, and the second day of every month in our calendar is named *Bhaman* and is consecrated to him.

In our age when there is the painful danger of our being driven towards the abyss of non-existence due to a nuclear holocaust, may this short prayer which offers us hope be the guiding principle of our destinies (Yasna 60.5):

> May understanding overcome misunderstanding,
> Peace triumph over discord,
> Generosity overcome avarice,
> Reverence triumph over contempt,
> Truth over falsehood.

Khaetwadatham: This may be explained as self-sacrifice of service of mankind; it is losing our petty selves by serving God.

The disturbances which so frequently occur in the social order result in part from the natural tensions of economic, political and social forms. But at a deeper level, they flow from man's pride and selfishness, which contaminate even the social sphere.

Freedom acquires new strength, by contrast, when a man consents to the unavoidable requirements of social life, takes on the manifold demands of human partnership, and commits himself to the service of the world community.

In every religion certain verses are regarded as specially sacred. The most sacred verse in Zoroastrianism is said to be the Ahuna Vairya. The third concept in this prayer lays emphasis on the importance of service. After gaining knowledge and having filled the heart with love, the fulfilment and the crown of human life should take the form of service of mankind. It is this spirit of service,[5] which crowns human life with perfection.

1 *Yasna* 54.1.
2 *Ibid.*, 46.14.
3 *Ibid.*, 53.8.
4 *Shayast ne shayast*, 15.9.
5 *Yasna* 62.10.

Zoroastrianism enjoins active service, and not contemplation away from the world, as the duty of man.[1] In this world of joy and sorrow, happiness and misery, life would be intolerable if it were not for the sympathy, kindness and love of fellow-men.[2] Unbearable is the burden of life when one is unaided. One cannot yearn for anything more ardently than to serve man with generosity and effectiveness. Life is incomplete when man lives for his own self, oblivious of the needs of others. The person who brings light into the lives of others himself receives light.[3]

To a Zoroastrian it is this principle of selflessness which forms the basis of a wedded life. Wedlock is a sacred union of two persons, where sympathetic understanding and absolute self-sacrifice ought to reign.

At another level it is this principle of *khaetwadatham*, which leads to communion with Absolute Reality. Zarathushtra himself offered his very life and being as a sacrifice to God.[4] It is when one is imbued with the determination to serve,[5] that the soul is transported into the realms of light.[6] The divine enraptures us, as we all have the spark of divinity within us. The deep urge of the inner self to relieve the distressed [7] leads to a merger with God.[8] BERGSON states that when this union takes place there is boundless joy, an all absorbing ecstasy. God is there and the soul is in God.[9] This spiritual experience is creative, as it brings about a change of consciousness.

Ashaonim: Zoroastrianism is suffused with the concept of *asha*. *Asha* is the divine plan. It is the immutable eternal law of God, according to which the universe has come into being. The cosmic process is not unintelligible chaos, but a pattern, an order which directs evolution. This cosmic process progresses towards its fulfilment by following the law of *asha*. *Asha* is the very foundation of Zoroastrianism. And yet, so lofty is it in depth, that it is difficult to define. Only sublime inspiration could have drawn from Tennyson a comprehension of its essence:

> That God who ever lives and loves,
> One God, one law, one element,
> And one far-off divine event
> To which the whole creation moves.

Such is God's creation. The infinite plan encompasses the totality of God's creatures, from the highest to the lowest. God intended creation to be the

1 *Yasna* 51.9.
2 *Ibid.*, 34.15.
3 *Ibid.*, 43.1.
4 *Ibid.*, 33.14.
5 *Ibid.*, 34.15.
6 *Ibid.*, 33.10.
7 *Ibid.*, 51.1.
8 *Ibid.*, 31.16.
9 H. BERGSON, THE TWO SOURCES OF MORALITY AND RELIGION, Eng. translation. (1938) pp. 196–197.

organ of His expression. He has not changed His plan from time to time, discarding one idea after another, until He devised the form of man. Evolution served to bring creation to its peak – Man. He is the ideal channel through which God speaks. Intelligence and God-consciousness are the attributes which make man cooperate with Him. Partaking of the divine nature, man knows of the inner life – and of the promised bliss if he follows the path of *asha*.[1] Man hungers for spiritual reunion, and holds God in his mind's eye as the true parent of the eternal law.[2] The summum bonum will be attained when all men act in full accord with the law, the law that forms the basis of all life.[3] The pathway already lies within him; the power to walk that path lies there also. Man has the right to be free from any limiting experience.

There is something sublime in PLATO's description of God – "That truth is his body, and light his shadow". In Zoroastrianism, the law of *asha* exalts truth, and equates truth with God. Truth or righteousness is the secondary connotation of *asha*. Hence the prayer:

O Mazda, grant that I perform all actions in harmony with righteousness and acquire the wisdom of the living mind, so that I may bring happiness to the soul of the universe.[4]

The righteous attain the highest gifts – truth, wisdom, perfection, immortality. But if we take to righteousness only in the expectation of a future reward, such an action becomes denuded of righteousness. He who passes the fiery test of truth,[5] chooses to follow God's path [6] and so belongs to Him. He furnishes himself, while there is time, with a store of righteousness, for the great journey his soul will have to undertake one day.

Those who overcome evil in their own persons and around them in the world prepare the way for the coming of the Kingdom of Righteousness, Zarathushtra has laid the foundation of the Kingdom of Righteousness, and has assigned man the stupendous task of building and establishing and completing it. It is left to man to bring that day near or keep it at a distance.

CONCLUSION

The essence of Zoroastrianism has an elevating impact on the dignity of the person, by the way in which it strengthens the seams of human society and imbues the everyday activity of man with a deeper meaning of life. It offers man the light and the strength to measure up to his supreme destiny. But this has to be attained through one's own efforts.

1 *Yasna* 31.3.
2 *Ibid.*, 31.8.
3 *Ibid.*, 33.1.
4 *Ibid.*, 28.1.
5 *Ibid.*, 30.7.
6 *Ibid.*, 30.5.

Zoroastrianism is a religion of action, and the Prophet's message emphasizes the importance of right action for furthering the divine plan.[1] Everything in a Zoroastrian cries out for action. Thought is noble, but action is
nobler. To live is to act and work.

The law of *asha* implies a regular and ordered progress in all manifestations. The divine seed is in us, but it must be nurtured and permitted to
mature. Nothing under heaven is complete and perfect, but we ought to
strive for perfection. Progress is the Zoroastrian watchword and the most
salient trait of the Zoroastrian character. It is the prerogative of every man,
and he ought to realize that he has the capacity to raise himself above his
animality and attain his full spiritual stature.

The aim of Zoroastrianism is to lift mankind to a new level; the world is
the scene of his spiritual evolution. The purpose of life is that man shall
know himself, his divine origin, his almost incredible potentialities as a
child of God and a co-worker with Him. The outward thrust of the Eternal
is nudging man on to his manifest destiny.

But doubting man pauses, ponders, hesitates,...and is lost. Only when
he lets the divine flame within him spark upwards will all doubt be inciner-
ated. And how can this be? Only through action. The springs of life are all
within. This is the secret of life. An integral part of this is the power of
choice. Man alone can choose, make decisions. This is echoed in the teachings of the Prophet. Man has been endowed with intelligence which enables
him to attain the state of interaction between the human and the divine.
But first, he has to know who he is and what he is. He is on a voyage of
self-discovery. His progress in the world will depend on the wisdom of his
deliberate choices.

Gautama Siddartha awakened to this truth and resolved to become the
Light-Bearer. The realization of *Nirvana* came to him, and, he preached that
it could come to any man who desired it.

As the eternal message of the Buddha lives, so does Zarathushtra's voice.
TAGORE says, "He was the watcher in the night, who stood on the lonely
peak facing the East and broke out singing the paeans of light to the sleeping world when the sun came out on the brim of the horizon".[2]

Zarathushtra's religion is not alone a matter of academic interest, nor
merely the guide of a community of a hundred thousand. It is addressed to
all humanity, without limitations of space or time. But today it is in Zoroastrian hearts that its conflagration blazes as the symbol of it ever burns in
their temples.

NEHRU has said, "It is remarkable how the Parsis, as they have been called,
have quietly and unostentatiously fitted into India, make it their home,
and yet kept quite apart as a small community, tenaciously holding on to
their old customs... They have prospered in business and many of them

1 *Visparat* 15.1.
2 R. TAGORE, THE RELIGION OF MAN, (1961), p. 51.

are the leaders of industry in India. They have had practically no contact with Iran and are completely Indian, and yet they hold on to their old traditions and the memories of their ancient homeland." [1] It is to their adopted homeland, India, that they hold allegiance. The spirit of service and the love for freedom deeply embedded in the Zoroastrian character urged them to throw off the fetters of foreign rule in India. Imprisonment, confiscation of property, humiliation...all was willingly accepted.

These are the Zoroastrians who have cast themselves headlong onto the path of *asha* – the Ocean of Righteousness...When a disciple asked the Sufi mystic Janayad of Bagdad: "I am told that you possess the pearl of divine knowledge, either give it to me or sell it to me". Janayad answered: "I cannot sell it for you have not the price thereof, and if I give it to you, you will have gained it too cheaply, you do not know its value. Cast yourself headlong, like me, into this ocean (of God) in order that you yourself may find the pearl." [2]

1 N. Sen, Wit and Wisdom of Nehru. (1960), pp. 441–42.
2 R. Nicholson, Mystics of Islam. (1914), p. 34.

Jesus as a Message for our Day

by

The Rev. Bishop A. J. SHAW
Methodist Bishop of Southern Asia, Bombay[1]

My topic is the relevance of Jesus as a message for our day. In our world today a kind of civilization is emerging which in many ways is different from the civilizations of previous generations.[1] Science, technology, ideas, varied loyalties, and visions have their own strong influence in transforming our present day life. A stormy situation, either in the form of war, or as racial, social, or economic upheavals, casts shadows of gloom and despair. The world seems to be experiencing pain, which may either be death pangs or birth pangs. The bewildering and disturbing changes that are rapidly taking place in our times confound people who do not know how to respond to them. Among these changes are states of political uncertainty, economic instability, and social unrest. Never was man so well-informed and so terribly confused. He is rich in knowledge but poor in wisdom. In the midst of scientific inventions and technological developments modern society is increasingly becoming depersonalized. Man's sense of loss and the cheapness of his life in a technological age call for a reaffirmation of individual worth, not alone but in community. The individual man spends his time in factories, schools, offices, theatres, business places, local, national, and international organizations and conferences, where he has to make innumerable, multifarious and quick decisions.

For all this a new man, a man loved and guided by a superhuman power every moment of his life is the need of the hour. It is this kind of man alone that will untangle the tangled world of our day. But how can such a man be produced? He needs spiritual renewal, a constant reintegration not only of his body and mind but also a spiritual tool for his poor soul. This is why Jesus emphasized that a man should be born over again. The word of Jesus Christ, his Gospel, as it is found in the New Testament, has relevance to our day, especially its ends of renewing man, broadening his outlook on life in all its aspects, and a developing beautiful attitude in him. The beauti-

---

1 Delivered extemporaneously at the Birla Academy, October 24, 1968.

ful Beatitudes of Jesus, given in the 5th chapter of the Book of Matthew, aim at building up spiritual maturity in all those who understand them, and who follow those wonderful teachings in their day-to-day lives. Here are given the eight steps which are essential in helping anybody become a new man: humility, mourning for lost ones, spiritual meekness, spiritual appetite, mercifulness, purity of heart (that is, freedom from selfishness, jealousy, hatred, enmity, fault-finding, etc.), peace-making, and finally readiness to suffer for all just and righteous causes.

The Christian must believe that Jesus not only taught these beautiful attitudes but lived them himself, and so in order to develop these qualities of life one has to keep before oneself Jesus as the ideal and perfect example to be emulated.

There are a few aspects of the message of Jesus, the New Testament, which have relevance to the world today, a scientific and technological age desperately needing new men and women. These aspects are, firstly, acknowledging the sovereignty of God, with just earnestness. God is the basis of all ethical principles. If God is not just to man in his day-to-day life then all hope is lost. Jesus envisages the coming into being of the Kingdom of God, the establishment of God's reign. He asks man to pray for this kingdom, and work for it and conform his will to God's will. The prayer which he taught his disciples says, "Thy kingdom come, Thy will be done on earth." We need to know his will and do his will in every sphere of our life and in all our relationships.

The significant thing is that Jesus emphasized exclusively moral considerations. He asked men to repent and submit themselves to the moral discipline which would prepare them for final judgment of a strictly ethical nature. He was so emphatic about ethical matters that he did not really give much importance to ritualistic and ceremonial religion. He was not sparing in his words of condemnation of the orthodox religionists who, he said, did all their works to be seen of men. He advised his disciples to pay attention to their words but not to follow their practice, for he said they say one thing and do another. Jesus believed that man could not be good and could do nothing unless he was in constant fellowship with God.

Communion with God, he maintained, would consequently bring man close to his brother man, in his love and concern for him. Jesus himself served the needy, the downtrodden and the rejected people. He had love and compassion for them, he took a towel and basin and washed the feet of his disciples. He taught that those who serve others were the greatest of all in the Kingdom of Heaven. His disciples then and all through the ages have followed his example and served humanity just for the love of their Lord and Master.

Although the teachings of Jesus have political and economic implications they were centered on the question of right and wrong in an absolute sense. In the Sermon on the Mount he said what I tell you is that anyone who nurses anger against his brother must be brought to judgment. If, when you are bringing your gift to the altar, you suddenly remember that your brother has a grievance against you, leave your gift where it is before the altar. Go immediately to make your peace with your brother and then come back and offer your gift. Love your enemies and pray for your persecutors. You must therefore be all goodness just as your heavenly Father is all good. Where else should such teachings do the most good except in our human relations, in our economic and political dealings, in the world in which we rub shoulders with one another, confronting all sorts of problems as issues of life. True worship of God should result in loving others as we love ourselves.

This leads us to the second feature of the ideal of Jesus as conforming to the will of God; the love that God has for man, whom He created in His own image and made the master of all his creation. By the power of this great divine affection man was inspired to reproduce God's great love for man. The distinguishing quality of this love lies in its inadequate distribution. Such a love determines our attitudes and is the sole test of right action and regulates all our human relationships. St. Paul, the greatest missionary of Christ, defines this love as follows. "Love is patient, love is kind, and envies no one. Love is never boastful, nor conceited, nor rude, never selfish, not quick to give offense. Love is not resentful, does not gloat over falsehood but delights in truth. There is nothing love cannot be. There is no limit to its qualities, its hope, and its endurance." Such a love never comes to an end. It is concerned with the best interest of a neighbor. Until men and nations love their neighbors as they love themselves there can be no peace in the world. To Jesus, the neighbor was anybody who needed help. This inclusive quality of love is not limited to those who love us but is also intended for those who hate us and persecute us. This love Jesus manifested in its highest and noblest form when on the cross he prayed for his enemies and persecutors saying, "Father, forgive them for they know not what they do."

In the modern world men have grown much closer now than they ever were before. Nations are actually very close neighbors of one another. For peaceful relations among them there has to be understanding based on the type of love we are talking about. The opposite of love is enmity; hatred; personal, national, and international jealousies, which, especially in this age of nuclear energy would lead the world to self-destruction. Christ, therefore, in the present new world, in our age of technological development, confronts the people with the challenge to undertake a creative venture in human relations so that the ethical love of God can be expressed in the current circumstances.

The Essential Brotherhood of Mankind: A Hindu View

by

His Divine Grace M A D H A V G O S W A M I M A H A R E J
President, Gauriya Math, Calcutta

I heartily welcome the organizers of this symposium in their attempt to explore an impartial and liberal approach to different views of religious faiths in this world, and to find out how world fellowship of the different religions or a unity of hearts amongst human beings can be promoted.

There are two ways of approach – (1) The sincere, real and practical approach having relation to the actual condition and nature of human beings and (2) an idealistic approach having little or no practical value and merely indulging in the luxury of high-sounding words. If we sincerely want to obtain a real and abiding effect, we should face facts boldly. The fact is that there exists no 100 percent identity amongst individuals. Each is a conscious unit having independence of thinking, feeling and willing. Individuals, as a result of their different actions, achieve separate environments and paraphernalia. Every individual has his peculiar nature, distinct from any other. So, obviously individuals will vary in their opinions and tastes. This is quite natural, and it is an unnatural thing to attempt forcibly to encage individuals in one fold, faith or particular ideology. Accordingly, cultivation of tolerance of others' views is essential for world peace and unity. Indian sponsors of religion appeared to have that insight and tolerance, for very many independent views have cropped up in India and have flourished simultaneously. Want of tolerance makes us sectarian, and that spirit motivates the forcible conversion of others, which brings turmoil and unrest in the world.

Religion should give equal scope to all individuals for their respective spiritual development according to their attributes. Indian saints have classified the nature of human beings in three broad groups – *sattvika*, *rajasika* and *tamasika*. *Sattvika* people are wise, sincere, generous and non-violent. As such they have an altruistic mentality and render disinterested service. *Rajasika* people are egoists. However, they are active and do good to others with the motive of getting a return for their actions or of self-aggrandisement. They won't tolerate harm to themselves, they have the spirit of taking revenge. *Tamasika* people are indolent, out-and-out egoists and of violent temperament. They are indiscriminate in their pursuit of enjoyment, they completely disregard the interests of others and will do anything to fulfill their selfish desires. So *sattvika*, *rajasika* and *tamasika* people vary in their tastes, habits and nature.

For this reason, three forms of teaching religion have been prescribed for the three groups, according to their eligibility, and seeking to give them scope for gradual elevation. These three modes of teaching are related to the apparent self, and as such they are changeable.

There are still higher and higher thoughts of religious existence which transcend those three qualities and relate to the eternal function of the real self. If we want quantity we must sacrifice quality and if we want quality, evidently we shall have to sacrifice quantity. Both cannot be achieved at one time. However, the primary point to be noted here is that there should be tolerance amongst sponsors of different religious views, and respect for others' views, as well as equal scope, for their spiritual upliftment. Another point to be noted here is that we should have the patience to understand the underlying spirit of different religious faiths and not merely indulge in disputes regarding the ritualistic aspects of religions which will certainly vary in different parts of the world.

Nowadays we find lack of discipline rampant in every sphere of human life – political, social, economical and even educational. Student unrest is one of the most serious problems of the day. It is extremely difficult to proceed with constructive work when people are prone to indiscipline. To fight against disruptive tendencies and indiscipline, a radical treatment of the minds of the people is required. Here we feel the necessity of moral and spiritual values in human life. There are two ways of treating diseases – pathological and symptomatic. In pathological treatment the root cause of the disease is ascertained first, and then the remedy is prescribed. The process of symptomatic treatment may be easier but it does not have a lasting effect; it may give temporary relief, while treatment through the pathological process brings about permanent relief.

To determine the root of unrest we ought first to determine the meaning of the self. I strongly believe that ignorance of our real self is the cause of unrest, discord and anxiety. The real self is not the physical tabernacle. It is something other than the gross and subtle body. We consider the body to be the person, as long as we observe consciousness in it. The moment the body is bereft of consciousness, it loses its personality. "I" am "I" when the conscious entity, i.e. the entity that thinks, feels and wills is present in me, and "I" am "not-I" when it is absent in me. Hence, the entity whose presence and absence makes me, "me" and "not-me", respectively, must be the person.

This conscious entity (soul) is designated as *atman* in Indian scriptures. *Atman* is indestructible, it has no origin and no end. If we plunge deep into the matter, we can trace our existence with the Absolute Conscious principle whom we call Godhead, the Fountain Source of innumerable conscious units. The Godhead is termed *Sat-Chit-Ananda*, i.e. He is All-Existence, All-Knowledge and All-Bliss. Individuals are points of rays emanating from Him and as such one of His eternal coexisting potencies. Individuals cannot live independently. They are all interconnected and coexisting, though retaining their own individual characteristics.

It has already been stated that differences in individuals are unavoidable, as they are conscious units. Now the problem is to find a common ground and interest for the solution of these differences. A sense of common interest can be fostered among individuals, if they know that they are interconnected, are parts of one organic system and are the sons and daughters of one Father. Here is the task of all religions, to teach people that all beings of the world are closely interrelated. Although steadfastness or firm belief in God (*Nistha*) according to some particular faith, and eligibility of the individual, religious bigotry which begets enmity is condemnable, as it is against the real interest of the individual, and society. Real religion teaches love for one another.

Lord Krishna Chaitanya Mahaprabhu propagated the cult of all-embracing Divine Love which brings universal brotherhood on a transcendental plane. According to him forgetfulness of our eternal relation with the Supreme Godhead, Srikrishna, is the root cause of all afflictions. Srikrishna is God of all gods, Supreme Person having All-Existence, All-Knowledge and All-Bliss, Beginningless yet the Beginning of all and Prime Cause of all causes. The word "*Krishna*" means one who attracts all and pleases all by His Wonderful Enchanting Beauty, Majesty, Munificence and Supremacy, and this denotes the highest conception of Godhead with all perfection. He is the object of All-Love. So, remembrance of Srikrishna or God is the divine panacea of all evils. The easiest and most effective way of remembering God is chanting of the Holy Name which can be practised by all, irrespective of caste, creed, religion, age, health, economic, social and educational status, at any place or time.

In the Vedic cult we find the theory of the cycle of time within the period of infinite time, which has four stages in accordance with the predominance of religiousness and irreligiousness. The four ages are designated as *satya, treta, dwapara* and *kali*. In *satya yuga* (the first age of the cycle of time) wisdom predominated in men, and as such they were unaware of the transitory nature of the world, and thereby were not fascinated by it; concentration without interruption was possible and meditation (*dhyanam*) was prescribed as the common religion suitable for all. In *treta yuga* (next age in the cycle of time) when the spirit of activity predominated and people were attached to wordly objects, *yajna* (sacrifice) i.e., offering of the things of attachment to the Lord, was prescribed as the common religion to divert the attention of the people from material objects of attachment and turn their minds towards Him. In *dwapara yuga* (next and more degraded age) when people were addicted to worldly objects, *afchana* (worship of deities) was prescribed as the common religion for gradual attainment of concentration of the mind, by directing all the senses and objects of attachment to His Service. In the present age, *kali yuga* (the last and spiritually most degraded age of the cycle of time), when people are firmly attached to wordly objects, they are incapable of performing meditation, *yajna* (sacrifice) and *archana* (worship of Deities) rightly and as such chanting of the Holy Name of God is prescribed for them.

Today the world is taking tremendous scientific strides. Modern scientists are performing wonders. But in spite of their marvellous accomplishments and despite their pride in Twentieth Century civilization, it is puzzling to see that science is so much engaged in inventing destructive weapons and thereby imperiling the whole human race. Any moment there may be a conflagration and the whole world may perish. Saints[1] are deeply concerned as to how to avert such a calamity. Mere material scientific accomplishments are unable to save the world from such a danger. Of course, scientific inventions or achievements as such are not condemnable. Everything depends on the proper use of things. Science may be used for the good of humanity and also may be misused for the destruction of human civilization. It is imperative to consider the problem and diagnose the disease of conflicts and mutual distrust amongst nations and individuals. So long as nations and individuals have separate centers of interest, tension is inevitable. Nobody can avoid it.

This world is limited. When there are many claimants for one limited object, disputes amongst claimants are unavoidable. It is because of this that Indian saints differ from the leaders of the West or from the westernized leaders of our country, in their manner of tackling the problem of peace. In fact, genuine saints of the world are wise enough to see the fundamental defect in the attempt of the so-called best brains to achieve world peace. They assert with great emphasis that a practical solution of the problems is not possible so long as people do not change their present craving for sensuous enjoyment and greediness for mundane wealth, and direct their attention towards the Unlimited, the Infinite, the Absolute. The heads of different religious groups should clearly and emphatically point out and teach their followers the painful and perishable character of worldly objects and the futility of sensuous enjoyment. They should create interest in man for the worship of God which brings about real happiness.

Unless and until the eternal relationship of the people is known to them, and they realize that they cannot exist and be happy without the Godhead who is All-Bliss, the natural inclination of the people towards the Godhead and diversion of their attention from the material aspects of life cannot be

---

1 In Hindu terminology, a saint is a wholly dedicated living holy man.

effected. As long as people have the conviction that their only interest lies in material prosperity and sensuous enjoyment, discord cannot be avoided. More belief in the existence of God will be of great benefit to humanity, by restraining people from committing sins, and leading them to do good to others; they will have fear of punishment for bad deeds, and encouragement to seek reward for good deeds. Want of patience and tolerance originates from lust. Any activity which leads to the satisfaction of one's own gross and subtle senses is termed lust. Hindrance to the fulfilment of lust breeds anger and that brings conflict and malice amongst individuals and nations.

So long as people do not understand that they are inseparably connected, and until the activities of the people are God-centered, mere sentimentalism or fictitious ideas will not be able to foster real love amongst individuals.

If we know that the infliction of harm to other animate beings is detrimental to our own interest and will bring harm in return, we will not be encouraged to harm any individual, nay even any sentient being of the world.

If we can love the Absolute Whole, I mean the Godhead, we cannot have the impetus to injure any of His parts. So, according to me or the teachings of Lord Gaurange, Divine Love is the best solution of all the problems of the world.

Religion and World Problems

by

Dr. Harold F. Snyder
International Affairs Representative for South Asia,
The American Friends Service Committee, New Delhi[1]

When I arrived I picked up one of the many fascinating pamphlets which have been available to us and read for the first time a story from the life of Woodrow Wilson. He, one day, was told that his glasses were slipping down toward his mouth and he said, "Oh fine, then I can see what I have to say." I knew only a few moments ago that I was to say anything this morning so I am somewhat in the position of Woodrow Wilson. But I am delighted at this opportunity to say a very few words. I am not going to tell very much about Quakerism because after all we are one of the very smallest of the many sects and religions represented here and that would entitle us to just a very few seconds as compared to the size of other groups that have spoken. I would like, however, to take advantage of this opportunity to underline a few of the things already said, the many very wise and inspiring things which have been said and which seem to me to point toward the main purpose of this discussion on the relevance of religion to the world today. I remind you that the relevance of religion to the world today is spelled out in the problems listed for discussion yesterday afternoon but which have been held over for further discussion this morning. They are: poverty in the midst of plenty, racial and religious prejudice and discrimination, the disaffection of youth, the cult of violence, and the causes of war.

The little sect or denomination to which I belong, Quakerism, is rooted in the idea that there is "that of God in every man." This was the phrase used by George Fox. It was taken from the older religions. Many of you, in speaking of the beliefs of your religions have brought out the same point. To Quakers this means that the ultimate blasphemy is war, because in destroying man, man is destroying God. And therefore Quakers are traditionally pacifists. But that pacifism is not just a negative manifestation. It is against an evil, war, but we do believe also that this requires of each of us that we not only abstain from war and from killing but that we enter into

[1] Delivered extemporaneously at the Birla Academy, October 24, 1968.

the service of man. Since so many of you have said exactly the same thing, from the point of view of your denominations I think that we can take heart that it will be possible for us to find common cause and to move towards a discussion of the relevance of religion for the world today.

I think we are all grateful, however, for the emphasis that several of you have placed upon the negative aspects of this question, beginning, I think, with Dr. DITZEN, who spoke about the irrelevancy of some religions to the world today, the irrelevancy of much in Christianity to the world today. The fact is that so many of our churches and religions, although I suppose, we can speak only for Christianity, have left the big questions of war and peace, poverty and youth, and injustice aside. In each great war the sanction of the major religious organizations has been found for that war and perhaps there is a little beginning of a movement in the other direction in the fact that so many American religious leaders now find it impossible to support the war in Viet-Nam, now find it necessary and consistent with their religious beliefs to support the groups which are working for racial equality and justice in the United States. Therefore, we do have a beginning, perhaps, here in our own Christian group, of a recognition that these problems of the world cannot wait, that we cannot live our good Christian lives without facing them.

When we come to the question of violence, as has been said so many times so beautifully here: there, too, how can we possibly deny that religion has been irrelevant to a problem with which the very fundamentals of religion are concerned? When you look at the life of Gandhi and Buddha how can one justify the use of war and violence? And yet, by and large, as I've lived here in Asia for two years, I find comparatively few of the religious leaders in Asia giving frontal attention to this problem, although more and more are doing so, and more and more are seeing the relevance between what is happening in terms of communal conflict in India, for example Hindu-Muslim conflict, and their religious beliefs. They see them as a denial of their religious beliefs. And yet communal conflict is growing. A Muslim scholar reported at a meeting I attended the other day that in the year 1967 there were more deaths in India from communal conflict, from Hindu-Muslim conflict, than in the combined nine years preceding that time.

So, while we can speak only of the irrelevance of Christianity, I think we might at the same time suggest that all of us from the point of view of our religions take a look at the irrelevances as well as the relevances of religion for the problems of the world today.

I will close by citing one statement by a Quaker leader, with which a number of you, I gather from the many fine things that have been said, would agree from the point of your own religions. WILLIAM PENN, the founder of Pennsylvania, and one of the early Quakers, said, "True Godliness does not turn men out of this world. It helps them to live better in it. It excites their endeavor to mend it."

Religion in an Age of Scientific Achievement

by

Venerable MAHASTHAVIRA N. JINARATANA
Mahabodhi Society of India, Calcutta

There are at present a number of higher religions, which may broadly be classified thus:

A. Buddhist: (i) *Theravada* in Ceylon, Burma, Thailand, Laos and Cambodia with some adherents in Assam, Tipperah, West Bengal and other places in India, in Chittagong, Comilla, Noakhali etc. in Pakistan (ii) *Mahayana* in Japan, Korea, China (now officially extinct in mainland China), Nepal and Viet-Nam. (iii) *Tantric* or *Vajrayana* in Tibet (Including refugees in India, Sikkim, Bhutan and Mongolia.

B. Jainism in India

C. Sikhism in India

D. Judaism, Christianity, Islam and Zoroastrianism.

E. Hinduism with many sub-sects.

A man's religion is determined rather accidentally, by his birth in a particular family, following particular beliefs, customs, ceremonies and forms of worship. The practical test of a religion is in its success or failure in helping human beings overcome sin and suffering in the phenomenal universe. A human being cannot realize the reality unless and until he frees himself completely from his innate selfcentredness (i.e. desires (*tanha*) along with I-ness). The Upanishads teach "*Tat tvam asi; so'ham*" – "thou art that"; that (*Brahman*, the Reality) is yourself; I am that (*Brahman*). The Reality in Buddhism is termed *Nibbana* in Hinayana and *Bodhi* (full enlightenment) in Mahayana.

As stated above, the primary object of a religion is to guide human beings to overcome sin and suffering. The very first discourse of Lord Buddha was to lead human beings out of the sufferings, concomitant to existence in this mortal world. He enunciated the four truths (*ariyasaccas*) thus: *dukkha* (suffering), *dukkhasamudaya* (origin of sufferings), *dukkha-nirodha* (cessation of suffering) and *dukkha-nirodha-gamini-pratipad* (the way of ending the suffering). The way is then explained thus:

1. *sila:* Right Speech; abstention from false-speaking, malicious talk, rough talk, frivolous talk; right action; abstention from killing, stealing, transgressing through lust or adultery; right means of livelihood; right exertion; avoiding unoriginated evils, removing originated evils, developing unoriginated good, increasing unoriginated good.

2. *citta:* Self-awareness of the physical body, feelings, mental states, and teachings; right meditation; right resolution.

3. *panna:* Right view, i.e., accepting the doctrine of Buddha.

CONSTITUENTS OF A LIVING BEING ANALYSED

A living being is composed of matter (*rupa*) and mind (*nama* or *citta*). By *rupa* is meant the physical body made of five elements, viz. earth, water, fire, air and space. The first four are inseparable, i.e. earth cannot be conceived without water, heat and air, likewise the other three elements. In other words, everything in this world is a composite (*samkhara, samkhata*).

It is worth while to say a few words about the Buddhist philosophical outlook. It should be dealt with, according to the Buddhist system, under three heads. These are *dukkha*, which has been outlined above; *anatta* and *anicca*.

Anatta means unreality, and it has a very specific significance.

Before the Buddhist conception of soul or self is discussed it is necessary to state the view of the early Upanishads and Vedantic school of thought. According to them, every living being has an individual soul (*jivatman*), which is pure and remains untarnished by his deeds, good or bad. It serves, however, the purpose of carrying the *karmic* effects of the present life to its future existence. This *jivatman* is identical with the Great Soul (*Brahman*), the Absolute Reality. It is something like air put in a colored bottle. The air merges in the other air when the bottle is broken. In Buddhist philosophy this Vedantic conception is criticized as illogical, because two elements of a contrary nature such as air and glass can never remain together. Likewise, a pure soul cannot remain in an impure body. Hence, it is not possible that a pure soul can exist in an impure body. In Buddhist philosophy it is explained thus – every being is composed of five constituents (*khandhas*), one of which is *samkhara* (impressions). It is this *samkhara* which passes at the time of death to a new being appropriate to the *karmaic* effects. For attaining the summum bonum the new being, if a human being, must depend on his own exertions to attain emancipation (*mukti*). No guru or spiritual preceptor can help his disciple to gain it. All that he can do is to guide him in the right path. This idea is expressed in the Dhammapada (stanza 160) in these words: "The Self is the lord of self, for, who else could be the lord? By a fully controlled self, one obtains the lordship, which is difficult to obtain."

In his last discourse, the Mahaparinibbanu-sutta (II. p. 100) given just before his departure from this mortal world, Buddha said to his disciples,

"Be a shelter to yourself, a refuge, none else can be the refuge." This was followed by his laying emphasis on the practice of *sattipatthana* (self-awareness).

From all that has been said above, it is evident that a Buddhist has to depend on his own exertions to realize the Absolute Reality.

The third of the three headings basic to Buddhism is *anicca* (impermanence) By *anicca* is meant that all worldly existences, whether of living beings or objects, are temporary and disappear after a certain period of time. In Buddhist philosophy this period of time has been explained elaborately. A bare idea of it is being attempted here. The time factor has been conceived as an infinitesimal point of time (*khapika*). The human body and mind undergo change every moment. The change is not ordinarily perceptible unless a week or a month passes. The finger-nails are growing every moment but they become apparent only after some time. Take, for instance, a seed. It does not sprout on a stone. It has to be placed in suitable soil where the conditions are made appropriate by fertilizing the soil. The seed is called in Pali *hetu* (cause) and the prepared soil *paccaya pratyaya* (conditions). The seed disintegrates within the soil, changes every moment, becomes a protoplasm and then sprouts. By further nourishment it becomes a tree and ultimately produces fruit. This fruit again gives rise to another tree. It is on this analogy that Buddhist philosophy explains the rebirth of the being. As a matter of fact, there is no death or rebirth. It is a continuous process, having no termination. Between death and rebirth there is theoretically no gap; it only appears to common man as a drastic change. By following the *atthangika-magga*, *satipatthana* and various other meditational processes a monk or a nun can put an end to the continuity of existences by attaining *Nibbana*, the Absolute. This is the teaching of Lord Buddha.

From what has been stated above, it will be clear that Buddhism was and is both a cultural and a religious movement. As a cultural movement it may also be pointed out that it had a missionary spirit. It had no scruples against propagating the religion among foreigners and indeed among all people irrespective of caste or creed. It is because of this catholic spirit that Buddhism could spread over Eastern and Central Asia. Another remarkable feature of this cultural movement was to allow the Buddhist scriptures to be translated into any language. Buddha had the foresight to give the dictum: "*sakaya niruttiya Buddhavananan apunitum*" and so today there are Buddhist scriptures in Sinhalese, Burmese, Thai, Tibetan, Mongolian, Chinese, Japanese and, recently, English. A few texts have been found in defunct languages like Khotanese, Uigur etc.

THE PRESENT PROBLEM

The problem that has been confronting the younger generation today is that in their eyes a religion serves no purpose for human welfare. What is needed most today for a good human life, they seem to think, is science and technology. Science is the captain and technology the rank and file. It is an undeniable fact that science and technology have conferred immeasurable benefits on the human race. The question is, can these material benefits give full satisfaction to a human being, composed as he is of matter and mind, spirituality and physical body? What many are now discovering is that science and technology cannot fully satisfy human inclinations.

The present craze for science and technology is to utilize atomic energy. So long as study and research about this energy was confined to scientists, it was fully appreciated by the people, but unfortunately it has passed into the hands of the technicians who have contrived it as an unthinkable means of destruction and devastation of the human race. It is now being controlled by the politicians, who are interested only in enlarging their empires and enjoying all the material benefits at the cost of others. Even today one shudders at the thought of the havoc created at Hiroshima by the atom bomb, and the whole world can now be converted into a Hiroshima.

THE ROLE OF RELIGION

Now we have to consider to what extent religion could be helpful in solving this problem. In this connection it has to be noted that *dharma* or religion has two aspects: the formal aspect and the essential aspect, the historical aspect and the spiritual aspect. The formal or historical aspect is represented by the organized form of religion which is also the popular form. The popular form of religion is based on local traditions, customs, rites and rituals. This form of religion has reference to the social, economic and even geographical conditions under which it came into existence. So this form of religion may change from time to time and place to place. Certain practices that are quite useful under one set of circumstances may become obsolete under another set of circumstances. What is in keeping with one situation may become an anachronism in another situation. So under new circumstances, in new situations, old forms may give place to new forms. What is true of other human institutions is also true of the institutional form of religion.

Here it has to be borne in mind that it is the institutional form of religion that gives rise to differences among various religious groups and communities. Much innocent blood has been shed in the name of this form of religion. Even wars have been fought. So is it not desirable that we dispense with this form of religion? It is neither desirable nor possible to do so. We must try to understand the significance of these differences in an historical perspective. This understanding will enable us to appreciate the differences and not quarrel about them.

This does not mean that we have to overlook or compromise with forms and observances which would not come up to the moral standard of man. If there are such forms and practices they have to be abandoned. Religious forms and practices worth the name must have a healthy influence on the moral and spiritual life of man.

Unlike the formal aspect, the essential or the spiritual aspect of religion does not undergo change according to the vicissitudes of life. For instance, we cannot say that yesterday it was *maitri* or love that brought about peace among man, and today it is *vera* or hatred that would do the job. They do not change their value under any circumstances. They are eternal verities.

How to know the spirit as distinct from form, how to separate the grain from the chaff, how to distinghuish *dharma* from *adharma?* We have it in a discourse of the Buddha, which he gave to Mahapajapatigotami, his foster mother. She was the first member of the Bhikkhuni Order. After joining the Order, she went to the Master and said, "I have joined the Order in advanced age. There is no time for me to study the *dharma* in detail. Therefore, please teach me only the essence of it." On that occasion Lord Buddha said to her – "Whatever leads to the destruction of passions and evils and the cultivation of virtues; whatever gives light and wisdom, peace and happiness, should be regarded as *dharma*, and whatever is of the opposite nature should be regarded as *adharma*."

These are pregnant words, full of meaning. In them we have a sure criterion with reference to which *dharma* can be ascertained as distinct from *adharma*. It was on this aspect of *dharma* or religion that Lord Buddha laid emphasis in the course of his ministry.

Today there is much confusion regarding the values of life. In some quarters all importance is attached to material value. So a revaluation of the values of life has to be made so as to have an integrated view of life. Along with his material progress man has to make an earnest effort to attain to his full spiritual stature. For this it is necessary that we have a clear understanding of the spirit of religion, the essence of religion as distinct from its formal side.

Today with the invention of nuclear weapons the very existence of man is threatened. Wars cannot solve problems. On the contrary they create more and more problems, bringing untold misery and suffering. In this connection Lord Buddha has said: "Hatred never ceases by hatred. By love alone it ceases. This is an eternal Law."

Man is a combination of body and spirit. He has to work for both material and spiritual well-being. A synthesis of science and religions has to be brought about. Then only can this earth be a happy place for man to live. Scientists are playing their part well. Let religious leaders fulfill their mission.

A Rethinking of Christianity

by

Dr. TETSUTARO ARIGA

President, Kobe College, Kobe, Japan; Observer, Second Vatican Council[1]

I. MAN IN THE MODERN WORLD

The first half of the Twentieth Century witnessed two world wars as well as great progress in science and technology. What seemed to promise a universal brotherhood of peace and prosperity turned out to be a tool for war and destruction. In spite of the formation of the United Nations the world is still split and at war against itself. Our civilization is finding itself caught in a great contradiction between plausible unity and actual disunity, between the possibility of better understanding and the deepening of misunderstanding, among people, among social groups, and among the nations.

The whole world is thus facing a serious crisis. However, we also realize that our society itself is today in a process of disintegration, from which process the individual person cannot escape. Man is indeed falling to pieces, he is losing himself; he cannot find his own identity, personality, subjectivity, and even "existence." The problem of the world is in the last analysis the problem of man. And man is asking anew the most basic of all questions: "What is man?"

This present day problem of man cannot be understood apart from the impact of Western civilization upon the rest of the world. And the main factors that make up Western civilization may historically be traced back to Greco-Roman and Judeo-Christian sources. Elements of Greek culture and Hebraic religion have been combined in various and intricate ways, and even the formation of Christianity owed much to ideas of Greek and Latin origin, though it claimed to be the fulfillment of Old Testament prophecy.

It is, therefore, impossible for us to ignore Christianity as we take up the problem of man in the contemporary world. We have to ask: How much and in what way have the influences of Christianity contributed to the inte-

---

[1] Presented in absentia

gration and/or disintegration of modern man and his society? Then and thus does Christianity become our common problem. It is not something that should be taken for granted, dogmatically or traditionally, but it is something that needs to be re-examined both in reference to the past and with a view to the future of mankind. No fair-minded Christian is able to escape the urgency of the task. To be sure, there has been no lack of self-criticism, radical or moderate, on the part of western Christianity through the centuries. But Christianity is in our days finding itself in a new situation. It is being faced with challenges coming from the very civilization it has helped to develop. It is finding it necessary to deal more squarely than ever with the non-Christian religions and cultural traditions of the world. It must undertake a fresh rethinking of the content and message of its own faith.

It is, however, not the Christian religion alone that is being challenged by the contemporary civilization of science and technology. All religious values and claims are made objects of either doubt or attack wherever scientism and materialism penetrate. Christianity can no longer stand alone. Its problems cannot be solved without reference to the problems faced by many other religions. A new attitude and a new approach should be found by Christians if their religion is ever, not only to maintain itself, but to bring some positive contributions to the growth and maturity of mankind. For in the present age the religions of the world are inevitably brought into a relation of mutual dialogue in an unprecedented way.

II. THE PROBLEMS OF CHRISTIANITY

Since the Eighteenth Century attempts have been made to seek Christian unity in the face of the rival claims for the ultimate truth made by various churches and sects. The theological discussion on the "essence" or "genius" of Christianity was continued until the twenties, and then a more realistic approach was proposed, which took the form of the ecumenical movement. The World Council of Churches was thus formed, and its first assembly was held in Amsterdam in 1948. On the Roman side, Pope John XXIII called the great Ecumenical Council (Vatican II) in 1962, which was continued by his successor Paul VI until the fall of 1965. Between the churches and de-nominations, especially between Catholics and non-Catholics, new roads of communication are now being built for the sake of better understanding and cooperation. Both the World Council and the Vatican have also developed programs for re-examining Christianity's relationship to non-Christian religions. This does not mean that all ecumenial problems are now being settled. It would be truer to say that problems are being discovered, or in many cases, rediscovered. Many a venture, along theoretical, practical, and organizational lines, is still needed for the solution of those problems.

The above is a rough description of the recent phenomenon of Christianity. But we have now to ask a more "essential" question, as to whether the problem of unity and disunity and that of closedness and openness may be traced back to the very structure of Christian thought itself. This was the theme once taken up by ERNST TROELTSCH in his book DIE ABSOLUTHEIT DES CHRISTENTUMS (1902). The discussion thus started has been interrupted for many years by the rise and prevalence of the theology of the Word of God, but our time seems to be requiring a resumption of it. The problem is not simply academic but very keenly existential especially for the present writer, as a Christian theologian in an Oriental environment.

Genuinely religious concern is rooted in the experience of encounter with the unconditioned and ultimate. There can be no religion without a sense of absoluteness of what it believes to be true and saving. Christianity is no exception. But this sense of absoluteness does not necessarily justify an exclusive claim to the ultimate truth. Each religion has its unique basis and structure. Of course it is academically possible to compare religious concepts and doctrines as concepts and doctrines. But we do not know the ultimate *religious* criteria for evaluating the religions of the world. The only possible religious criticism of a religion is self-criticism. It is highly probable that the criteria religions find in themselves are similar to each other; nevertheless, the criterion of each is primarily for its own self-judgment, and only analogically for judging other religions. The sense of absoluteness should make one's mind open and humble rather than closed and exclusive.

Here is a problem which touches the very kernel of the Christian religion. For in its most basic structure we find a dialectic between particularity and universality. Unlike the Greek conception of "being", from which "ontology" could be developed, the Hebrew conception of *hayah* is dynamic, active, and concrete. The ultimate of the Hebrew Bible is "I am" (*'ehyeh*), or "He will let be" (*Yahweh*) not the *to on* or *to ontos on* of a Plato. It was only later, in Hellenistic Judaism and early Patristic thought, that God and *to on* came to be equated. Originally, the Biblical God was personal (*'ehyeh*) and creative (*Yahweh*), and between Him and the people of Israel a covenant relationship was established at Mt. Sinai. This covenant character is very basic, not only to the religion of Israel, but also to Christianity, which is believed to have been founded on the New Covenant.

The logic of the Judeo-Christian religion therefore has its aspect of particularism; the particularism of election, covenant, and the consequent *achal*-structure. The other aspect of the logic, however, contains moments of universalism: the divine creation and government of the whole world, humanistic ethical imperatives, and the divine recognition of each individual person in his destiny. Jesus of Nazareth both in his proclamation of the Kingdom of God and in his own life and death, revealed the meaning of love (*agape*) in a most profound way. Here is a universalism of love breaking through the barriers between the nations, races and classes. However, insofar as it works in and through the *ecclesia* as a community of the New Covenant, Christianity is still a religion of particularism. A tension between universalism and particularism thus belongs to the very nature of Christianity itself. If only a proper dialectical relation between the two is maintained, it will be possible for the universality of love to be realized in the particular and concrete. Actually, however, the particularism of the *ecclesia*-structure has been combined with, and conditioned by, various contingent factors of socio-historical origin. These factors tended not only to make the Christian church institutionally demarcated and closed, but also to split it into a number of churches, sects, and groups. Furthermore, they tended to foster the degeneration of the universalism of love into an imperialism of power and conquest, with the result that in Asia and Africa people still remember Christian missions as in one way or another associated with Western colonialism.

The self-criticism of Christianity, then, seems to point to a purified dialectical structure of love in which the universal and the particular work together in fruitful interaction, rather than to a vague universalism dissociated from all particularism. For the basis of Christian thought is not to be sought in the general concept of being, but in one's encounter with the "I am" and "He will let be". Early in the history of Christianity, however, the influence of Greek ontology began to make itself felt by identifying the Biblical God with Being (*to on*) or the True Being (*to ontos on*). It should be noted that this identification had its antecedent in Hellenistic Judaism, in Philo especially. And down the centuries the Hebraic-Biblical and the Greek-ontological have acted on each other for the formation of western culture. On the one hand ontology helped to bring out the universal imports of what was recorded in the Bible as happened, given, said, or done. On the other hand the concept of *hayah-Yahweh* intimated a new dimension of being, rather, beyond being. Greek ontology, together with the Biblical faith in God as personal creator, thus brought forth a super-ontology. From the Hebraic-Christian viewpoint, it may be more appropriate to call it *hayah*-ontology. However, it seems just as important to characterize it as super-ontology, because it brings into the horizon of Christian thought the contrast of being and non-being. By creation all things have been brought into "being" out of "non-being" or "nothing". He who has thus brought all things into being is neither abstract being nor a being as existent, but the creative ground and power of the being of all things existent. As such, he is beyond the reach of all ontological concepts. There is no way to define this ultimate reality but in negative terms. Or it may be hinted at by symbolic terms or paradoxical expressions. Apophatic theology therefore is not necessarily an alien element in Christian thought. If one meets Christ in the heart of the unutterable "not-being", it should be called a Christian experience. The ontological-apophatic method, however, helps to find in it the dimension of depth, where distance and nearness are in paradoxical unity.

Since the apophatic method is universally applicable and has actually been employed by mystical thinkers of all religions, there may be provided by it a ground for the meeting of thinkers of different religious convictions for the sake of a better mutual understanding. If, for instance, Buddhists and Christians come together for a colloquium on such a basis, the "compassion" of the Buddha and the "love" of Christ will be found to be very near and akin to each other. The "particularism" of Christianity is not thereby lost but is so purified that the particular and the universal work together in a dynamic sort of dialectic.

III. MATURITY OF RELIGION

Self-reflection and self-criticism make a religion humble and open, rather than narrow and arrogant, as long as it is rooted in the experience of the ultimate in a unique way. For the experience has the two aspects of "givenness" and "search". The ultimate reality reveals itself to man, but man is not able to grasp the full meaning of the revelation. Givenness, if genuine, does not make the believer complacent but rather incites him to search for the truth in which he has already been granted a share. Since divine revelation is always unique to each religion, man's search for the ultimate truth cannot be made in the same way in all religions. Nevertheless, since the ultimate truth cannot but be one, it is possible for us to say there is common search for truth in all genuine religions. If so, it will also be possible for the members of different religions together to be engaged in study and discussion and even meditation. It should be regarded as a sign of maturity that a religion has developed such an attitude of openness and readiness to learn, not only from its own sources, but also from other religions.

And it is only where this attitude of common search for truth prevails that a common endeavour of all religions for the betterment and integration of human society will be possible. In this age of history where the dignity of man is taken for granted and yet so much ignored, and where both man and his society are brought into a rapid process of disintegration and degeneration, all great religions of the world are naturally concerned about the phenomenon. But this is a problem that they should all cooperate to tackle, for which task only mature understanding and thinking will give them proper qualifications. What is most needed today is not simply cooperation on the secular, cultural and scientific level, but cooperation with a deeper religious foundation. Nothing short of it will be equal to the problem of man, because it is basically a religious problem.

There are in this world prejudices, hatreds, inequalities, rivalries, violence and wars. At their roots they are all religious problems; religions therefore cannot be indifferent to them. Undoubtedly more common action is needed for their solution, but actions which do not come from deep meditation and prayer cannot be truly effective in the spiritual transformation of man for the maturity of his humanity. What is needed most is not self-sufficient contemplation but hard thinking and reflection coupled with prayer and meditation, always in faith, hope and love.

"Are the religions relevant?" is a question often asked by religious people themselves. They should rather ask themselves whether they are honestly and earnestly trying to make their religions relevant. And the beginning of this effort will only be made by a self-examination of and self-reflection on the history and content of their own religions. History reveals to their embarrassment what share the religions have had in the fostering of prejudices and hostilities. This should make man humble and penitent, but not frustrated. As long as the eternal source of light is still shining above the clouds, he need not despair of the darkness below in which he finds himself. Instead of blaming and accusing each other, the religious of the world should seek to turn people's eyes to that Light Transcendent. Again speaking on behalf of Christianity, the best positive contribution it can bring to the renewal of mankind will be to bear witness to that love revealed by Jesus Christ in its purity, in which the most universal works in and through the most particular.

A Baha'i Viewpoint

by

Dr. H. M. MUNJE
The National Spiritual Assembly of the Baha'is of India, Kanpur

What a happy coincidence that this unique Conference is being held this year when we, the Baha'is all over the world, are celebrating the Centenary Year of the proclamation of Baha'u'llah, The Divine Founder of the Baha'i World Faith.

It was in 1867 that Baha'u'llah (literally: The Glory of God) sent out His holy invitations to all the rulers and religious heads of the world asking them to unite, in the name of God and for the sake of humanity, and thus lay the foundation for understanding the universal harmony of the entire human race He said:

"O people! consort with the followers of all religions in a spirit of friendliness and fellowship."

The Universe is wrapped in an ecstasy of joy and gladness. The scriptures of past dispensations celebrate the great jubilee that must need greet this most great day of God. Well is it with him that hath lived to see this day and hath recognized its station. ... Seize your chance, inasmuch as a fleeting moment in this day excelleth centuries of a bygone age. ... Neither sun nor moon hath witnessed a day such as this.

It is heartening to note that this Conference of ours is in keeping with the spirit of the Baha'i faith in this age.

The most important and emergent question of the world today is a planetary solution for the whole of mankind, for a living peace and justice in action.

The failure of highly vaunted schemes, spiritual despair and heartless intrigues are everywhere evident. What is the disease mankind is suffering from? What are its cures? Can we do something in this?

The importance of statesmanship, the increase of godless movements and the weakening of the pillars of religion has brought about an unprecedented crisis, unprecedented because it is a world crisis, demanding a universal solution on all levels and in all walks of human life.

Shoghi Effendi, the Guardian of the Baha'i faith, wrote: – "The world is in truth moving on towards its destiny. The interdependence of the peoples and nations of the earth, whatever the leaders of the divisive forces of the world may say or do, is already an accomplished fact. Its unity in the economic sphere is now understood and recognized. The welfare of the part means the welfare of the whole, and distress of the part brings distress to the whole." The revelation of Baha'u'llah has, in His own words, "Lent a fresh impulse and set a new direction" to this vast process now operating in the world. The fires lit by this great ordeal are the consequences of men's failure to recognize it. They are, moreover, hastening its consummation. Adversity prolonged, world-wide, afflictive, allied to chaos and universal destruction, must needs convulse the nations, stir the conscience of the world, disillusion the masses, precipitate a radical change in the very conception of society and coalesce ultimately the disjointed, bleeding limbs of mankind into one body, single, organically united and indivisible.

Indeed, the lessons of two world wars have not sufficed to bring mankind to its senses. We are numbed with fear and do not wish to dwell on the awesome reality of atomic warfare. Philosophies, economic systems and politicians have led us nowhere. It is crucial for mankind to find out whether religion has the answer. Hence, the question of its relevance to modern society; the economic plight of the world and the injustices we see everywhere. How powerful is religion to revive the failing fortunes of a harassed humanity?

A WORLD IN TRAVAIL

"The world is in travail and its agitation waxeth day by day", said Baha'u'llah. "Its face is turned towards waywardness and unbelief. Such shall be its plight that to disclose it now would not be meet and seemly. Its perversity will long continue. And when the appointed hour is come, there shall suddenly appear that which shall cause the limbs of mankind to quake. Then and only then will the Divine Standard be unfurled and the Nightingale of Paradise warble its melody."

"How long will humanity persist in its waywardness? How long will injustice continue? How long is chaos and confusion to reign amongst men? How long will discord agitate the face of society? The winds of despair are, alas, blowing from every direction, and the strife that divides and afflicts the human race is daily increasing. The signs of impending convulsions and chaos can now be discerned, inasmuch as the prevailing order appears to be lamentably defective."

"The vitality of men's belief in God," Baha'u'llah has testified, "is dying out in every land; nothing short of His wholesome medicine can ever restore it. The corrosion of ungodliness is eating into the vitals of human society; what else but the elixir of His potent revelation can cleanse and revive it?"

THE ROLE OF RELIGION

"Religion is the greatest instrument for the order of the world and the tranquillity of all existent beings. The weakness of the pillars of religion has encouraged the ignorant and rendered them audacious and arrogant. Truly, I say whatever lowers the lofty station of religion will increase heedlessness in the wicked, and finally result in anarchy."

THE RELEVANCE

"The all-knowing Physician hath His finger on the pulse of mankind. He perceiveth the disease, and prescribeth, in His unerring wisdom, the remedy. Every age hath its own problem, and every soul its particular aspiration. The remedy the world needeth in its present-day afflictions can never be the same as that which a subsequent age may require. Be anxiously concerned with the needs of the age ye live in, and center your deliberations on its exigencies and requirements."

ONENESS OF THE HUMAN RACE

"The Baha'i Faith upholds the unity of God, recognizes the unity of His prophets, and inculcates the principle of the oneness and wholeness of the entire human race. It proclaims the necessity and the inevitability of the unification of mankind, asserts that it is gradually approaching, and claims that nothing short of the transmuting spirit of God, working through His chosen mouthpiece in this day, can ultimately succeed in bringing it about. It, moreover, enjoins upon its followers the primary duty of an unfettered search after truth, condemns all manner of prejudice and superstition, declares the purpose of religion to be the promotion of amity and concord, proclaims its essential harmony with science, and recognizes it as the foremost agency for the pacification and the orderly progress of human society. It unequivocally maintains the principle of equal rights, opportunities and privileges for men and women, insists on compulsory education, eliminates extremes of poverty and wealth, abolishes the institution of priesthood, prohibits slavery, asceticism, mendicancy and monasticism, prescribes monogamy, discourages divorce, emphasizes the necessity of strict obedience to one's government, exalts any work performed in the spirit of service to the level of worship, urges either the creation or the selection of an auxiliary international language and delineates the outlines of those institutions that must establish and perpetuate the general peace of mankind."

Baha'u'llah wrote hundreds of books while in prison and in exile. He wrote and sent letters to the principal priests of all religions and to top leaders in various departments of human life, and a proclamation in 1867 to all the kings, emperors and rulers of the whole world, summoning them, one and all, to the Divine Banquet of world peace through living world unity in all the inter-dependent walks of humanity in its entirety. Among these are (1) Spiritual Unity, as a Foundation, (2) Social Unity, as the Ground Floor, (3) Economic Unity, as the 1st Floor, and (4) Unity on the Governmental level as the Dome of the Super-structure of an Enduring Planet-Wide Most Great Peace.

This being a Spiritual Summit Conference, I shall say a few words about the spiritual solution offered by the Baha'i faith for world unity and peace through divine love.

All prides, prejudices and chauvinisms must be forgotten once for all, for Baha'u'llah says: "The Tabernacle of Unity hath been raised. Regard ye not one another as strangers. ... The whole world is but one country and mankind its citizens. ... One people of the World! Of one tree are ye all the fruits and of a single branch the leaves."

All religions are fundamentally one. It is only the outward and non-essential aspect of religion which is changed by the Divine Will in accordance with the evolving necessities of human beings living in every age.

Religion must be the cause of the unity of the entire human race, or else it is not worth the name. It is not religion which separates man from man and divides humanity. It is our misunderstanding based on misinterpretation of the divine scriptures that has played havoc. Hence, it is obvious that we should come to a universal understanding and nothing less. Herein lies the realization of our true aims and objects.

We should first come together, understand each other on a global scale and try to adjust with one another and co-ordinate all our affairs. Then and then alone we will be guided by the Divine Plan to merge into the mighty ocean of the love of God and His infinite mercy and be as one soul and one body living with the breath of God and functioning in complete harmony to His pleasure.

Religion must be in full harmony with human reason and science, or else it is mere superstition. On the other hand, science must be controlled universally by God-fearing men for the benefit of the whole of the human race and its richest services should be utilized in the establishment of paradise on earth.

Of course the golden age when men will truly be able to live as brothers in the same family is still far away. We have only to look about us to see how tragically true this is. Indeed we often fear the forces of destruction by uncontrolled powers of science and politics. We see young people in every country asking the question, "What should we all do to prevent a universal suicide which we are going to commit?" In conclusion let me once again quote Baha'u'llah who spoke in unequivocal terms about the harmony between all religions of the world and the working together of all the peoples on this planet:

That the diverse communions of the earth, and the manifold systems of religious belief, should never be allowed to foster the feelings of animosity among men, is, in this day, of the essence of the faith of God and his religion. These principles and laws, these firmly established and mighty systems, have proceeded from one source (God), and are the rays of one light (Divine). That they differ one from another is to be attributed to the varying requirements of the ages in which they were promulgated.

And last but not least, Baha'u'llah says: "O people! Consort with the followers of all religions in a spirit of fragrance and fellowship."

The Obligation of Religion in our Era

by

The Reverend Toshio Miyake
Senior Minister, Konko-kyo Church of Izuo, Osaka, Japan[1]

"The Relevance of the World's Religions to the Present-day World" is the theme of the Spiritual Summit Conference here at Calcutta, India, under the auspices of the Temple of Understanding, Inc. This conference proposes to study and discuss how the world's religions can cope with the various problems of the recent-day world; for instance, those of poverty in the midst of plenty, food, population, racial and other discrimination, causes of war, human alienation, etc.

At this conference the study and discussion ought not to end in fruitless idealistic talking. The reason is that religion does not mean idealistic thought or idealistic philosophy, but real practice in daily life for the sake of "relieving and being relieved", that is, the actual devout action itself.

This conference, therefore, should not be satisfied with writing out, through mutual talks among the conferees, a mere idealistic answer to the above-mentioned problems. It should not be confined to mere preaching on everybody's spiritual attitude to cope with the situations mentioned above. As for me, I think we should debate and clarify the part the world's religions should and can play in pointing out the causes of these problems, in eliminating these causes and eventually in solving the problems.

Of course, I will not confound educational work with political activities. This conference should not be a so-called cathedral educator who speaks only idealistically of the foundation of world peace, if it aims to build the foundation of world peace through mutual understanding and cooperation of the world's religions. The conference should be not only a good educator who has a strong will to achieve world peace, but also should be a powerful man of action who aims to build up the foundation of world peace, because only a powerful man of action can be a good educator and a good leader. The powerful man of action, who aims to establish the foundation of world peace, can only foster in everybody's mind a firm spiritual

---

[1] Presented in absentia.

power strong enough to ascertain the cause of the above-mentioned situations, and a strong practical power to lay the foundation of world peace. Generally speaking, mere words or thoughts cannot educate a person. Practice is the true mainspring of education.

Naturally the educational work of The Temple of Understanding, Inc. must be distinguished from political activities, for it will prove to be fruitless if it becomes confounded with political activities. I don't think I am the only person who is afraid of it.

Now there is a serious question whether capitalistic and socialistic societies really have the ability to solve the various problems of the present-day world; those of poverty, food, population, racial or other discrimination, war, human alienation, etc. Today's advanced nations are industrialized societies, and capitalistic and socialistic societies are two modifications of industrialized society which are based on scientific technology. Such societies will necessarily become societies of technocracy, the so-called "supertechnological society."

The solution of the problems of the present-day world owes a great deal to the progress of scientific technology, but as is generally agreed, the advancement of scientific technology, on the other hand, also makes the problems of the present-day world more grave and serious, especially those of human alienation and destruction of all humankind. Therefore, both societies, capitalistic and socialistic, will be compelled to modify or revise themselves many times to solve the problems. But their revision naturally has its limits.

Such being the case, it may safely be said that neither society has the ability to solve the problems. The reasons for this should be examined scientifically and objectively, apart from the viewpoint of any given ideology. In due course, the time will come when a third and new social system will be a subject of our discussion. Can the world's religions be allowed to assume an indifferent attitude? I think they have to take an active part in the process from their respective standpoints, because their participation in this work has a close connection with building up the foundation of world peace.

Many people say that the way to world peace and human happiness lies in the doctrines of the world's religions and that religion is their very basis. But when we ask whether the religions of the world are playing an active part in the solution of the problems which must be solved before we can establish world peace and realize human happiness, we are compelled to answer "No". The answer will remain in the negative so long as we religionists, do not carefully consider these problems as well as tackle the various problems arising in capitalistic and socialistic society.

Though many reasons for a negative answer are conceivable, we feel the following tendencies, observed in religious circles as a whole, are the main ones:

1) Religionists for the most part are concerned only with the relief of individual souls, not with worldly and material problems in daily life.

2) They are apt to take it for granted that when they must be concerned with worldly and material problems, their aim should be to relieve the daily lives of individual persons, and that the great social problems should be left in the hands of politicians.

3) Each religious sect or denomination considers its own doctrines to be absolute and is apt to dismiss the doctrines of any other sect or denomination. Furthermore, it is apt to be too proud to think of mutual understanding and cooperation among the world's religions.

The history of humankind is changing rapidly. The above-mentioned problems are all caused by the rapid change of historical society. It will be impossible for politics and scientific or technical progress alone to solve them. If each religious sect or denomination does not realize this fact and try to play an active role in their solution, they will remain permanently unsolvable. This is why "The Relevance of the World's Religions to the Present-day World" is so important a theme.

If my way of thinking is correct, the religions of the present-day world must continue to be concerned with relieving the daily life of each individual, because only by repeatedly performing this can the relief of the individual soul be accomplished. The relief of each individual, in the actual phases of his daily life, has a great deal to do with the various social problems with which we are confronted, because the solution of the latter alone can perform the former. Only if we find the solution of the social problems, can the problems of the daily life of each individual be solved. Thus, man can barely be saved. We must not lose sight of this.

It is needless to say that the solution of all great social problems is beyond the abilities of any single religious sect or denomination. Such a great task can be performed only by mutual understanding, cooperation and mutual participation of all the religious sects and denominations of the world.

Therefore, it is not too much to say that this conference is a very timely attempt because of its intention to clarify the relevance of the world's religions to the present day world through mutual understanding among them.

At this conference the first thing we must do will be to humble ourselves and consider why all the traditional religions have been powerless to solve the problems before us. Secondly, we must seriously consider casting off the superficial skin of the present religious institutions, as we work together, for by cooperating on these significant tasks we shall contribute much to improving mutual understanding and cooperation among the religions of the world. Examining ourselves humbly and wishing to cast off our skins is an indispensable basis for this.

Mutual understanding and cooperation are not mere means to an end with man. They are inherent in man. Why? In the doctrine of Konko-kyo the relationship between God's existence and man's existence can be expressed as follows: Kami (God) exists within man and man exists within Kami.

Here we must be careful not to misinterpret. "Kami exists within man", means that the existence of man is requisite to that of God, and the former is the basis or the ground of the latter. God reveals Himself in the midst of the actual life of man through man's prayer to God.

The function of God is to save man in response to his prayers. Such a function of God is not his only function. It is realized only through the existence of man who prays to God for mercy. The passage through which God, the Absolute, make His appearance is man's prayer to God. This is what "Kami exists within man" means.

On the contrary "Man exists within Kami" means that God's existence is the basis or the ground of man's existence. Man can exist because he is supported, brought up and helped by God. Moreover, man's existence is based on that of his fellow creatures. With us human beings, "we exist within God" is no less true than "we exist within our fellow creatures." The existence-relation in this sense, between God and man and between man and his fellow creatures is the basis upon which mutual understanding and cooperation between God and man and between man and his fellow creatures is founded. Through such twofold relationships man is helped, becomes prosperous and happy, and at the same time God's earnest desire is fulfilled. It is especially to be noted that such relationships do not deny God's absoluteness in the least. On the contrary they make it clearer.

Mutual understanding and cooperation in international relationships and interreligious relationships are as important and indispensable as those in relationships among human beings. For the realization of world peace and human happiness all the nations of the world must cooperate with one another beyond so-called nationalistic egoism. The same is the case with the various religions of the world. They must not confine themselves to their own shells, but try to understand one another better and cooperate with one another for a common purpose, for realizing world peace and human happiness. That is what religion should be. Only thus will the nations prosper and the various religions be able to fulfil God's great desire for establishing world peace and saving human beings. All religionists must have a devout and broad-minded heart to embrace the world and all human beings, including those of other religions.

The Temple of Understanding is desirous of establishing a world body of religions by repeatedly holding such Spiritual Summit Conferences as the present one, by promoting mutual understanding among the world's religions to enlighten the people of the world and by building up the foundation of world peace. I strongly feel that the establishment of such a world body of religions is an attempt which deserves admiration. I will do my best to cooperate in any attempt of the same nature and it is earnestly hoped that the authorities of The Temple of Understanding will make an untiring effort towards this goal.

SECTION II

TOWARDS INTER-RELIGIOUS COOPERATION

The Founding of the Congress of Religions, Ceylon

by

AL HAJ S. M. A. RASCHID
Patron, The Congress of Religions, Colombo, Ceylon[1]

In the name of Allah, the Merciful, the Beneficent. Ten million thoughts pass through my mind. Ten million thoughts which passed through the minds of a few people dedicated to bringing about amity, peace, and good-will in the name of religion. The message I give you is the way in which we established the Congress of Religions in Ceylon; a small country, a country which represents the heartbeat of the world, because if you look at any common map you will see that Ceylon is in the center of the globe. As such it acted as a heart of religion.

We were just three; one who was threatened with excommunication, before Vatican II, for his outspokenness about the approach of religion towards solving man's problems. The other was a Theosophist, a man who was accused of making a synthesis of all religions. The third man, very ironically, was a man who was equally outspoken. His outspokenness brought about the accusation that he was a communist, a man who was an atheist, a man who tried to promote religion but was himself an atheist. These three different people put their heads together to give actual effect to the thoughts, to the feelings that have come throughout the ages of man in the name of religion.

In this very country where we are assembled, in 300 B.C., Asoka said, "No man reverences his own religion unless he reverences other religions also." Then we have a man, Mohammed, who said, in the 8th Century, A.D., in Sura II, verse 266, "There shall be no compulsion in religion." In the 12th Century we have St. Francis of Assissi who said, "Lord, make me an instrument of thy peace. Where there is hatred, let me sow love." That was in the past. Just a few years ago, a man, a common man like you and me, was the first martyr, not for religious tolerance, but for religious equality. That was none other than Mahatma Gandhi. It is in the fitness of things, I think it is the divine will, that we are assembled here, in the country of the first man to lay down his life, not for religious tolerance but for religious equality.

1 Delivered extemporaneously at the Birla Academy, October 26, 1968.

These were the spirits which moved us in Ceylon. Our task was not a very easy one. You may say, "Oh, Ceylon has just 10,000,000 people. It is a very small country, therefore it was easy for the Congress of Religions to be established, and it was possible for them to function, for the whole world to talk about. But we can't do that in any other part of the world, with any other nation." Our problems were much greater than the problems that confront other nations. Just two years before we established the Congress of Religions, there was, not in the name of religion but in the name of language, mass murder, looting, arson, and other crimes. All that in a country which for over 2,500 years cherished and loved religious and social tolerance. We were disturbed. We were terribly disturbed. It was a result of that event in 1958 that we thought that the time had come for us to establish the Congress of Religions where we could not merely *Save* the nation from evil because religion throughout the ages has saved mankind. But in the process of saving mankind from evil it has saved mankind from realizing the good things on earth; a decent living, homes, something to eat, and something to sleep on. There is no doubt that it saved the nations from evil, but it also saved them from receiving the good things on earth. Therefore we substituted the word *Serve* the nation.

We thought, at the Congress of Religions level in Ceylon, that we would serve the people. How did we achieve this? In a very small way. We started off by agreeing in advance that there should be tolerance, that there should be amity, that we should bring all the religious leaders, both the laity and the clergy, together and whenever there was anything to be done, that it be done using religion as a base. The only form of communication that we have today is on a religious basis. Any other form of communication would be on a negative basis. If we tried to approach our problems from a political, ideological, or social communication chord I am afraid we would have too many people against us. But if we were to use the spiritual channel of communication, nobody could object to us. It was in that context that we used the spiritual channel of communication in establishing the Congress of Religions.

We are not a mere organization, doing nothing tangible. On the very eve of my departure from Ceylon we presented to the national government a demand, in the name of the Congress, for a just wage as a measure of social justice. We also demanded from the government minimum standards of housing and sanitation. We also demanded from the government, mark my words, we were demanding from the government, that religious education, both primary and secondary, should be readily available. The Prime Minister of Ceylon has accepted these demands and we are sure they will be implemented in the near future, if not by this Prime Minister, by the future Prime Minister.

So, we are functioning in a very tangible way. It is in that context that you, each one of you, have to function, Go back to the place you come from.

It may be a lane, it may be a street, it may be a village, it may be a city, it may be a state. Irrespective of what it is, go back with this noble message, of establishing small Temples of Understanding. You may think the problems are very great. They are not. If each one of you thinks it is a worthy cause, there will be hundreds and hundreds of small Temples of Understanding, which in the near future could be federated under the aegis of the Temple of Understanding in Washington, D.C. Go back and establish it.

I can give you an example of how it can be done. As I said, there were three people who thought of the Congress of Religions. They were not readily accessible to the masses because one was supposed to be a communist, the other a Theosophist, and one was about to be excommunicated from the church. One of us became President of the as yet non-existent Congress of Religions. The three of us became officers; we had no members. It was then that we thought of a membership, of an organization. You can do that. Be the live-wire of the movement; in whatever name, in whatever way it is done. Go back. It is not a formidable task. Each one of you go back, establish a small atomic (an atom can explode today and wipe out the world) Temple of Understanding which can create and recreate the world. Go back to your country. I would appeal to the Temple of Understanding that the religious leaders who are represented at this Conference be brought into the general working body of the Temple of Understanding. Eventually when these small Temples of Understanding are established, the Temple of Understanding in Washington can take the initiative in formulating a world federation of religions or a united religious organization.

The Congress of Religions- Ceylon; A Report

by

OLIVER L. ABEYSEKERA

General Secretary, Congress of Religions, Colombo, Ceylon

EDITOR'S NOTE: The Congress of Religions in Ceylon serves as an example of what can be done within a single country, where the religions in the past have had little communication. As the report indicates, the Congress of Religions has faced both the potentials and the complexities of genuine interreligious communication (among Buddhism, Hinduism, Islam and Christianity) in a realistic and productive spirit.

This report was presented in absentia.

The Congress of Religions was formed about five years ago for the purpose of fostering harmony, understanding and tolerance among adherents of the World Religions in Ceylon, thereby opening up a way for the creation of an integrated society serving the Nation through religious harmony.

In a message to the Congress, on the occasion of its inaugural Convention, the Governor-General of Ceylon, Mr. William Gopallawa said:

This effort is a most laudable one and the time for making it most opportune. The rapid changes taking place today as a result of progress in science and technology have made it necessary for man to wage a continuous battle in order to see that spiritual values are not overwhelmed. If man is not to become a victim of his own creations, it is necessary that the clamour of worldly achievement should not lead to the discarding of spiritual truths. It is therefore to religion that we must turn if the proper progress and development of mankind are to be ensured. All religions are equally useful for this purpose, and all religions must therefore unite to see that spiritual values are preserved. It is with this firm conviction that I sincerely wish all success to the Movement that is being inaugurated today for the achievement of religious harmony in this Island of ours, which is so dear to all of us alike, whatever religion we may profess.

The Aims and Objects of the Congress of Religions, as embodied in its Constitution, are four in number. They are:

1. To establish and maintain an Inter-Religions Council composed of religious leaders of the community to resolve acrimonies and allay suspicion among religious denominations.

2. To sponsor action that promotes mutual understanding between religious denominations.

3. To sponsor action that promotes religious amity based on such mutual understanding.

4. While in no way undermining the value of sectarian or secular social service, to sponsor a form of service possessing a spiritual background, that also galvanizes the energies of the community as a whole.

In order to implement these objects, the Congress of Religions organized itself into four distinctive units. They are: The Inter-Religions Council, The Cultural Unit, The Social Action Unit, and the Administration Unit.

I. THE INTER-RELIGIONS COUNCIL

As it is not possible to establish religious amity and harmony where there is antagonism and suspicion, it became necessary, in the first instance, to resolve inter-religious antagonisms and allay any suspicions that may have existed between religious denominations. For this purpose an Inter-Religions Council was established at national level to deal with such acrimonies and suspicions.

The body of members who form this Inter-Religions Council is comprised of acknowledged leaders of the various religious denominations, whose responsibilities and prestige are sufficent in themselves to cope with religious acrimonies and suspicions.

One important procedural decision that was arrived at, at the first meeting of the Inter-Religions Council was as follows:

In view of the particular set-up of the Council where religious denominations are represented through the heads of various denominational bodies, the question of arriving at decisions needs to be carefully considered. Members representing these denominational bodies may be bound by their own organizational decisions. It is therefore felt that any conclusions arrived at by the Council should be based on the accepted formula agreed to by all members, and not on the basis of a majority decision.

The types of problems that are dealt with by the Inter-Religions Council are:

1. Countering attempts to persuade persons to change a particular religious viewpoint through undue influence of either material benefits or mental conditioning or both.

2. Ensuring just distribution of vocational opportunities among the citizens of the country free from religious bias.

3. Ensuring equal opportunities for worship and religious teaching to all religions.

4. Ensuring adequate educational opportunities to the adherents of all religions in this country for their religious and secular education.

Up to now, several problems have been discussed by the Council and settled amicably.

2. THE CULTURAL UNIT

In order to further the second and third objects of the Congress, Cultural Units were formed with the responsibility of promoting understanding and religious amity through cultural relationships between religious denominations.

In order to promote understanding, the Cultural Unit organized public meetings and film shows aimed at developing an appreciation of the fact that every world religion has valuable cultural expressions and a worthy moral heritage.

At such meetings, while each speaker representing a particular religion speaks on the subject from the point of view of his own religion, no comments are made on what has been expressed by previous speakers representing other religions, nor are there any comments from the audience, the members of which are expected to arrive at their own conclusions.

Among the themes that have already been presented at such meetings are:

1. "The Family and its Social Significance."
2. "Parental Responsibility."

Apart from such public presentations, the Cultural Unit of the Congress of Religions organizes discussion groups among the members of the Congress in order to encourage dialogue between religious denominations. Here the members present participate actively in the expression of ideas with a view to determining areas of agreement, and also *accepting areas of disagreement*. As dialogue of this kind requires a consciousness of brotherhood and the eschewing of prejudice, such discussions are not open to the public. The dialogue is the common search for the good which each religion now possesses separately and is not a compromise on the fundamentals which each one accepts.

We of the Congress of Religions consider all religions to be fragant flowers of varied hues in a spiritual garden, and each member has the right to choose the flower which he considers the best.

In order to promote religious amity, the Cultural Unit celebrates the festivals of the World Religions, in public, in a non-religious way.

The Congress does not involve its members in the rituals of any religion. In order to honor such occasions, a lecture by a distinguished exponent of that religion is presented. The topics of the lectures that have been given on these occasions thus far include:

1. "The Social and Political Philosophy of Buddhism and the Task of the Buddhist."
2. "The Responsibilities of a Christian in Contemporary Ceylon."
3. "The Significance of Hindu Religious Festivals."
4. "Some Unique Features of Al-Koran."

A further expression of this same idea of amity, which the Congress sponsors, is participation in the celebrations of special events in the life of religious institutions or religious leaders and also participating, as a mark of respect, in the funeral obsequies of religious leaders.

3. SOCIAL ACTION UNIT

We have in Ceylon today two distinct types of social service. Firstly, there are the Denominational Social Services, which are based on spiritual values and reach a high standard of expression. However, the weakness in this type is that, in a multi-religious community, such social services do not galvanize the community or neighborhood as a whole.

Secondly, there is the State-sponsored social service, which, though enlisting the cooperation of the community as a whole, lacks the quality that comes from spiritual expression.

The Congress of Religions, while accepting the value of both these types of social service, advocates a third type of service which is of an inter-religious character, based on the perennial spiritual virtues common to all religions. This type of social service is, in our opinion, able to galvanize the community as a whole.

At the Annual Convention of the Congress, held in October, 1967, certain proposals relating to family life, adolescence, and adult society were discussed under the theme "The Conservation of the Moral Values of the Nation." A joint declaration embodying these proposals and accepted by the Council of the Congress was signed by leaders of religious denominations and community organizations in the country.

We are now working out a program to bring these proposals direct to the community, in towns, villages and neighborhoods.

In order to convey to you an idea of the type of proposals adopted, I quote below two representative examples:

1. Proposal No. 1 – the Home:

"The home must be considered a basic human need as it is vitally necessary for the stability of the family, the fundamental unit of society. The home creates the environment in which the family discharges its moral and spiritual functions as a basic unit of society. The morality of the home is stabilized by adequate housing and a just wage."

2. Proposal No. 17 – Social Responsibility:

"We suggest that Social Responsibility Units on an inter-denominational basis be established to focus attention on current problems affecting community life, such as the elimination of corrupt practices and lapses in administration, which particularly affect the less privileged members of the community. Such Social Responsibility Units can coalesce on a national basis, giving a social direction to spiritual endeavour."

4. THE ADMINISTRATION UNIT

The Administration Unit of the Congress of Religions performs two functions. While it carries out the administration of the Congress affairs through its officers, it also attends, at the same time, to the development and the extension of the movement.

Authority for the general administration and the management of the affairs of the Congress is vested in the General Council which is the governing body of the Congress. It is composed of members of the parent body, representatives of the branches of the Congress and Representatives of organizations affiliated to the Congress.

The Executive Committee which performs the administrative functions, is responsible for the management and the administration of the affairs of the Congress, subject to the overriding decision of the General Council.

CONCLUSION

Taking into consideration the fact that a detailed report of all the activities of the Congress of Religions and its branch organizations would make a very bulky document, I would like to confine myself to the outlines that have been enumerated above and conclude by saying that since its inception, a few years ago, the membership of the Congress continues to grow rapidly, year after year, persuading us that this world idea which we represent and which is right for our times is also ripe for our times.

Further information about our activities can be readily obtained by writing to the General Secretary, Congress of Religions, 75, Dharmapala Mawatha, Colombo 7, Ceylon.

Introduction to the Manner of Communications Between the World's Religions

by

The Reverend John C. Haughey
Associate Editor, America, New York

I would like to begin my remarks by putting them in the context of the beautiful words of Dr. Huston Smith last night. As you recall, he divided the ages of man into three; the primitive, the axial, and the modern. I would like to submit some additional prolongations to those remarkable ideas. I think, first of all, that we could perhaps divide the ages of man into a fourth age, as yet unnamed, depending on how the religions of man react to the new phenomena that are about us. I think, secondly, that what is a constant in all four ages and moves one age into the other is a difference in communications. As Dr. Smith remarked, we moved from the primitive groups, in which man was only in contact with what is called a primary group, into a new age when man was in contact with a further grouping which we might call a secondary grouping. The changes upon the religions themselves were crucial and cataclysmic, as the religions of man moved from an eternal focus into a more ethical one. I would submit that the ages of man moved from the axial into the modern, perhaps at a stage a little bit earlier than the age of enlightenment, and that the reason why the human course of events moved from the axial to the modern was largely due to the invention of the printing press in the sixteenth century. Once we had the printing press we had a new means of communication and man could therefore be in touch with a new world of ideas. Prior to that he was only in touch in a face-to-face way with ideas. I think we are moving into a fourth age. I think the fourth age, like the first three ages, is going to crucially and deeply affect the religious history of man.

What I would like to talk about this morning is the shape and meaning of this fourth age, not in any theoretical way but in a very practical way. I think that the harbingers of this new age were the invention of the telegraph in 1844 and the telephone in 1876. These two simple scientific devices made it possible for man to transcend his geographical confinement and be in communication with men that he did not see. Even more important, and more immediate in the twentieth century, the development of the motion picture technique in 1903, of radio broadcasting in 1920, and the massive development of television in 1948 bring us foursquare into a new age of communications between man and man. With these three new inventions we get what we call mass-communication. The results on religion should become obvious as I spell this out.

More important perhaps than the telephone and the telegraph, the television and the radio, and the motion picture industry is the whole new world of communication satellites. This new world is only three years old and within the next decade it is going to transform our universe into something that I believe very few of us are prepared to think about. Since it will transform our universe, it is capable of disfiguring, or of developing, inter-religious communication.

The whole communications satellite system which will cover the globe within the next decade will make of the world a village, and will make of each of us global villagers, in the MARSHALL MCLUHAN sense of the term. As you know, the communications satellite is just that; it is a satellite which marries space-age technology to the whole technique of mass-media developed in the last century. A satellite is a sending-center, a fixed platform that bounces signals from transmitting centers onto receiving stations. It moves in perfect harmony with the terrain over which it has been launched. It has been called a little switchboard in the sky, which rids man of the need of laying miles and miles of cables in order to be in communication with man.

For example, Pope Paul, last month in Bogota, Colombia, talked simultaneously to and was seen simultaneously by 125,000,000 people, because of the communications satellite, off which his speech was bounced. In Mexico, the Olympic games were seen simultaneously by 1,000,000,000 people, live, as a result of the communications satellite. The education system of every country is about to be seriously transformed by this system of satellites. The Federal Communications Commissioner of the United States, Mr. HYDE, came to India and spoke to the Communications and Education Minister of India, Mr. RAM SINGH. They spoke in specific terms about the launching of a domestic satellite for India which the two of them estimated would touch and reach 92% of the Indian population. This is the world, not in the future, but the world tomorrow, which is going to necessitate, for religious man, a whole new series of imperatives. It is about these imperatives that I think this conference must become sophisticated and it is about them that we must talk practically, because these imperatives give us the program which lies before us, which if we do not do it, will not get done.

I think the name of this fourth world will depend on us, the religions of the world. It will either be an inter-confessional world, a trans-confessional world, or a post-confessional world, depending on whether we, the religions, are in communication with one another. The new communications techniques force us into new religious postures, if we care to assume them.

What I mean by an inter-confessional world is a world which makes use of the mass-media to be in communication, religiously, with one tradition over against another tradition; where the religions will be in dialogue with one another by means of the mass-media, overcoming their ignorance of each of the other rich religious traditions in the world. They will be escaping from the cold war of ignoring one another which has been our history up to this time, conditioned as each of us is to existing in a geographical enclosure which has now been made needless as a result of the communications satellite. The world therefore will be named according to our reaction and our response to these new phenomena. It could also be called a trans-confessional world, in which the religions of man will be the object of commentary by the technicians of the satellite communications system. Man's beliefs will be observed, noted, talked about.

Or, the much more likely and frightening situation is that the new means of communication will make our world post-confessional, because of the fear of communications experts to touch on the sensitive point of the religious beliefs of man. Rather than touch on this sensitive point, the communications technicians can very easily ignore the religions of man, remain silent about them. The result will be a new secularization of life, promoted by those very mass-media in which no form of transcendence will be acknowledged, by the very means whereby man hears about the meaning of man.

It therefore remains for us to grow sophisticated about the phenomena within reach of all of us. It is up to us whether or not this world will be trans-, or post- or inter-confessional.

I think that there are three imperatives laid before us. One is theological, one is procedural, and one is practical. The theological imperative which is laid before us is this. We have to catholicize or universalize the religious traditions in which we each find ourselves. What I mean by catholicity is the gradual extrication of the religious tradition from the limitations which surround it. Those limitations are historical, national, cultural and conceptional. The process of catholicity or catholicizing religious elements brings our particularity and parochialism into a wholeness or a universal possibility of communication. Each of the religions must take seriously the imperative to universalize its particular tradition, by changing the conceptional framework within which it has gone into that tradition.

For example, in the Judeo-Christian tradition the imperative, which has been fairly successfully met, is to take the revelation of a universal human experience and remove it from the mythic context in which it is communicated to us. I am thinking in this particular case of the Adam and Eve story. When you disengage the mythic elements from the meaning behind those elements you have universalized a human experience, and added the revelation to that experience so that it can be communicated to a universe. Or take the process of catholicizing worship, which moves it away from magic, from the phenomenal, partly from the external ritual, to a more interior and yet socially meaningful event. I think that if a religion does not respond to the imperative of catholicity it will gradually find itself becoming an object of curiosity and eventually a museum piece, a stage along the long road of man's history which becomes more and more curious to man. The imperative for each of our religions is catholicity.

The second imperative, which I call procedural, has been called in the West ecumenicity. Each of the religions places itself in dialogic relationship to the other religions, each religious element is examined, refined and deepened. The ecumenical process makes the treasures of each religion capable of being appropriated by the rest of the religious traditions of man.

The third imperative which weighs heavily upon us, and upon this very privileged group brought together by the Temple of Understanding, is the need for a catalytic agency through whose instrumentality the first steps of inter-religious communication on a worldwide scale might take place. This agency, obviously, would see itself as servant of the communications function and would not, therefore, exist for its own sake. It would react flexibly to the new communications possibilities which we find facing us in 1968, rather than woodenly. Its executive membership would be made up of those who were representative of the world's religions.

I would like to cite some immediate, practical steps which can be taken by each of you in this room but can be engineered in a more effective way by this catalytic agency, the Temple of Understanding. Each of these steps takes seriously the imperative of interreligious communication and goes, propelled by that imperative, to different population layers of the universe.

One of the first steps which would be taken, by this catalytic Temple of Understanding would be to approach the academic community which, as you know, is a worldwide phenomenon. In approaching the academic community it would promote the idea of a world university. The idea of a world university does not mean building or creating any new university. It means that each of the departments, the salient departments of sociology and anthropology, history, theology and philosophy would be compenetrated by the faculties and the resources of six, seven, or eight other universities from other parts of the world whose peculiar competence is in some other religious tradition. Consequently, the University of Baghdad, compenetrated with Harvard University's sociology, anthropology, etc. departments would be twice as strong as Harvard's present department. Multiply that by eight; the University of Ceylon, the University of Moscow, one of the universities in Taiwan, one of the universities in the Islamic nations, and you get the idea of an inter-religious communication at the academic level whereby graduate students and faculty would be interchanged, and we would be gradually overcoming the ignorance which we have of the other beautiful religious traditions of man, through the competence of the academic communities.

A second step, given these new communications phenomena, would be for the Temple of Understanding to send an exploratory committee to Unesco to investigate, the plausability of a council of the religions under the auspices of UNESCO. It would seem that UNESCO would be an appropriate agency for such a world council of the religions, since it represents a world force, but does not itself represent any one of the religions. Such an association would seem not only a good thing but a necessary thing, since at the root of most political disharmony is the religious ignorance that we have of one another.

A third step which each of us can do something about, and the Temple of Understanding can do something very effective about, would be to convince the many private corporations and foundations of the crucial need for endowing a center where the various religious leaders of the world can "live-in" for brief periods of time so that they may come to an appreciation of, a sympathy for, and a knowledge about, the other religious traditions. It is the religious leadership's ignorance of the other religious traditions that makes this cold war go on and on and on: and it must be terminated soon, for the interests of all religious men. I believe it is clear that each of us here, and the Temple of Understanding in particular, can provoke the centers of spirituality and monasticism in the universe to seize the initiative in amassing the erudition necessary for the religions to engage in dialogue. I suggest that it would be a good thing if each of these centers of spirituality and monasticism were to open itself formally to men of other religious traditions, to go and live in those centers. Nothing would do more for inter-religious dialogue than an ecumenical approach to monasticism. All have so much to lose by staying apart, so much to win by coming together, that it would be a tragedy if apartness continued to be order of the day.

The next step involves the many international youth organizations that exist across the globe. Each of us, and the Temple of Understanding in particular, could promote the idea with these international youth organizations, that they should put themselves of an inter-religious footing, at least for *ad hoc* conferences, so that the various religious traditions of man might come under the bright examining light of the young mind and thus encounter all of the beautiful things that come from that mind and might be enriched by such an examination. I would suggest that each of us can be supportive of the attempts of the young to communicate across the boundaries of varying belief systems.

Finally, it seems to me the heaviest imperative of all that lies upon the shoulders of all of us is to be in professional contact with the communications-media men, to make them see the need to assign a high priority to man's religious convictions. We ought to convince the communications personnel of the preferability of man speaking for himself about his religious beliefs, through the media, rather than being spoken for, or spoken about, or observed.

Another point is what can be done on a national scale about interreligious dialogue. Ceylon has been a beautiful example of what can be done if we concentrate our gaze on a national perspective, and the inter-religious harmony or disharmony within a single nation.

In conclusion, it would seem to me that the immediate task of the catalytic agency, which is and can continue to be the Temple of Understanding, is the creation of a pool of the existing materials which are of major importance in the religious traditions of mankind. I am speaking primarily of a repository of the world's scriptures, and the various materials which are authentic, authoritative, and of major importance, and which have been developed over the course of time and perfectly describe the various elements of each of the traditions.

A second imperative upon the Temple of Understanding is not just the creation of such a pool of important religious material but making it an active pool, a distribution center, if you will, whereby material can be sent out across the world, so that the people of one tradition can see and hear the meaning attached by other traditions to the religious beliefs of men.

The most important task of all is for some agency to take seriously the fact that the world will be in touch on a global scale, through the satellite system. But to be in touch with the universe means there has to be a content which you can hear and about which you can think. We must begin to develop those materials which can be bounched off the satellites, and which materials will communicate the religious meaning to a universe.

It seems to me that this is the most crucial task for this agency, right now to take seriously the development of communications material which will make religious communication a reality.

APPENDICES

The First Spiritual summit Conference

Calcutta, India, October 22–26, 1968

The Spiritual Summit Conference was convened in Calcutta under the auspices of the Temple of Understanding, Inc., Washington, D.C., U.S.A. It brought together thirty-two distinguished spiritual leaders of ten world religions – which among them have 2,500,000,000 adherents – Buddhism, Christianity, Confucianism, Islam, Judaism, Hinduism, Sikhism, Baha'i, Zoroastrianism, and Jainism.

Meeting with the religious leaders were: a panel of distinguished scholars; representatives of youth; and more than forty members of the Board of Directors and Friends of the Temple of Understanding, headed by Mrs. DICKERMAN HOLLISTER, President and founder, and Mrs. B. K. BIRLA, of Calcutta, Chairman of the International Committee. There was also a large and sympathetic attendance of believers in understanding who came from every part of India. FINLEY P. DUNNE, Jr., Executive Director of the Temple of Understanding, was general chairman.

The opening session, held in the garden of the Birla Academy of Art and Culture, was attended by more than 600 persons. Principal speakers were Mrs. BIRLA, the hostess of the Conference; Mrs. HOLLISTER; His Excellency SRI DHARMA VIRA, Governor of West Bengal, who extended official greetings. Messages of good will were read from many notables, including Mrs. INDIRA GANDHI, Prime Minister; the President and Vice President of India; The King and Queen of Sikkim; PAOLO, Cardinal MARELLA, President of the Vatican Secretariat for Non-Christians, and U THANT, Secretary General of the U.N.

Most of the sessions were held in the capacious auditorium of the Birla Academy. On the morning of Friday, October 25, the entire Conference crossed the Ganges River by steamboat to the Calcutta Botanical Gardens, to join in prayer for peace and the salvation of mankind. Another meaningful event was a reception given by Mr. and Mrs. B. K. BIRLA at their residence, "Basant Vihar."

An evening session, held in the Grand Hotel, featured addresses by Mrs.

HOLLISTER, Mrs. BIRLA, and Professor HUSTON SMITH of Massachusetts Institute of Technology.

On October 24, more than 1,000 persons at Hindi High School heard an inspiring program of speakers who included: Dr. DITZEN, Dr. SMITH, AYMERO WONDMADGNEHU, Princess POON, Mrs. THONDUP, Swami LOKESHWARANANDA, Dr. VAHIDUDDIN, PIR VILAYAT KHAN, RABBI WAXMAN, Dr. WEI TAT and Dastoor N. B. MONOCHEHR HOMJI.

The final session under the chairmanship of Dr. DITZEN culminated in the passage of a Declaration calling for concerted efforts to encourage further communication among the world's religions. It was also resolved to celebrate in 1969 the 500th anniversary of Guru Nanak, founder of Sikhism.

OFFICIAL PARTICIPANTS IN THE SPIRITUAL SUMMIT CONFERENCE

REPRESENTATIVES OF THE WORLD'S RELIGIONS

CHRISTIANITY:

The Rev. PIERRE FALLON, S.J., Calcutta, representing the Vatican Secretariat for Non-Christians; The Rev. Dr. LOWELL R. DITZEN, Director, The National Presbyterian Center, Washington, D.C.; Dr. HAROLD F. SNYDER, International Affairs Representative for South Asia, the American Friends Service Committee; Rev. AYMERO WONDMADGNEHU, Director of His Imperial Majesty's Private Cabinet for Religious Affairs and Administrator of the Ethiopian Orthodox Mission, Addis Ababa, Ethiopia; THOMAS MERTON (Brother Louis), Abbey of Gethsemani, Trappist, Kentucky; Bishop A. J. SHAW, the Methodist Church in Southern Asia; Mrs. SANFORD KAUFFMAN, Church Women United, National Council of Churches of Christ; Sister BARBARA MITCHELL, Manhattanville College of the Sacred Heart, Purchase, New York; ROLAND GAMMON, New York, Unitarian-Universalist Church.

BUDDHISM:

H.S.H. Princess POON DISKUL, President, World Fellowship of Buddhists, Thailand; Mr. AIEM SANGKHAVASI, Secretary-General, World Fellowship of Buddhists; Dr. REIMON YUKI, representing Lord ABBOT KOSHO OHTANI, NISHI HONGANJI, Kyoto, Japan; Venerable PIYANANDA MAHA THERA, President, Buddhist Vihara Society, Washington, D.C.; Dr. HAKUJIN MATSUO, NISHI HONGANJI, Kyoto, Japan; Venerable MAHASTHAVIRA N. JINARATANA, Mahabodhi Society of India, Calcutta, Mrs. GYALO THONDUP, Darjeeling.

HINDUISM:

Swami CHINMAYANANDAJI, Chinmaya Mission, Bombay; Dr. V. RAGHAVAN, University of Madras; Professor AMIYA CHAKRAVARTY, State University of

New York; SWAMI MADHAV GOSWAMIJI, Gouriya Math, Calcutta; SWAMI LOKESHWARANANDA, Ramkrishna Mission, Narendrapur.

ISLAM:

Dr. SYED S. VAHIDUDDIN, University of Delhi; PIR VILAYAT INAYAT KHAN, Ecole Internationale de la Méditation, Paris; AL HAJ S.M.A. RASCHID, Colombo, Ceylon.

JUDAISM:

Rabbi MORDECAI WAXMAN, Temple Israel, Great Neck, New York; Dr. EZRA SPICEHANDLER, Hebrew Union College School of Archaeology and Biblical Studies, Jerusalem, Israel.

CONFUCIANISM:

Dr. WEI TAT, College of Chinese Culture, Taipei, Taiwan.

ZOROASTRIANISM:

Dastoor N. B. MINOCHEHR HOMJI, Bombay; HOMI B. DHALLA, Bombay.

JAINISM:

Miss VATSALA AMIN, Divine Knowledge Society, Bombay, representing MUNISHRI CHITRABHANU.

SIKHISM:

SARDAR SHER SINGH "SHER", representing S.S. SANT CHANAN SINGH, Amritsar.

BAHA'I:

Dr. K. M. MUNJE, National Spiritual Assembly of the Baha'is of India, Delhi.

SPECIAL COUNSELLORS:

Dr. HUSTON SMITH, Professor of Philosophy, Massachusetts Institute of Technology; Dr. STUART MUDD, Professor of Microbiology Emeritus, University of Pennsylvania, Vice-President, World Academy of Art and Science; Dr. EMILY HARTSHORNE MUDD, Professor of Family Study in Psychiatry Emeritus, University of Pennsylvania; The. Rev. JOHN C. HAUGHEY, S.J., Former Professor of Theology at Georgetown University, Associate Editor, "America."

STUDENTS:

ARTHUR SHRIBERG, Teachers College, Columbia University, Assistant Director, International House, New York; Miss BARBARA HALL, American University, Washington, D.C.; TOM HOPKINS, National Taiwan University,

Taipei; Miss SUSAN HYDE, Wheaton College, George Washington University, Washington, D.C.

THE TEMPLE OF UNDERSTANDING:

Mrs. DICKERMAN HOLLISTER, Greenwich, Conn., President; Mrs. B. K. BIRLA, Calcutta, Chairman, International Committee and Member of the Board; ASHA MIRCHANDANI, Bombay, International Committee; The Rev. LOWELL R. DITZEN, Washington, D.C., Member of the Board; Mrs. HAROLD HOLMYARD, Greenwich, Conn., Member of the Board; Mr. C. J. MILLS, Byram, Conn., Member of the Board; Mrs. WALLACE O'NEAL, Pinehurst, N.C., Member of the Board; Mrs. ROBERT E. PABST, Westport, Conn. Member of the Board; Mrs. CARROLL STUCHELL, New York, N.Y., Member of the Board; Mr. FINLEY P. DUNNE, Jr., Washington, D.C., Executive Director, and General Chairman of the Spiritual Summit Conference.

THE FIRST SPIRITUAL SUMMIT CONFERENCE
Calcutta, India, October 22–26, 1968

A DECLARATION

I. We, members of the world's religious faiths, with their two-and-a-half billion adherents, assembled in the first Spiritual Summit Conference, under the auspices of The Temple of Understanding, having here demonstrated that inter-religious communication is possible and fruitful, see these factors as significant for the present and for emerging world of tomorrow;

We see that science, technology, political and industrial forces, with all their powers, have so far not been able, either alone, or in combined effort, to produce the kind of world that all men desire.

We believe it is time for all peoples and nations, including the leaders of our major secular institutions, to recognize the relevance of the world's religions to the fate of man in the present century.

It is our judgment that the religions themselves must now actively seek increased communication with one another and together speak to our total human community and assist in creating the conditions for the better world. The prejudices and misunderstandings that have stood between us in the past must give way to a climate of understanding of co-operation.

II. Therefore, we challenge the leaders of the several world faiths to take creative initiative in forming a strong international, inter-religious world body. We recognize that the development of such an instrument will require the elevated thought, prayer, study, patience, firm vision and conciliation of many dedicated men and women. But this Summit Conference sees such a Council as a necessity in this 20th Century. We are aware of developments of inter-religious communication, as in Ceylon, Japan and other nations. We are convinced that such fine steps should now be developed on a world wide scale.

As a move toward this end we instruct The Temple of Understanding to consult with the leaders of the several world religions, looking to the calling of another Summit Conference in 1969 to weigh the desirability of creating such an inter-religious world body. The intention is that authorized representatives of the several world religions shall be present as delegates.

We further recommend that all delegates, leaders and participants to this 1968 Summit Conference receive progress reports.

Further, as a more immediate step, it is our mandate that the Temple of Understanding implement the guidelines for inter-religious communication, namely; The Academic Community; The Family of Nations; The Private Corporations and Foundations; The Centres of Spirituality and Monasticism; International Youth Organizations; The Communications Media; and that it create pools of information on the world religions and develop facilities to create materials for the mass media.

The Temple of Understanding, Inc.

Founded in 1960 by Mrs. DICKERMAN HOLLISTER of Greenwich, Connecticut, the Temple of Understanding, Inc., is a nonprofit corporation dedicated to education about the world's religions, and to the proposition that education will bring an understanding on which the religions may build a future of cooperation and mutual respect.

Its programs, of which the Spiritual Summit Conference in Calcutta was an example, are financed by private contributions. It plans eventually to construct a world center to be known as the Temple of Understanding.

The administrative offices of the Temple of Understanding, Inc., are at 1346 Connecticut Avenue, Northwest, Washington, D.C. Its officers, Board of Directors, International Committee and International Scholars Advisory Committee are listed below:

BOARD OF DIRECTORS

Mrs. DICKERMAN HOLLISTER
President
Greenwich, Connecticut

The Rev. LOWELL R. DITZEN
Vice President
Washington, D.C.

Rabbi SAMUEL M. SILVER
Treasurer
Stamford, Connecticut

Mrs. JOHN A. CLARK
Secretary
Greenwich, Connecticut

FINLEY P. DUNNE, Jr.
Executive Director
Washington, D.C.

Mrs. CHARLES H. BABCOCK
Winston-Salem, North Carolina

Mrs. B. K. BIRLA
Calcutta, India

GIBSON F. DAILEY
Princeton, New Jersey

LATHROP DOUGLASS
New York, New York

Miss ELIZABETH GEMPP
St. Louis, Missouri

THOMAS B. GILCHRIST, Jr.
New York, New York

JAMES V. GOURE
Potomac, Maryland

Mrs. HAROLD HOLMYARD
Greenwich, Connecticut

Hon. ARTHUR LEVITT
New York, New York

Robert C. LIVINGSTON
New Canaan, Connecticut

Mrs. BERTIL MALMSTEDT
Omps, West Virginia

CHARLES J. MILLS
Byram, Connecticut

Mrs. FREDERICK S. NICHOLAS
Malvern, Pennsylvania

Mrs. WALLACE W. O'NEAL
Pinehurst, North Carolina

Mrs. ROBERT E. PABST
Westport, Connecticut

Mrs. WILLIAM H. REA
Pittsburgh, Pennsylvania

Mrs. JOSEPHINE RICHARDSON
New York, New York

MAURICE M. ROSEN
Philadelphia, Pennsylvania

H. E. Mr. ZENON ROSSIDES
New York, New York

Mrs. CARROLL D. STUCHELL
New York, New York

FRANK E. TAYLOR
New York, New York

Mrs. WILLIAM L. VAN ALEN
Edgemont, Pennsylvania

Mrs. JAMES VAN DIJK
Tunbridge, Vermont

Mrs. E. SIDNEY WILLIS
Greenwich, Connecticut

INTERNATIONAL COMMITTEE

Mrs. B. K. BIRLA, Chairman
Calcutta, India

Dr. SARVEPALLI RADHAKRISHNAN
Honorary Member
Madras, India

Dr. TETSUTARO ARIGA
Nishinomiya City, Japan

Miss NORMA E. BOYD
Washington, D.C.

LADY CHAPMAN
North Sunderland, England

Dr. CHANG CHI-YUN
Taiwan, Republic of China

Mrs. GORDON CLEMETSON
Tunbridge Wells, England

His Holiness, the DALAI LAMA
DHARMSALA, India

H.S.H. Princess POON DISKUL
Bangkok, Thailand

Mrs. STEPHEN M. ECTON
Tokyo, Japan

The Very Rev. PIERRE FALLON, S. J.
Calcutta, India

Bishop SHINSHO HANAYAMA
Tokyo, Japan

H. E. Sir MUHAMMAD ZAFRULLA KHAN
The Hague, Netherlands

Miss MARY MACAULAY
London, England

ASHA MIRCHANDANI
Bombay, India

Dr. STUART MUDD
Philadelphia, Pennsylvania

Lord ABBOT KOSHO OHTANI
Kyoto, Japan

Mrs. E. Kenneth Sandbach
Sydney, Australia
Dr. Ezra Spicehandler
Jerusalem, Israel

James M. Tompkins
New York, New York

INTERNATIONAL SCHOLARS
ADVISORY COMMITTEE

Dr. Tetsutaro Ariga
Kobe, Japan
The Very Rev. Monsignor
William W. Baum
Kansas City, Missouri
Dr. Amiya Chakravarty
New Paltz, New York
Dr. Chang Chi-yun
Taipei, Taiwan
The Rev. Lowell R. Ditzen
Washington, D.C.
Bishop Shinsho Hanayama
Tokyo, Japan
H. E. Sir Muhammad Zafrulla Khan
The Hague, Netherlands
The Rev. Dr. Harry C. Meserve
Grosse Pointe, Michigan

Dr. Stuart Mudd
Philadelphia, Pennsylvania
Dr. F. S. C. Northrop
New Haven, Connecticut
The Rev. George Pera
Greenwich, Connecticut
The Venerable
Mahathera Piyananda
Boston, Massachusetts
Rabbi Samuel M. Silver
Stamford, Connecticut
Dr. Wen Yen Tsao
Johnson City, Tennessee
Dr. T. K. Venkateswaran
Denver, Colorado

Glossary

The following terms have been briefly defined according to the specific religious tradition or traditions in which they are primarily used. These have been indicated in abbreviation as follows:

Bud – Buddhism	Jain – Jainism
C–T – Confucianism–Taoism	Jud – Judaism
Chr – Christianity	Sikh – Sikhism
Hin – Hinduism	Zor – Zoroastrianism
Is – Islam	

Agape (Chr) – selfless love for neighbor.

Ahimsa (Bud; Hin; Jain) harmlessness; the vow of noninjury to life.

Anekantwad (Jain) – the recognition of all particular religious viewpoints as relative.

Aparigraha (Jain) – doctrine of non-acquisition; non-attachment.

Atman (Hin) – the Self; the unity of the self and *Brahman*.

Bhakti (Hin) – devotion; the devotional way of attaining release.

Brahmacarin (Hin) – one who is in the student stage of life.

Brahman (Hin) – the absolute universal Being; the One.

Dharma (Bud; Hin) – duty; religion; one of the four ends of man. (Pali: *dhamma*).

Dukkha (Bud) – the understanding of human existence as suffering or pain caused by change and impermanence.

Gathas (Zor) – the hymns written by Zarathustra expressing his revelations of God (Ahura Mazda).

Gita (Hin) – a dialogue between the Lord Krishna and the warrior-prince Arjuna found in the Mahabharata, concerning the fundamental religion and ethics of Hinduism.

Guru (Hin; Sikh) – teacher; spiritual guide who has attained insight.

Halachah (Jud) – details of Rabbinic law, generally based on Scripture.

Hinayana (Bud) – the tradition emphasizing self-purification by following the Noble Eightfold Path toward enlightenment or *Nibbana*; see *Theravada*.

Hsiangs (C–T) – hexagram symbols representing the sixty-four possible combinations of the *Yin-Yang* in sets of six.

Jen (C–T) – the basic Confucian principle of virtue as humanity, "human-heartedness," benevolence.

Jivan mukta (Hin) – one who has attained spiritual release.
Janna (Hin) – knowledge; the knowledge way of attaining release.

Karma (Hin; Jain; Sikh) – deeds or action, in past and present incarnations, having determinative effect in the destiny of the individual.
Karuna (Bud) – the principle of compassion, charity, kindness, love, tolerance.
Koran (Is) – the fundamental scripture of the faith; revelations of Allah as recorded by the prophet Mohammed.

Mahayana (Bud) – the tradition emphasizing the attainment of enlightenment for the sake of helping others achieve the same.
Mantra (Hin) – a sacred syllable, word or verse; embodiment of a deity or cosmic force in sound.
Manu (Hin) – the mythical first man of the universe to whom are attributed the fundamental moral and societal prescriptions of Hinduism.
Mara (Bud) – the personification of evil and delusion.
Metta (Bud) – the principle of love; universal love.
Mishnah (Jud) – explanations of the Written Laws of Moses, originally given as Oral Law, but later reduced to written form.
Moksha (Bud; Hin) – release from the karmic cycle of rebirth; the final end of man.

Nama-rupa (Bud) – understanding of human existence as interaction of mind and material substance.
Nibbana (Bud) – realization of release from the world of suffering, from *samsara*. (Sanskrit: *Nirvana*).

Prajna (Bud) – the concept of intuitive wisdom.
Prakriti (Hin) – the basic material substance of the universe; primal blind energy.
Pralaya (Hin) – the period of quiet and inaction following the dissolution of the universe; separation of *purusha* (consciousness) and *prakriti* (matter, energy).
Purusha (Hin) – pure consciousness; also used to refer to the principle of self or the plurality of selves in the universe.

Sadhana (Hin) – a course of spiritual discipline.
Sadhu (Hin) – one who has renounced all worldly things; an ascetic.
Samsara (Bud; Hin) – experience of the phenomenal world; life understood as flux and change.
Sanhedrin (Jud) – Court of justice.
Sat-Cit-Ananda (Hin) – existence, consciousness, bliss respectively which together express the universal Absolute.
Shari'ah (Is) – the traditional sacred law.
Sufi (Is) – one who practices asceticism and tends toward mystical experience within the Islamic faith.
Sutta (Bud) – the Buddha's teaching in the form of a discourse or sermon; also one of the three main divisions of the canons of Buddhism.

T'ai Chi (C–T) – the Absolute Reality of which the phenomenal universe is a manifestation.
Talmud (Jud) – the principle literature of post-Biblical Judaism.
Theravada (Bud) – the way of the elders, equivalent to *Hinayana*.
Torah (Jud) – the Written Law, the basic legal code of Judaism (usually referring specifically to the Five Books of Moses).

Tripitaka (Bud) – the canonical division of the Buddha's teaching into three books: *Vinaya* (Code of Discipline), *Sutta* (Discourse) and *Abhidhamma* (Philosophy and Psychology); usually called "Three Baskets" (Pali: *Tipitika*).

Upanishads (Hin) – the last portion of the Vedic literature expressing the essential philosophical doctrines of the Vedas.

Varna (Hin) – position in social order; caste.

Vedanta (Hin) – the essential teachings of the Upanishads, and the philosophical schools of commentary based upon them; literally "end of the Vedas."

Vedas (Hin) – the ancient Sanskrit scriptures.

Vinaya (Bud) – the Buddha's teaching concerning moral discipline; also one of the three main divisions of the canons of Buddhism.

Yahweh (Jud) – the personal, proper name of God.

Yin-Yang (C–T) – the interacting polar opposites whose rhythmic interchange constitutes the Tao.

Zazen (Bud) – the Zen Buddhist practice of sitting meditation.

Index

DATE DUE